MARIE CURIE

MARIE CURIE

Robert Reid

New York

SATURDAY REVIEW PRESS/E. P. DUTTON & CO., INC.

For Nancy Reid

Contents

Acknowledgments

In preparing this biography I have been helped in many ways by relations, colleagues and co-workers of Marie Curie, as well as by some who, in the early years of the century, worked in the enthralling period of chemistry and physics following the discovery of radioactivity. As I write, knowledge of radioactivity is seventy-seven years old and the numbers who worked on the subject in the fruitful ten or twenty years after its birth, are dwindling. Sadly, three who made significant contributions in the field, one a chemist, one a physicist, and one a medic, and who gave me their time and help, died before the book was complete. I gratefully acknowledge my debt to them all.

The opinions expressed in this book are of course my own; I was freely allowed to form them because of the generous access to documents given me, particularly by the Laboratoire Curie. There I drew on the considerable skill and patience of Mme M. Bordry, the archivist of the Laboratoire, who was always ready with help and support. Members of many other institutions willingly gave me assistance and I wish to thank, among others, the staffs of the Académie des Sciences, the American Institute of Physics, the Bibliothèque Nationale, the Bodleian Library, the British Museum, Cambridge University Library, the Carnegie Corporation of New York, Columbia University Library, the Fawcett Library, the Glowna Library of the Uniwersytetu Marii Curie-Sklodowskiej, the Library of Congress, the Muzeum Marii Sklodowskiej-Curie of Warsaw, New York Public Library, the Royal Institution, the United Nations Library of Geneva and Yale University Library.

For their constructive comments on the manuscript I am grateful, as always, to my wife Penelope, to Diana Crawfurd and to J. E. Stanfield. I have greatly valued the work of my skilful

Acknowledgments

and tactful editors, Philip Ziegler and John Knowler. For their helpful comments on parts of the manuscript I am indebted to Mrs Malcolm W. Davis, Jozef Garlinski, Dr G. E. Harrison, Professor Francis Perrin and Dr J. Vennart.

I wish to thank the following for allowing me to use manuscript material in their possession or to which they hold copyright: Columbia University Library, Laboratoire Curie, M. Maurice Curie, Mrs William Brown Meloney, Professor P. H. Fowler, Yale University Library: and the following for permission to make quotations from their publications: Librairie Félix Alcan, for extracts from *La Radiologie et la Guerre* by Marie Curie; Cambridge University Press for extracts from *Rutherford* by A. S. Eve; Éditions Bernard Grasset for extracts from *Souvenirs et Recontres* by Camille Marbo; Doubleday & Company, Inc. for letters from *Madame Curie* by Eve Curie, translated by Vincent Sheehan, and Curtis Brown Ltd for extracts from *Pierre Curie* by Marie Curie.

MARIE
CURIE

Chapter 1

Polish Childhood

Maria Sklodowska was born in a small apartment in one of the cobbled streets leading from the red brick battlements of the city walls of Warsaw. On one side of the entrance to the house in Freta Street is a plaque commemorating her birth – on November 7th, 1867. On the other side is another plaque with a short list of names of the People's Army Staff who fell there fighting in 1944 in the Warsaw Rising. These memorials, side by side, illustrate well the two national qualities the Poles keep very dear and which they hold up to new generations who might otherwise forget too easily: first, pride in the struggle for a national identity, and second, pride in intellectual achievement.

No generation of Poles during the past few centuries has avoided the struggle for the existence of the nation. Maria Sklodowska, later to be known as Marie Curie, was one of a generation which accepted it as a fact of everyday life. Just as today the old city has memorials to those who died trying to preserve it for the Poles themselves, so too the Warsaw of the 1860s kept its memories and shrines. As children Maria's brothers and sisters had to walk only a few steps from their door to the site of the old Barbican in the city walls and the spot where, in 1656, the citizens of Warsaw were cut down defending their homeland from the invading Swedes.

The Swedes were one of many armies to have tramped backwards and forwards over Poland. Muscovites, Teutonic knights, Austrian infantiers, Tsarist cavalry, Prussian lancers and Nazi stormtroopers are only some of those who have seen this piece of Central Europe as legitimate territorial pickings. Implicit in the acts of plunder have been either the inferiority or the dispensability of the people whose territory it was. Bismarck had a certain hypocritical compassion for them. He wrote to his sister in 1861, 'Hit

13

the Poles till they despair of their very lives. I have every sympathy for their position, but if we are to survive, our only course is to exterminate them.'[1]

Hitler had a similar attitude, but with no pretence of compassion. In 1940 one of his Polish provincial Gauleiters, preparing the ground for the concentration camps, aped his attitude: 'Not even an inch of the land we have conquered will ever belong to a Pole again. Poles can work for us, but not as rulers, only as serfs'.[2]

The first of these statements was written six years before the birth of Maria Sklodowska, and the second six years after her death. During her years in Poland, masterful attitudes were no different; only the master differed. In 1867 Russia was the master.

Poland had emerged from the eighteenth century as a nation partitioned piecemeal among its neighbours, Austria, Prussia and Russia. In what was left of central Poland, now named the Congress Kingdom, the so-called King of Poland was in fact the Emperor of Russia himself. Russia, like every other nation that sat hard upon Poland, was a hated conqueror, no matter what its professed intentions for Polish self-determination. In 1830 Russia had beaten down a Polish military revolt with unrestrained brutality. Again in 1864 an uprising had ended with the cropped heads of five Poles dangling from a public scaffold on the hill outside the Warsaw citadel.

The Sklodowski family fought as well as any patriots in defence of the homeland. Maria's grandfather, Jozef, had been 26 when he took part in the 1830 fracas, and several of his seven healthy children saw both blood and suffering in their generation's fight. Jozef's third son, Zdzislaw, had held in his arms the bleeding body of the revolutionary leader, Colonel Marcin Borelowski, and watched him die. Jozef's eldest daughter, Boleslawa, like so many young women in this country where female inferiority was not so readily assumed as in other European countries was deeply embroiled. Acting as an undercover agent for the insurgents, she helped organise the family home into a little hospital, to which she guided wounded rebels and nursed them until they were fit enough to be smuggled to the Austrian border.[3]

But the generation that produced Maria Sklodowska's generation became cowed. The Russian boot had been heavy for too long. Only the stories of glory remained. Jozef Sklodowski's eldest son, Wladislaw, was in any case a more conventional and submissive man than most of the others in his family. To him and to many other Poles it was obvious that Russia was too powerful and too ruthless a neighbour. Freedom for Poland would come only when Russia condescended to give it. Wladislaw elected to compromise with the system. Like his father before him he set about getting himself a Russian scientific education in Russia, in Russian.

He pushed himself slowly up the Russo-Polish academic ladder and into a job teaching physics at a Warsaw school. During this steady progress in a conservative career he found himself a girl, a teacher as might have been predicted, who had similar interests in music, poetry and science, and who would clearly make a devoted wife within the constraints of the strictly limited combined income they could expect as teachers.

When Wladislaw met her, Mademoiselle Boguska was the principal of a small girls' boarding school in Freta Street. She was dark, handsome and quite masculine in appearance; Wladislaw in his way was somewhat feminine with his light eyes and thin whiskers. But together they made an imposing pair, and posing for a photograph as they did, among the young ladies of the school, with their straight backs, bobbed hair and corseted waists, they looked every inch the typical Victorian parents radiating the sternness, and conventions of that rank.

They spent their early married years on the first floor of the Freta street house. As principal of the school Madame Sklodowska had been allotted rooms there. The whole establishment – school and apartment – was tiny, so that what family life there was, was much of it conducted in public, and much of it to the accompaniment of girlish screams or the patter overhead of feet on deal floorboards. They had status, but few tangible rewards. The fruits of love, however, were plentiful.

During five of the eight years she taught, administered and lived in Freta Street the young wife was pregnant. A son Jozef, named after his grandfather, had at last followed three girls: Sofia, Bronislawa and Helena. In the early spring of 1867 she found herself pregnant yet again.

The few years that followed were the most stable, and the happiest they were all to have together. The parents were a self-controlled (perhaps over self-controlled) pair who ran the family efficiently and with little demonstration of either anger or physical affection. Sklodowski imposed his Victorian father's sense of propriety. He admired intellectual achievement particularly of new scientific kind, and the strict observance of external morality. Sklodowska imposed her Victorian mother's sense of uncomplaining duty. She accepted the woman's role in family affairs, and displayed an intense religious devotion. And they lived their lives in the subdued but effective atmosphere of a police State.

When her time came early in the winter term of 1867, Madame Sklodowska as on the four earlier occasions, had to bear her labour pains while the school carried on around the improvised delivery ward. Sheets, pillows, swabs and innumerable jugs of hot water which inevitably accompanied the event in those days, were carried in over the heads of small girls. Maria Salomee, as she was to be christened, was born in the bedroom of the Freta Street apartment on November 7th without any undue complications. Her arrival did however force Sklodowski to face the problem of his income. What had once supported a pair of schoolteachers with modest tastes, was no longer adequate for a family of seven. Within a few weeks they had moved to a nearby Warsaw high school for boys, where an apartment was provided and Sklodowski could combine his post of professor of mathematics and physics with a job providing a second income: school under-inspector.

These few years saw the slow but calculated effects of Russian pressure acting on the beaten-down nation. The most ruthless period of Russianisation of Poland had begun in 1867, the year of Maria Sklodowska's birth. The planned programme affected every aspect of Polish life. The Polish law courts were disestablished. The words 'Vistula Land' were substituted for 'Poland' on maps of the Congress Kingdom. Not only was Russian turned into the country's official language, a start was made on a policy of replacement of Polish officials by Russian immigrants.

Maria was six years old when Sklodowski was forced out of his supplementary school post of under-inspector, and he was made to give up his school lodgings.

There were several moves about the city before Sklodowski found a job – a position little more than a boarding house keeper. He took an apartment where he could lodge boys of school age and give them tuition.

Again the family lived among the cries of strange voices, but here the young owners of the voices had also to be accommodated. Maria, as the youngest member of the family, had to sleep on a couch in the dining-room and be clear of it by six every morning so that the place could be got ready for the pupils' meals.

She was a timid child, small and nervous, but old for her years, they said. They probably meant that she had a logical turn of mind, that might have seemed a certain coldness to those who did not know her well. It was part of her inheritance; her father passed on to her not only his rational mind and his preciseness, but also an introspective nature and a ready acceptance of convention. From her mother she derived her sense of duty and also, her total refusal to compromise. In her mother this immensely strong trait showed itself most forcefully in her religious attitudes. The intensity with which she took her daily doses of Catholicism deeply impressed the little girl. In the well-attended city churches Madame Sklodowska publicly displayed uncompromising goodness and dutifulness. Maria deeply admired her mother for these characteristics.

No child could possibly avoid religion in Warsaw in the 1870s. Its influence was everywhere apparent, and is still obvious to anybody walking the streets of Poland today. Within a few yards of Maria's birthplace, for example, was the Baroque Dominican Church, white and noble, where she could peep in and watch white-robed friars pushing mops over the black and white tiles; immediately opposite was the Church of the Holy Ghost: over-decorated with carvings and guilded monuments; and down the streets sloping from Freta gently to the Vistula, she could pass the Church of the Nuns of the Holy Sacrament, with the low and red-roofed convent alongside, and in and out of which glided black clothed figures of her own sex looking serene and good. But for Maria the mystical experience was soon to come into conflict with rationalism. Whether rationalism or mysticism would prevail was determined by a series of tragic events in the family's life. Maria was deeply impressed by the amount of time her mother spent on her knees in a church pew apparently in intimate contact with her Maker. It was also clear to her that there was a barrier to intimacy between herself and her mother. Deference of children to their parents was the custom, and they addressed their elders in the third person. But in this family the distance and the problems ran deeper. Quite suddenly Maria noticed that her mother began to avoid kissing or even embracing the children. Her mother suspected, rightly as it turned out, that she was suffering from the first symptoms of tuberculosis.

This coldness within the family might in the 1870s have seemed cruel and unnecessary, whereas it was a wise practice in advance of its time. But the effects of being kept at a distance by the mother she 'passionately admired' were deep; Maria was never afterwards able easily to accept physical closeness.

A lesser but still important problem for Sklodowski was that poverty was creeping up on him, and was now suddenly made acute by having to find money to send his wife to expensive sanatoria in France. Worse was to come, however, when an outbreak of typhus among the pupils spread to the Sklodowskis. Among its victims was the eldest child, Sofia, who died early in 1876. And very soon Mme Sklodowska's tuberculosis began to show itself in more distressing symptoms. Earlier lethargy gave way to fatigue, the muffled cough was more frequent and the blood on the handkerchief was frightening to the older children who understood what the stains meant. In an age familiar with the disease, the prognosis was all too easy. She was dead within two years of her eldest child. For the second time in her short life Maria sat with what remained of the family and watched a Catholic priest leave a death-bed.

Whether the Victorian attitude to death was healthy is an uncertain subject for psychologists and psychiatrists to debate. What is certain is that the age which made a necessity, even a fetish, of mourning, with black-curtained windows, black-veiled women and black-edged notepaper, also unconscionably prolonged the agony. The new loss was catastrophic to Sklodowski himself. Among the children, the youngest, Maria, now ten years old, was most deeply affected. The period of mourning was allowed to drag on for several years and the effect clung to both father and child for too long.

It was this unnecessarily drawn out event which caused the rationalism she had learnt from her father to conflict with the mysticism to which her mother had introduced her. Maria was unable to understand logically what it was that had so deeply touched and influenced her mother. The death, she now saw, was making her father a prematurely old man. The wasteful effects of the tragedy finally tipped the scales. Religion lost. Three or four years later she rejected it completely. Unusually at such an early age, she became what T. H. Huxley had just invented a word for: agnostic. She had taken a step which led her more easily in the direction of science.

All her life Maria suffered from agonies of shyness and timidity. When little more than a baby she was made to stand in front of her class and recite her newly-acquired Russian for the benefit of a stern-faced Russian-speaking inspector of schools; the trauma of this mild experience stayed with her all her life. The timid manners and fragile reactions were in fact only outward symptoms of deeper nervous troubles. There were times when she broke under the strain.

The first occasion, from which she had to be nursed carefully back to health, was when she was 15 years old. She had had the first steps of her education guided by the many teacher-members of her own family, and had then passed through small private educational establishments, and finally through the State system in Warsaw. She emerged triumphant with a gold medal.

But the effort to succeed took its toll. She was always peculiarly but typically reticent in describing the pressure which brought on what doctors, lacking any better diagnosis, called her 'nervous breakdown'. Maria herself preferred to call it 'the fatigue of growth and study'.[4] Whether the collapse was due to the pressures applied by an academic family demanding academic success, or whether there was some organic cause, it was serious enough for Maria to be sent away from home. For the better part of a year she was packed off to the south and to relations in the country with no commitment to study. Leading the enforced idle life of a convalescent she wrote to a school-friend,

I may say that, aside from an hour's French lesson with a little boy I don't do a thing, positively not a thing – for I have even abandoned the piece of embroidery that I had started. . . . I have no schedule. I get up sometimes at four or five (morning, not evening!) I read no serious books, only harmless and absurd little novels. Thus, in spite of the diploma conferring on me the dignity and maturity of a person who has finished her studies, I feel incredibly stupid. Sometimes I laugh all by myself, and I contemplate my state of total stupidity with genuine satisfaction.[5]

These are not the sentences of an immature girl. She had never been a child's child. Even at fifteen she identified with adult behaviour, and observed both it and childish behaviour with an adult's eye.

Until this break from Warsaw her life had been ruled by belief in the superiority of learning and intellectual activity. These were the values exalted by both her mother and her father. It was a strait discipline for an adolescent, and she suffered pangs of conscience when she was not following it. It was so different a life from that of the people she was now living with. She sampled the rustic frivolities and she loved them. There were *kuligs*, the regional barn dances, and there she swept into mazurkas and waltzes with the young men who came in from Cracow, and saw the dawn in with the same spirit as that of the blooming young girls who were her contemporaries. There were the sleigh rides and tumbles in the snow, the gasp for breath at the first view of the mountains and the satisfaction of the still panorama of rolling plains.

But for Maria Sklodowska at the age of 15, these days of

pleasure and enjoyment were an interlude in life, and not life itself. Working inside her was a spirit which told her that the greatest rewards of life were those to be worked for with the mind. Sleigh rides and 'absurd little novels' were other people's idea of life's enjoyments. They were not hers. Though she had yet to decide what was.

Chapter 2

Positivist Girlhood

She returned to Warsaw plumper, a rather plain snub-nosed 16-year-old. Beside her elder sisters, with their long flowing hair and maturer manners, she cut an ugly duckling figure. Both her sisters, in the family tradition were planning teaching careers and brother Jozef was studying medicine. Boys' secondary schools in Poland taught as principal subjects Russian, Latin and Greek and successful credits in these subjects gave students the right either to apply for university entrance or to sit entrance examinations at any of the technical high-schools in the Russian Empire. However, there was not even a remote chance of higher education for women. No classical languages were taught at girls' secondary schools and so, automatically, Polish women were excluded from gaining entrance qualifications to universities within the Empire. The only solution was to leave the country and take a degree at a foreign university. Bronia, Maria's elder sister, was determined to do this. The only barrier was the continuing Sklodowski problem: money.

Maria saw herself following her elder sisters into teaching. What better method of financing it than practice with pay, there and then? They would set up as private tutors in Warsaw.

They were not the first nor the last aspirant academics to think in these terms. More depressingly they were not the only young people in Warsaw in 1883 seeking the same solution. The city had a glut of adolescents who were hoping to pay for an education by giving one to somebody else less fitted to tackle the Russian educational hurdles. The Sklodowski family, particularly its youngest member, spent much time waiting at home for customers who rarely came. She wrote:

Nothing new at home. The plants are healthy, the azaleas are in flower. Lancet (the dog) sleeps on the carpet. Gucia, the seamstress, is making over my dress, which I have dyed; it will be suitable and very pretty. Bronia's dress is finished and looks very nice. I have written to nobody; I have so little time, and even less money. A person who knew of us through friends came to inquire about lessons; Bronia told her a half-rouble an hour, and the visitor ran away as if the house had caught fire. . . .[1]

But at 16 Maria still herself had plenty to learn. In spite of the obvious obstacles to original and hence possibly revolutionary thought in Warsaw, new ideas and philosophies were developing which were particularly appealing to the young. Twenty years after the bitter and bloody failure of yet another revolution, reaction had set in. The new generation, Maria's, began to look on the heroic gesture, the march into battle armed with nothing but a farm scythe, simply as romanticism which could not possibly improve Poland's future. And these thoughts were developing when intellectual ideas in the rest of Europe were undergoing profound changes. Science was emerging as a new force; its various subdivisions, together with what many people regarded as some frightening economic theories, were throwing up ideas that had implications far beyond the apparently narrow subjects themselves.

Maria Sklodowska grew up into an intellectual scientific age dominated by the revolutionary gospels of four men: Marx, Freud, Einstein and Darwin. All would have importance for either her work or her life in general. But at this moment the thoughts of just two of them were impinging on hers.

The first, Darwin – the young man who went to Cambridge to become a clergyman, and whose great work was interpreted as being a denial of God – was also being variously interpreted in Poland. Herbert Spencer's interpretation of Darwin's theory of natural selection, 'the survival of the fittest', was seen by many of the young bloods, swept on by the magnificence of Darwin, as a scientific reason why the old Polish policies for the Poles were bound to work against the nation in the end. Poles, so the new thinking went, must reconcile themselves with the existing conditions, then stabilise, then improve their lot.

It was time for the old Polish self-romanticism to end. From here on thinking ought to be with the head and not with the heart. Realism and logic should be paramount. The fittest would survive.

The logic of this appealed to Maria Sklodowska. On long walks in the countryside her father and her grandfather had explained nature in terms of reason. Why should human behaviour not submit itself to similar logical processes? Just at the time Maria returned to the capital, a few young Warsaw enthusiasts were getting together to try to develop these ideas. They called themselves 'positivists', greatly influenced by the writings of the French philosopher, Auguste Comte, whose works on *Positive Philosophy* had appeared from 1830 to 1854. Comte, who gave sociology its name, filled the young Poles with new hope that a scientific discipline might solve their society's problems.

Poland under the Russian boot was intellectually isolated and the infiltration of these new ideas were challenging and radical. One group which organised itself to cultivate these ideas called itself the 'Floating University' – a grand name for a parochial little institution. Like all educational processes carried on in Poland outside the Russian system it had to be done in secret, and those who took a role in it did so with a real risk to themselves. The 'University' lecture halls were top-floor apartment drawing-rooms, safe from the eyes of the State police; the 'professors' included not only genuine teachers, who risked their careers, livelihoods and a winter in Siberia, but also half-qualified enthusiasts, many of them with half-developed and sometimes half-baked ideas.

The curriculum reflected the ill-developed ideas of the 'University's' founders. It included, to be sure, subjects such as anatomy and natural history: but it also added in for good measure, a pleasant piano recital, a little poetry reading, or perhaps a short travel lecture. But what was perhaps most interesting about this educational pastime was its acceptance of women's right to a place in it. It was only in the year of Maria Sklodowska's birth that the first women's suffrage society had been founded in England, and twelve years later that John Stuart Mill had published *The Subjection of Women*. Yet here already in Poland the mainstay of the student population of this avant garde, if faintly ridiculous, University were female – mostly teenage girls with few responsibilities and time on their hands, young married women with little else to interest them, and the young daughters of successful bourgeois parents.

However, the sense of sampling forbidden fruit gave them a zeal which one observer, the novelist Stefan Zeromski, observed with a certain enchantment.

There were gathered there progressives and mad patriotic girls, but I didn't see any scholars there. Daughters of Warsaw. I was ravished by their way of dressing: modest and elegant in the Warsaw style . . . It's the first time I've ever seen sensible girls to whom you can speak without any of the usual conventional nonsense. They were . . . so young, so natural and with good and pure smiles on their faces. They talked to you without either blushing or simpering and couldn't have wounded you with an ambiguous word.[2]

Maria Sklodowska's was one of the well-scrubbed faces drawn into these circles. With her eldest sister and her friends she climbed the stairs to the attic lecture rooms, and suddenly found, to her delight, that great new horizons of knowledge were open to her.

Maria had intense powers of concentration and a remarkable memory. Whoever was responsible for guiding her choice of literature Maria's notebooks showed a catholic taste: she sampled Dostoevsky, Heine, Musset, Sully-Prudhomme, and many others, often in the original languages. Some of her own Polish writers, too, such as Henryk Sienkiewicz (later to win the Nobel Prize and author of *Quo Vadis*), and Boleslaw Prus (once a pupil of her grandfather), were using the novel as a means of expressing their views on Poland's social progress. Prus, who acquired his intense scientific interests in much the same fashion as Maria herself, was also greatly influenced by the positivist movement.

When a bullet strikes a wall, it halts and generates heat. In mechanics this process is called the transforming of mass motion into molecular, of what was outward into an inner force. Something like this happened in Poland after the cruel quelling of the insurrection. The nation as a whole woke up, ceased to fight and conspire, and began to think and to work.[3]

The analogies were obscure at times, but they were exciting. And the application of positivism was personal and relevant to a young adolescent. Positivism was quite clear about what its progress implied: the emancipation of women, sexual equality in education, anti-clericalism, the end to discrimination against Jews, the abolition of gentry and class traditions, and education for the peasants. This was the liberal credo of the youth of the 1880s. Give or take a few nouns, it is not much different from what will be the liberal credo of the youth of the 1980s.

Maria grasped at these ideas and their promises. After one Floating University session she followed her sister into the local photographer's studio. There they posed shyly for photographs. Maria appears as a girl still plump, but getting prettier, competing bravely alongside her adult and svelte eldest sister. Across it, full of enthusiasm for what she had discovered, she wrote to a friend who had shared the new experience, 'To an ideal positivist – from two positive idealists'.

Positivism had its view of how social problems should be dealt with: but there were quite different views that could not easily be dismissed, and Maria must have come face to face with some of them. The great apostle of positivism at this time was the writer Alexander Swietochowski. He edited the periodical *Prawda* and used it to publicise views on subjects from social economy to medicine. It was this magazine that introduced the latest works of Marx and Engels to an eager young Polish readership. *Das Kapital* had been published in Russian in 1873. The Marxist movement had developed in Poland among the workers in the growing manufacturing industries. The positivist attitude of reconciliation with Poland's existing situation and of providing scientific solutions was, in Marxist terms, acceptance of servitude by the bourgeoisie and collaboration with the occupying powers. No two ideologies could have been more opposed.

For an informed and sensitive young lady, now 18, in a small city such as Warsaw the issues were unavoidable and certainly perturbing. For the time being Maria had pinned her colours to the banner of positivism. If the Tsar's secret police knew of the Floating University then it did not worry them much. But the new Marxist socialists and the spectre of revolution attracted the ruthless Russian hand. Maria watched the new socialists suffer for their pains. Two hundred were taken into custody. Public executioners were again soon to be in action. After a series of trials seven men were led to the traditional spot on the slope between the Warsaw citadel and the River Vistula, not far from Freta Street, and shot. Their leader, Ludwik Warynski, was said to have died in prison of starvation.

The Russian subjugation of Poland created a whirlpool from which revolutionaries and martyrs would rise to the surface again and again. This was predictable. What was not predictable was the extent to which women in Poland felt that they could compete on equal terms with men and, if necessary, be revolutionaries and martyrs. Maria Sklodowska was one of these. So was a small dark-haired young Jewess, three years younger than Maria called Rosa Luxemburg. Like Maria, Rosa had a bent for natural sciences. And like Maria, the sight of the social conditions of the peasants and the workers in Poland led her to think hard about the means that ought to be available to change these conditions. Like Maria she too left Poland to do her revolutionary work. Having adopted Marxism, and despising the national pretensions of Poland, her life was too close to violence, and ended with her murdered body floating down a Berlin canal.

There are too many differences between Maria Sklodowska and Rosa Luxemburg to make a prolonged comparison worthwhile. But what is certain is that some of the pressures, the experiences and the observations that propelled Rosa in the direction of Marx were similar to those operating on Maria about the same time. At the age of 18 Maria's mind was nothing if not malleable and the next few years would be crucial in determining whether, as was very possible, it was shaped by the writings of this other whiskered Victorian gentleman, who had scribbled so busily in the warmth of the British Museum Reading Room.

The immediate direction of Maria's future was decided by money or, as usual in her family, the lack of it. Her father was, as she described him, 'now aged and tired'. In fact he was 53, prematurely old and worried – worried about money for his daughter's education, and worried about providing for his own retirement. Maria, he decided, must now try to lead an independent life. Teaching, the family profession, would have to support her. But, without qualifications, the only possible way was to become a governess.

Late in 1885 she accepted what she thought would be a suitable post. Maria Sklodowska carried to the end of her life the memory of her unhappiness as she climbed into a railway compartment on Warsaw station, knowing that it was to take her many hours' distance from the family she loved. As she sadly watched the figures on the platform diminish then disappear, she had no idea whether those new horizons of knowledge that had been opened to her, those readily acceptable ideas of emancipation, and those contradictory social theories, would also diminish from view and disappear. For the moment she had to face the problem of paying her way.

Chapter 3

Breaking the Bonds

The first governess-ship was a failure. The family of lawyers to which Maria went had values entirely different from her own family. There were strained relations between the lady of the house and the young governess. Maria was treated, she felt, like a prisoner. But she had come for independence and that is what she would show. She squared up to the mistress and told her that she could not endure the situation any longer. The rest of her opinion on this lady and her household she put on paper in a letter to her cousin, Henrika Michalowska.

Since she was exactly as enthusiastic about me as I was about her, we understood each other marvellously well. It was one of those rich houses where they speak French when there is company – a chimney-sweeper's kind of French – where they don't pay their bills for six months, and where they fling money out of the window even though they economise pettily on oil for the lamps. They have five servants. They pose as liberals and, in reality, they are sunk in the darkest stupidity. And last of all, although they speak in the most sugary tones, slander and scandal rage through their talk – slander which leaves not a rag on anybody . . .[1]

This was the first record of her strength of will and her habit of exerting it. The habit was to develop: so was the will.

The next new family, the Zorawskis, were like the last, wealthy, but unlike the last, qualified for approval by the sharp eye of the critical young positivist. She wrote to Henrika Michalowska:

February 3rd, 1886.

I have now been with M. and Mme Zorawski for one month; so I have had time to acclimatise myself in the new post. Up to now all has gone well. The Zorawskis are excellent people. I have made friends with their eldest daughter, Bronka, which contributes to the pleasantness of my life. As for my pupil, Andzia, who will soon be ten, she is an obedient child, but very disorderly and spoiled. Still, one can't require perfection . . .

In this part of the country nobody works; people think only of amusing themselves; and since we in this house keep a little apart from the general dance, we are the talk of the countryside. One week after my arrival they were already speaking of me unfavourably because, as I didn't know anybody, I refused to go to a ball at Karwacz, the gossip centre of the region. I am not sorry, for M. and Mme Zorawski came back from that ball at one o'clock the next afternoon. I was glad to have escaped such a test of endurance, especially as I am not feeling at all strong just now.

There was a ball here on Twelfth Night. I was treated to the sight of a certain number of guests worthy of the caricaturist's pencil, and enjoyed myself hugely. The young people here are most uninteresting. Some of the girls are so many geese who never open their mouths, the others are highly provocative. It appears that there are some others, more intelligent. But up to now my Bronka [*Mademoiselle Zorawska, aged 18*] seems to me a rare pearl both in good sense and in her understanding of life.[2]

Maria Sklodowska, at the age of 18, had already adopted rigid stances. The narrowness of her upbringing could not allow much else. She herself was fully prepared to give, and indeed did give a full working day despite the fact that she was nervous and never physically strong. She worked with Bronka for four hours a day and with ten-year-old Andzia for three.

The Zorawskis were a good-looking family. Bronka and Andzia were a particularly handsome pair. Three sons were being educated in Warsaw and there were two younger children. The father managed a large estate, farmed a considerable acreage of beet and had a holding in the factory that turned it into sugar. Maria found him old-fashioned – perhaps like her father – and sympathetic. Madame Zorawska was less easy, had a temper and showed it frequently, but she had been a governess once herself and struck up a good working relationship with the children's new teacher. She most certainly could not have found any fault with the young girl's conscientiousness; indeed, it almost verged on the puritanical. Even Zorawski's fashion of life, relatively restrained considering their affluence, was a shade too relaxed for Maria Sklodowska.

She wrote to Henrika:

April 5th, 1886.

I am living as it is customary to live in my position. I give my lessons and I read a little, but it isn't easy, for the arrival of new guests constantly upsets the normal employment of my time. Sometimes this irritates me a great deal, since my Andzia is one of those children who profit enthusiastically by every interruption of work, and there is no way of bringing her back to reason afterwards . . .

. . . Conversation in Company? Gossip and then more gossip. The only subjects of discussion are the neighbours, dances and parties. So far as dancing is concerned, you could look far before you would find better dancers than the young girls of this region. They all dance perfectly. They are not bad creatures, for that matter, and certain ones are even intelligent, but their education has done nothing to develop their minds, and the stupid, incessant parties here have ended by frittering their wits away. As for the young men, there are few nice ones who are even a bit intelligent. . . . For the girls and boys alike, such words as 'positivism', 'Swietochowski' or 'the labour question' are objects of aversion – supposing they have ever heard the words, which is unusual. The Zorawski household is relatively cultivated.[3]

Henrika was by now very familiar with cousin Maria's views on the proper subject matter of conversation for intelligent young women. She was, it seems, equally familiar with the state of Maria's nerves. In the same letter Maria wrote of the difficulties she was having with Andzia, her 10-year-old pupil:

Today we had another scene because she did not want to get up at the usual hour. In the end I was obliged to take her calmly by the hand and pull her out of bed. I was boiling inside. You can't imagine what such little things do to me: such a piece of nonsense can make me ill for several hours. But I had to get the better of her . . .[4]

Her body always reacted physically to these efforts to dominate others. When it was essential that her will should triumph, she triumphed: but at a price.

However, her social conscience did not allow her to let up for long. She found in the village of Szczuki, where the Zorawskis lived, the perfect situation to practise the idealist social principles she had so excitedly absorbed in Warsaw. She decided to try to set up a school for the peasant children from Zorawski's beet farms, and workers' children from the sugar factories. She planned this although she was committed to seven hours' coaching each day with the Zorawski children, and another additional hour with a workman's son she was preparing for school.

The Zorawskis agreed to her evangelical scheme and even to their eldest daughter helping with the teaching, though they were well aware that the enterprise was against the law; should the Russian authorities discover what was going on there were likely to be police reprisals. So, in addition to her regular daily commitments Maria now took on ten peasant children for two extra hours. She taught them in her own room, to which they were able to climb without disturbing the Zorawskis, by a separate stairway from the courtyard. By December of 1886 the number of her class had risen to eighteen, and on Wednesdays and Saturdays she was sometimes with them for five hours.

During this period of her life she saw the true nature of the inequalities in the way of life in the country where she lived. She moved in and out of the peasant hovels which contained families of ten, twelve or more children with nothing warmer than an atmosphere of hopelessness. She knew the names of the beet-factory workers who, no matter with what paternalism, were exploited over by far the greater part of the fraction of the 24 hours that made up a day, to produce profits which were used to widen the gap between themselves and their employers.

Maria Sklodowska had had both the education and experiences

which would easily have turned her into what her compatriot Rosa Luxemburg became. If ever an educated young woman was to turn to Marx, that time had arrived for Maria. But she did not. Her passionate nationalism, her love for Poland, clashed with the harshness of Marxism and its emphasis on internationalism. But there was something else more important that distracted her. Quite simply, she had discovered science.

In spite of her heavy workload, in spite of her nervous ailments and her hypochondria, Maria had immense reserves of both physical and intellectual energy. Her work left her with most of the long winter evenings free; they were not to be frittered away, and certainly not in the fashion favoured by the girls of her own social class. She had been educated to the habit of self-education, and this is how her free time was to be spent. Positivism had left her with a wonderful menu of scarcely touched dishes; it had introduced her to new aspects of European literature, to Polish literature, and to natural science, and sociology. She made her own eclectic choice of what would be good for her. Her reading during this period included the first volume of Daniel's *Physics*, Spencer's *Sociology* (in French), and Paul Ber's *Lessons on Anatomy and Physiology* (in Russian).

Most of all she was excited by physics and mathematics. She had the concentration and persistence to take her beyond the first flush of their novelty. In the small room reached by the outside staircase, in this remote Polish village, she effectively started what was to be her life's work. And for the new passion she jealously kept every available spare hour. When an evening was occupied by duties in the Zorawski household she got up at six in the mornings to compensate. When she was called on for social duties she gave the time with a bad grace. Once when she was asked to make up a four at cards she deeply resented the innocent request as a wasteful intrusion into the time she could profitably have used acquiring knowledge. The passion was deep.

It was at this time that she heard that Bronia, her eldest sister, had taken the step that ultimately showed Maria the way to a different and a larger life. Bronia had conceived the idea of studying medicine. There was nowhere in Poland she could study and she had lighted on Paris. It was a breathtaking decision for the whole family. First, it would mean another family financial trauma. Second, the conception swept up and brought into the real world a vast horizon of dreams: dreams of culture, intellectual attainment, freedom and hope for a future. Paris was the distant symbol of so many Polish travellers' dream-like tales. And now they were on the doorstep to Bronia who had taken the breathtaking decision simply to reach out and touch the dream, and realise that it had substance.

Financial problems were not so simply solved. For some time now the plan between the eldest and the youngest sister had been that each would provide aid for the other. The time had come to put it into operation, and the youngest had to make the sacrifice. The money Maria was sending home would be siphoned off to Bronia in Paris. When Bronia qualified and was earning, the compliment would be returned: Maria could then choose how she would be educated.

To Maria the plan seemed idealist but practicable, and therefore admirable. But she had not reckoned with the principal enemy – time. Her own future seemed an age away. Before many months had passed, it must have seemed an eternity. The enclosed life of a village community, the restrictions imposed on a governess's life no matter how liberal the household, the limited range of daily contacts – and her own personality, nervous, critical, and easily isolated – soon changed initial optimism into bitter introspection. The undertone of her letters began to change. At 18 life had been heaven; at 19 it was melodramatically tragic. She wrote to cousin Henrika in December 1886:

... My plans for the future? I have none, or rather they are so commonplace and simple that they are not worth talking about. I mean to get through as well as I can, and when I can do no more, say farewell to this base world. The loss will be small, and regret for me will be short – as short as for so many others.[5]

Clearly, she took time out to stand over an imaginary grave as an imaginary coffin carrying her own body was lowered into it, mourned only by the salt tears of a few peasant children. There was nothing abnormal in that stage of her adolescent development. Nor for that matter in the next stage which added to both the melodrama and the tragedy. Its origins were firmly denied in the same letter:

> ... Some people pretend that in spite of everything I am obliged to pass through the kind of fever called love. This absolutely does not enter into my plans. If I ever had any others, they have gone up in smoke; I have buried them; locked them up, sealed and forgotten them – for you know that walls are always stronger than the heads which try to demolish them ...[6]

The obvious and correct reinterpretation of these sentences is that Sklodowska had fallen in love. The predictable object of the affection was the son of the house. Kazimierz Zorawski, the eldest child, was as good-looking as Maria's pupils. Fair-haired, with a trim moustache, he cut a dashing and fashionable figure, even twentieth-century in style, when he returned to the country from his Warsaw studies. Maria now had an intellectual equal of her own generation. He was fresh from the capital with all its news, and a link with its progressive attitudes. Moreover his subject of study was also her newly adopted one. And she to him was a significant addition to his customary country scene, undoubtedly intelligent if unguided, and unquestionably nubile.

The home background of Maria, the nature of her interpersonal relations, the rejection of physical contact, the strictly imposed code of public conduct between sexes which was expected by the middle class of their peers, combined to prepare Maria inadequately for this unnerving experience. As the young governess she was socially in an inferior position, which confused even further this already delightfully upsetting relationship. No matter what the details of the romance, it blossomed into full flower. Marriage was mentioned. Then the petals fluttered sadly to the ground. The reason given for the breaking of the liaison was that Kazimierz's parents expected a better match for their son and heir. Whatever the reasons, the relationship left its mark on Maria. It was her first love-affair and its end was painful. She did not have the opportunity for the experience again for six years.

For Maria the time still to be spent with the Zorawskis now had the cold look of a penal sentence. Already at 20 years old, she grew bitter. She was very homesick, missing her father – but at least with the consolation that he was missing her too. She wanted to get back to him, and back to what she now called 'my independence'. She told Henrika on December 10th, 1887, 'The poor man misses me a lot; he would like to have me at home; he longs for me! ... If the thing is at all possible, I shall leave Szczuki – which can't be done, in any case, for some time – I shall install myself in Warsaw, take a post as teacher in a girls' school and make up the rest of the money I need by giving lessons. It is all I want. Life does not deserve to be worried over.'[7]

The following March she wrote to tell her brother Jozef how much she was missing Warsaw, and how depressing was the old problem of never having money. The once gay atmosphere of the Szczuki household had disappeared, relations had soured, and the 'excellent people' of two years before had taken on different characteristics, which included persecution, real or imagined, of their young governess. She told Jozef, 'I say nothing of my clothes, which are worn out and need care – but my soul, too, is worn out. Ah, if I could extract myself for just a few days from this icy atmosphere of criticism, from the perpetual guard over my own words, the expression in my face, my gestures! ... If only I didn't have to think of Bronia I should present my resignation to the Zorawskis this very instant and look for another post, even though this one is so well paid.'[8]

Summer did not improve the situation. Her nervous problem recurred and she acknowledged the fact in a letter to her old school-friend Kazia in October. The news of Kazia's engagement was an excuse for some self-dramatisation and not a little self-pity. 'You tell me you have just lived through the happiest week of your life; and I, during these holidays, have been through such weeks as you will never know. There were some very hard days, and the only thing that softens the memory of them is that in spite of everything I came through it all honestly, with my head high.'[9]

Three years had now dragged by. The veneer over her sensitivities was nowhere near thick enough to protect her for this length of time. The marks left by the experience were deep and lasting. Now a gloomy bout of self-analysis set in. She wrote to cousin Henrika in November, 1888:

> ... I wonder if, when you see me, you will judge that the years I have just passed among humans have done me good or not. Everybody says that I have changed a great deal, physically and spiritually during my stay at Szczuki. This is not surprising. I was barely eighteen when I came here, and what have I not been through! There have been moments which I shall certainly count among the most cruel of my life . . . I feel everything very violently, with a physical violence, and then I give myself a shaking, the vigour of my nature conquers, and it seems to me that I am coming out of a nightmare . . . First principle: never let one's self be beaten down by persons or by events.[10]

Her contract with the Zorawskis was due to end in the summer of 1889. Through the cold and isolated early months of the new year she counted the weeks to Easter when she hoped for a decision on a new governess's post – in Warsaw. And, having landed the job, she impatiently counted the days through the spring until she could take her last backward glance at what she now labelled, 'this provincial hole'.

The job in Warsaw lasted for only a year and it passed by easily. At the end of that year she decided to go back to her father. The financial pressures on Sklodowski, and therefore on Maria, had eased. To supplement his pension he had taken on the directorship of a reformatory near Warsaw. The work did not please him, but to one who had spent each of the last twenty years worrying about how the next was to be paid for, the remuneration had its compensations. Maria herself was able to find work giving private lessons, so that the combined family income rose higher than it had for some years. Bronia in Paris could be financed by her father, and Maria began to put by for her own future.

Not least of the pleasures of being back in Warsaw was re-forging links with the friends she had known at the Floating University. Her exile in the country had separated her from them physically, and without their discussions of ideas and values she had grown confused and dispirited. Now she was back and they were still there, still bright-eyed and fresh-cheeked, still secretly meeting in little groups in quiet apartments, still full of hope and enthusiasm. Poland's future lay, for them, in her words, in the development of 'the intellectual and moral strength of the nation'.[11]

They were aims with which she could identify herself com-pletely. But during these months too her passion for science properly began to catch fire. 'Think of it,' she had written to Jozef in October 1888, 'I am learning chemistry from a book. You can imagine how little I get out of that, but what can I do, as I have no place to make experiments or do practical work?'[12] But now in Warsaw she found a place. Her cousin, Jozef Boguski, had founded what he called grandly The Museum of Industry and Agriculture. The title was designed to hide the fact that it was another of Warsaw's clandestine teaching establishments. It included a small laboratory with apparatus for simple experiments in physics and chemistry. With what time she could find on Sundays and in the evenings Maria could teach herself the simple manual operations of practical science: how to use a blowpipe and carbon-block, handle thermometers, play with gold-leaf electro-scopes, actually distil a clear liquid from a dirty mixture. She found satisfaction her textbooks had not led her to expect. In later life she wrote of these few months' experience,

Though I was taught that the way of progress is neither swift nor easy, this first trial confirmed me in the taste for experi-mental research. [13]

There were other factors too that heightened her interest. There were men in the laboratory with scientific travellers' tales, who spoke with familiarity of legendary nineteenth-century scientists. Her cousin, Boguski, could boast of having been assistant in St Petersburg to the great Russian chemist, Mendeleev. Another of her teachers at the Museum, Napoleon Milicer, had been a pupil of Robert Bunsen. They were distant but heady connections for a girl of sensitivity.

There were also other stimuli around, probing perfectly understandable latent responses. Kazimierz Zorawski appeared briefly during one holiday. Whatever contact was struck, whatever heartstrings were plucked and bitter recrimination or sweet explanations offered, there was no reconciliation. The humiliation remained. But Kazimierz too must have been affected. Warsaw citizens still remember that as an old man, professor of mathematics at Warsaw polytechnic, he used to sit quietly and contemplatively in front of one of the statues of Maria Sklodowska.

Many months had now passed since March 1890, when sister Bronia had written urging her to throw caution to the winds and come to Paris. Bronia, a practical and simple woman, was engaged to a medical student ten years older than her named Dluski. They could provide lodging for Maria in her first academic year at the Sorbonne. Bronia, her practical eye on exchange rates, had even suggested that her sister immediately change her savings into francs, since the rate was favourable. Maria hesitated, entered another brief period of gloom and self-analysis, then avoided a decision by offering the excuse that their father needed her there in Warsaw.

A year and a half later, Bronia, although now pregnant, wrote repeating the offer. Again the letter reduced Maria to introspection and depression, but this time accompanied by an attack of her familiar 'nerves'. It was more than a childish palpitation of excitement: she was close on being 24. Sklodowski wrote to Bronia that her letter had sent Maria into a state of fever. However within a few days Bronia had a typically abrupt letter:

> Now Bronia, I ask you for a definite answer. Decide if you can really take me in at your house, for I can come now. I have enough to pay all my expenses. If, therefore, without depriving yourself of a great deal, you could give me my food, write and say so.[14]

Again the letter was dramatic and not a little self-piteous in

39

the references to the 'cruel trials' the past summer had inflicted on Maria. But the words were token resistance. She had made the crucial decision. Within a few days she was bundling case and bags on to the rack of a third class railway compartment. There was just time to reach Paris for the start of the first quarter courses of 1891 at the Sorbonne.

The little man, her father, who stood on the Warsaw platform to watch the train steam out and wave a sad hand to the youngest of his family, must have wondered at the wisdom of his decision to let her go off like this. It was true she was no longer a girl and had a mind of her own. She was an odd mixture of things: of confused and confusing ideals: of shyness and stubbornness: of astuteness and naïvety. At 24 she was intellectually under-developed. Little else could be expected considering the inadequacy of her education. But she had fallen in love with the idea of intellectual achievement as an aim in itself.

Physically, Maria was still plump, her curves accentuated in the fashion of the day by a corseted wasp-waist. Her hair taken up on top of her head and brushed forward into a curly fringe. She was plain, but if the plumpness disappeared, she could expect to take on a more distinguished appearance. But what her ordinary bodily characteristics disguised was a quite singular quality in a woman conditioned by the educational system of the repressed country of the 1880s: that of ambition.

In a letter to her brother Jozef she had once written,

You will not be surprised to hear that I should suffer enormously, for now that I have lost the hope of ever becoming anybody, all my ambition has been transferred to Bronia and you.[15]

In fact, by writing of it she acknowledged its existence. But ambition for what? The future viewed through the train window on that autumn day was limited to one thing: a proper scientific university education.

It was environmental chance – strait upbringing mixed with sporadic education, financial embarrassment mixed with real and imagined social humiliations – that gave Maria Sklodowska her iron independence and her ambition. Chance could still have taken her on to a track quite different from that of the trans-continental steam train heading for France, and could still easily have diverted her back to Russian-dominated Poland. But what chance could now no longer do was alter her character; that was moulded and immutably fixed before she struggled with her bags on to a platform at the Gare du Nord.

Chapter 4

Paris

Paris was different. There was an intangible but unmistakable quality about the place. Henry James at that time described it as 'the good taste, as it were, of the atmosphere'.[1] Like its people Paris seemed free, vibrant and confident; these were conditions in short supply in Maria's native country. But she was already well able to judge the subtleties of both light and shade of the French character. The Frenchman's obsession with overt individual freedom was just as pronounced then as it is today, just as was the Frenchman's delight and failing, always to go behind the back of established authority, even to the extent of impinging on somebody else's individual freedom.

This insistence on the demonstrable libertarian spirit gave to the Paris of 1891, oozing as it seemed with the material prosperity of a confident, peaceful period, an air of gaiety and obvious frivolity. Maria Sklodowska arrived in this atmosphere like a daisy in a hot house. Everything was in such obvious contrast to her previous experience. The glimpses of bawdy behaviour beneath the flimsy covering over the society's surface were shocking to the newcomer from the sheltered background, but so were the physical attributes of the city breathtaking. It would be difficult for a visitor in 1891 to believe that only twenty years earlier a pall of smoke and a bitter stench of burning had hung over what remained of the Commune and ravaged Paris. Then English and American tourists had turned up, not to admire, but to stare at the scars and to pick over unusual souvenirs.

Now the scars were invisible. The face-lift that Haussmann had planned for the queen of capitals after the fall of the Second Empire had at last been completed and the beauty that resulted could not be denied, even by those who criticised the phenomenal expense of the operation. Haussmann's broad boulevards charmed the eye and the solidity and splendour of the buildings that flanked the boulevards testified to the capital's health.

Maria Sklodowska came from a background where outward appearances counted for little. Naïvely she was looking for what lay underneath the surface glitter. The libertarian spirit of this society provided, along with a sparkling exterior and some plain imperfections, a fertile soil in which creativity could grow. And she was looking to plant a few roots in it. Its remarkable products were all about, though not always immediately recognised for what they were. Only three years earlier César Franck had had his first symphony performed and heard it described as the death of classical harmony; yet within a few more years his statue was being raised and his monumental works described as 'cathedrals in sound'. Only fourteen years earlier Rodin's most mischievous critics had paid his power of observation of the human body its ultimate compliment by accusing him of casting *The Bronze Age* from a living man. Three years before that a journalist looking at a picture by Claude Monet had, with unwise intolerance, called it 'impressionism' and lived to see his one word given greater permanence than all else he ever wrote. Even journalism itself, the ephemeral medium which mirrored the ephemeral and apparently frivolous society, provided the soil for the growth of durable creativity. Had the Polish girl (as would have been quite out of character) bought one of the racily illustrated twenty centime weekly newspaper supplements on the Sunday after her arrival in Paris, she could have read in it short stories by Zola, de Maupassant or Prévost.

Ironically the cultural field Maria Sklodowska had chosen for herself, was, when she arrived in Paris, the one that was responding least to creative stimuli, from within or from abroad. The chances are that, had she had the benefit of up-to-date and informed opinion at the time that she left her home city, she would have ended up, not in Paris, but in Berlin, Heidelberg, London or Cambridge.

It was in France that biologists were most hostile to what was probably the most far-reaching single hypothesis of the century: Darwin's theory of evolution. No other advanced scientific nation dug its heels in in the face of the evidence with quite such resolution. The reason for the depths of the resistance is perhaps that it was chiefly French apple-carts that Darwin was upsetting. Cuvier, for example, believed in a historical genesis, and Lamarck insisted that animal and human characteristics acquired by one generation in its lifetime could be passed down to the next. Both theories would be discredited when the bare facts of Darwinism were faced.[2]

What was perhaps most surprising of all was that even the most outstanding French scientific genius of the century, Louis Pasteur, should have shown reluctance to accept Darwinism. But if Pasteur showed a tendency to scientific conservatism, his achievements provided ample compensation. Maria Sklodowska arrived in Paris towards the end of his life, when his phenomenal creativity was at an end. But he was still a beacon illuminating the whole of French science. As a chemist, bacteriologist and immunologist he had used series of simple and beautiful experiments to attack major scientific problems; his work had led to fundamental changes of thought that were to have a lasting influence on science.

Pasteur's spectacular triumphs applying biology to medicine were still fresh in mind. It was only six years since he had used extract from the spinal cord of a rabbit to inoculate a small boy infected with rabies. His calculated gamble had succeeded and the child had lived. In not much more than a year the lives of 2,000 men and women had been saved by the same method. But the work of Pasteur which affected most of his fellow countrymen and which many Frenchmen warmly welcomed as his greatest triumph was his staggering ability to turn his science to their money-making activities. In his lifetime much of Pasteur's work had been applied, and applied so well that it had had a magnificent effect on the French economy. His major discoveries in alcohol and vinegar fermentation, and in wine and silkworm diseases, were significant because, among other benefits, they created profits. It was on the wave of the shock reaction to France's defeat by Prussia in 1870 that Pasteur set out to investigate problems in beer manufacture and preservation in order to give France a brewing industry to compete with Germany's. In the end his success was such that T. H. Huxley guessed that the profits to France of Pasteur's applied science exceeded the cost of the war-time indemnity which the nation owed her conquerors.

There were many other examples of applied science and they could be seen with no difficulty as Maria Sklodowska's transcontinental steam train pulled into its Paris station in 1891. The single huge symbol of mechanical invention could not be avoided even by those who wanted to try: the Eiffel Tower. It was, as Gustave Eiffel himself described it, the 300 metre metallic flagstaff of the nation. That it was a magnificent feat of engineering was undeniable, that it was functional was questionable, and that it was beautiful was, to say the least, contestable. So vile did some Parisians consider its plan that an opposition 'Committee of Three Hundred', one member for every metre, which included such cultured inhabitants of the capital as Gounod, Dumas *fils* and de Maupassant, was rapidly formed; it failed to prevent the erection of the monster to its place of gross dominance over the city. When he saw it Edmond de Goncourt cried, 'Can any one imagine anything more outrageous to the eye of an old man of taste'.[3] Tasteful or tasteless, it was built with a purpose. It was the centrepiece of the grand Universal Exhibition of 1889 mounted to mark the centenary of the Revolution and, more significantly, to show the public what scientific industry could do for a modern nation.

The Eiffel Tower was the symbol, the rest was merchandisable reality. By the date of Maria Sklodowska's arrival, flickering gasjets had given way to incandescent mantles; electric lamps were already being installed along the boulevards; there was a gay new variety of colour in women's dresses, dyed by new compounds; three- and four-wheeled vehicles, driven by internal combustion engines, were appearing on the streets.

But these were the products of Science's hands; what Maria was looking for was Science's mind. Intellectual challenge had brought her to Paris, not its biproducts. And in one section of the city, she was told, she could learn to meet this intellectual challenge.

That first day when Maria Sklodowska walked along the streets on the hill above the river on which the Sorbonne stands she covered this tiny area of ground. It was not to disappoint her. She was to spend more or less the whole of the rest of her working life there. If her mind was not what Pasteur might call prepared, it was certainly in a most suggestible state. Then as now the *Quartier Latin* had a flamboyant, brash and predominantly youthful population. They crowded its pavements, littered its cafés and used its bookstalls as open-air reading rooms. When there was the chance of bizarre or eccentric behaviour, they displayed it. When the fashion in hair was short they wore it long; when the fashion was long, they wore it longer.

Eccentric behaviour was a garish top-dressing; it covered a functional society and disguised the depths. The intellectual climate of the *Quartier Latin* dominated the whole of France, and arguably the whole of Europe. The University of Paris which fostered the climate was the premier university of the country. Every day 12,000 of its members moved in and around its doors, absorbing its message and imposing themselves on the life in this square kilometre or so of left bank.

The front of the Sorbonne was covered with a mesh of scaffolding for its face-lift when Maria first approached it along the avenue of plane trees from the Place de la Sorbonne. Today a statue of Auguste Comte, the positivist philosopher, dominates this square. His bust rests on a plinth dedicated to 'Order and Progress'. Maria Sklodowska would have approved. She might not have approved of the two statues that guard the clock above the great pillared entrance to the Sorbonne: two graces, bosomy and timeless, with little else to do other than watch time pass by as they looked out over Comte's cropped head. Maria had no time for this image of womankind. She intended to compete with man on equal terms.

She spent the first few months of her new life in France with her sister and brother-in-law. Dluski had set up in medical practice in La Villette, a suburb about an hour by horse-bus from the Sorbonne. It meant that Maria could do a good day's work in a library or a laboratory, then withdraw to the reassuring shell of a real Polish room with its familiar knick-knacks strung here and there. It provided a comfortingly gradual introduction to new habits and new values. Besides, it was only a few steps from the Gare du Nord, the end of the umbilical cord that led to the east. If this new city threatened to overwhelm her she could live with the belief that it was a simple process to fling herself into a train aimed at Poland.

She had a single-minded objective: to learn. However, the odds were stacked against her making the best use of this faculty. She had had no *baccalaureat* preparation nor the seven years of *lycée* that went along with it. There were also other disadvantages to studying scientific subjects in Paris, many of which she could not be aware of.

At the beginning of the nineteenth century France could have claimed to lead the world in its science teaching: some of the highly successful German techniques of scientific organisation and research, then coming to fruition, had been built on French experience. But by 1870 the British journal *Nature* was calling 'Imperial France ... perhaps the most conservative in science of any country in Europe': and that meant the world. The first professor of industrial and agricultural chemistry was not appointed in France until 1876, and by 1890 there was only one chair of theoretical physics. The Ministry of Education invested very little in university science during this period and this was reflected in the style in which research was carried out.

But spartan scientific conditions were of no great matter to a first-year student with no scientific tradition to draw on. The tradition of student life in the *Quartier* was much more personally important. When, after only a short stay with her sister and brother-in-law, Maria made the decision to leave the Dluski apartment and move into lodgings near the university the life-style she could expect to take up was primitive and poor. It was shared by many others. There were thousands of students all around her living under almost identical conditions.

The garret she found was at the top of six flights of stairs; it was hot in summer, cold in winter. She carried coal for the stove up the six flights and shivered when the ration had burnt itself out. When in the first winter the temperature dropped so low that the water she carried up for her washbasin froze, she piled her coats on top of her blankets and climbed into bed, in no way warmed by the knowledge that in the dozens of garrets within shouting distance dozens of similar coats were piled in similar fashion on dozens of similar beds.

A myth has grown up about the poverty of her student days. She *was* poor, but so were most students. Her allowance from Poland was small and had to be divided between tuition fees, and the price of life in the garret. When the cost of fuel was high there was little left for food; the main protein cooked over her spirit stove was usually egg. In student history the omelette can probably claim to have sustained more educations than any other stimulant.

The effort of physical self-denial during that first year and the discovery of what it was like to be poor, and not merely to be the detached observer of somebody else's poverty, was a revelation. The life, she later wrote, was 'painful from certain points of view'[4] but there was something about it she actually discovered she enjoyed. The life had 'for all that, a real charm for me'.

In that first year she discovered that her physical needs were few. Her old egocentric 'nervous problems' disappeared – in spite of the fact that she was underfed. The new stimulant, and the new worry, was the intellectual challenge. She found that she could centre her whole life round the studies which the classrooms and the laboratories of the Sorbonne opened up to her; but she was also deeply troubled by the fact that, on many occasions in those first months, she was totally unable to follow the lectures, since often she could not follow spoken French, so different from what she had learned to read in books and papers. More important, she lacked the mathematics necessary for basic understanding of the physical sciences. There was a great gap from her Polish education, and it had to be filled. Before the year was out she was spending all her free time in the library; when this did not fill the gap she began to work into the night in her garret. And by the end of the year, when she still had feelings of inadequacy, she decided to stay on in Paris for more tuition in mathematics.

The single-mindedness with which she attacked her subjects

inevitably meant that she had to begin to live an almost un-relievedly solitary existence. In her classes there were no other Polish students. Her spoken French was still poor, and the French habit of mocking those who mutilate the language did not help the problem. Above all, she was a naturally shy and reserved creature. At no time of life did she welcome anybody calling her by her Christian name. At first she kept up a few relations with other Poles she met among the crowds of foreigners in the *Quartier Latin*; she would go on walks with them to slake a nostalgic thirst for Warsaw, or go with them to political gather-ings, where she could renew her old fervent interest in the nationalist cause or the positivist question. But politics were being pushed into the shadows by the deep interest she was de-veloping for scientific subjects. Soon these took over to the exclusion of everything else. By her second year she had severed almost every one of the personal relationships that might have distracted her from study.

What surprised her – and she was now 24 – was that the condi-tion of solitude she had deliberately imposed on herself was more than an adequate substitute for personal relations. 'All my mind was centred on my studies,' she wrote. 'All that I saw and learned that was new delighted me. It was like a new world opened to me, the world of science, which I was at last permitted to know in all liberty.'[5]

She had become addicted to learning, like a junky to heroin, and with some of the same alienation from the society she was living in. The notebooks she kept for her first courses are models of patience and obsessiveness. In a neat, controlled hand which never varied during the whole of her life, she kept an account of every precious scientific word injected so acceptably into her system. Lovingly annotated, physics and calculus notes in 1891 move on to elasticity and mechanics in 1892, and electrostatics and kinematics in 1893. Dates and numbers, carefully kept for each lesson, chart her progress from classroom to classroom under some of France's leading mathematicians and physicists: Brillouin, Painlevé, Lippmann and Appell.

As her second year passed and her comprehension of both the

language and her subject increased, so did the depths of her self-imposed solitude. But self-denial, she found, had its rewards; it was the characteristic that had made it possible for so many aspirant natural philosophers working in dour, bourgeois or Calvinist countries, where the tradition of devoted and hard work was admired, to rise to pre-eminence. Those who adopt it and benefit from its pleasures often tend to adopt a certain smugness along with it. Maria again, was no exception: 'If sometimes I felt lonely, my usual state of mind was one of calm and great moral satisfaction.'[6] She suffered the pain of self-denial for a great deal of the rest of her life so that she could enjoy its simultaneous rewards.

Nevertheless, aspiring to the loftier riches of the mind still left certain mundane problems. Her savings and her father's allowance gave her a budget of 40 roubles each month. When in the early months of 1893 Sklodowski learnt that Maria was proposing to sit for her degree in physics (*licence ès sciences physiques*), he was sent into his usual mother-hen-like flurry of worry as to how it could be paid for. He found it difficult not to worry over the future of his youngest child. When Maria was staying with the Dluskis, she had thrown herself into the spirit of a patriotic fancy dress party and draped herself in national colours as 'Poland breaking her bonds', and she wrote expecting him to approve. He did not. He worried over the possible consequences:

> I deplore your taking such active part in the organisation of this theatrical representation. Even though it be a thing done in all innocence it attracts attention to its organisers, and you certainly know that there are persons in Paris who inspect your behaviour with the greatest care, who take note of the names of those who are in the forefront and who send information about them here, to be used as might be useful. This can be the source of great annoyance, and even forbid such persons access to certain professions. Thus, those who wish to earn their bread in Warsaw in the future without being exposed to various dangers, may remain unknown. Events such as concerts, balls, etc., are described by certain correspondents for newspapers, who mention names. It would be a great grief to

me if your name were mentioned one day. This is why, in my previous letters, I have made a few criticisms, and have begged you to keep to yourself as much as possible. . . .[7]

Clearly Sklodowski adopted his most pessimistic Polonius stance because he was judging his daughter's involvements by the passionate interest she had shown in social and political activities before she had left Warwaw and which she might be tempted to continue on her return. He was not then aware how pronounced her swing of interests had become.

Kazimierz Dluski, the handsome thick-bearded brother-in-law watched with a certain interest and not a little amusement, when the girl came to his apartment. Supposedly *in loco parentis*, he recognised from the start that the chances of maintaining authority over the serious and self-willed girl were slim. He and Maria adopted a friendly scepticism towards each other, which probably kept the relationship all the healthier. She was irritated by his continuous chatter, his turbulent sociability and extrovert nationalist activity (he had had to take refuge abroad, having been suspected of taking part in an attempt on Czar Alexander II's life). He on his part made fun of her over-devotion to her academic ambitions and her tendency to self-dramatisation; he gently teased her by calling her life in the garret 'the heroic period' of her life.

Heroic or not, it was productive. The time came when Maria had to face the examination which would test whether she had mastered the language of physics, and also conquered the French language sufficiently to express the grammar of science. It would be a public demonstration of her abilities and, as on all similar occasions, she worried herself sick in anticipation at the thought of it. In letters to her family she fretted over her likely inability to meet her examination papers in anything like a prepared state. The sense of theatre and personal exposure in lecture halls and examination rooms caused her hands to tremble on even the least testing of occasions. That day in 1893 when she began her final examination was, she knew well, a test for life. Failure would mean return to Warsaw, and the governess-ship. Worse, it would be a public display of her personal inadequacies.

Typically, she had over-reacted. She emerged from the ordeal with more than her self-confidence secure. She took first place as *licenciée ès sciences physiques* – scarcely bad going for a nervy girl who three years before had had no formal scientific training. But her ambition to compete and to succeed did not end with her as front runner in this highly competitive field. The period of self-denial and solitude had reached its peak of productivity and therefore of pleasure. Looking back on these two years of intense loneliness she called them 'one of the best memories of my life'.[8] She had also seen from the brief periods she had spent in chemical and physical laboratories, how indispensable was a mathematical background to the development of a fruitful systematic approach to the newly developing sciences. She decided to take a degree in mathematics.

Her success in the physics degree meant that she could return to Warsaw for the long vacation of 1893. Whatever pangs of homesickness she might have had were surprisingly easily dealt with. The year to be given over to mathematics was eased by the award in Warsaw of the Alexandrovitch Scholarship given to outstanding students wanting to work abroad. It was worth six hundred roubles: enough to live on for more than a year. It removed the immediate financial difficulties that might have stood in the way of her return to Paris. It was even with a sense of relief that she got there. Immediately on her return in September 1893 she was writing to her brother Jozef: 'I hardly need say that I am delighted to be back in Paris. It was very hard for me to separate again from Father, but I could see that he was well, very lively, and that he could do without me—especially as you are living in Warsaw. And as for me, it is my whole life that is at stake. It seemed to me, therefore, that I could stay on here without remorse on my conscience.'[9] Ambition had now taken precedence over family ties. Within another six months she was again telling her brother: 'I regret only one thing, which is that the days are so short and they pass so quickly.'[10] And they were crowned with success. She emerged at the end of the academic year as a *licenciée ès sciences mathematiques*, this time occupying second place in the examination list.

She also emerged with a clearer idea of where the ambitious streak she recognised in herself might lead. It was strongly conditioned by the attitudes of the young professors and demonstrators in chemistry, physics and mathematics she was now meeting in her Sorbonne classes. These men were in turn strongly influenced by a scientific cultural tradition which was extraordinarily powerful at that period. It had as its central prop one hallowed dogma. Previous ages had never held this up for the young to admire: nor would future ages. But in the 1890s and for the years to follow, it was pre-eminent: that science should be *pure*.

Purity in science meant that the process of science should be carried out only with a view to the widening and deepening of knowledge. It should not be carried out with a view to its practical application to any particular problem. If it could be applied (and as it happens there is no fundamental research which is not sooner or later applied) then so much the better for mankind, but this should not be an original aim.

The attitude was widely held. It pervaded the whole of scientific thought, and it was not restricted to France. In Britain, for example, when Lord Rayleigh, the physicist, was presenting an address on behalf of the Royal Society to W. H. Perkin (who had made the first synthetic dye), he left his audience in no doubt that the sons of gentlemen scientists ought not to dabble in applied science. He excused Perkin's association with the coal-tar business by reminding them that they should not forget that 'this wonderful industrial and social development could have been initiated and carried on only through the methods that have been established for the pursuit of knowledge as a reward in itself and primarily for its own sake'. Applied science continued to be *infra-dig* in Britain for years. By the turn of the century Britain was importing the bulk of its dyestuffs from Germany. In 1914 British troops had to set out for battlefields in France wearing uniforms in shades of British-made dyes ranging from light olive to dark brown.

France's traditions were above all influenced by the ageing

Pasteur. Nobody could deny that his greatest work had been done with a practical aim in view, from inoculation against rabies to improving beer yields. Yet it was the intellectual achievement of his systematic scientific research, not its practical results, which was held up for emulation. Pasteur had gone to some pains to explain his credo to Napoleon III's aide-de-camp: 'Any scientist who allows himself to be lured by the prospect of industrial applications automatically ceases to be the servant of pure science; he clutters up his life and thinking with preoccupations which paralyse his faculty for discovery.'

If Pasteur's acquired bourgeois ambitions, his snobbery and his jingoism are not beyond criticism, at least his scientific values in the time in which they operated were unimpeachable. 'It is my opinion,' he said, 'that disinterested scientific thinking ought to be encouraged, because it is one of the prime sources of that progress in pure research without which there can be no progress in the application of science to practical production.'

These were the finest motives expected of scientists: and Maria Sklodowska learnt to admire them. The word which Pasteur and the French used to describe the characteristic was 'disinterested-ness'; she took it as her own. It was to be her highest form of praise: her watchword for all her future operations in science. It was to be difficult to justify at times, but she was to stick to it with the single-mindedness with which she clung to every other adopted precept.

The first stage of her ambition – to give herself a man-sized scientific education – had been achieved. She could now look over that brow of the hill to something great and challenging: to make her own contribution to scientific knowledge: but to *pure* scientific knowledge.

If the triumph of the years 1891–93 had been achieved by an iron self-discipline with the rigorous exclusion of personal relationships, then 1894, undoubtedly as a result of the success in the physics examination, allowed a slight relaxation. She was now 26 years old, and, as a result of the attic existence and an inadequate student diet, had lost some of the puppy fat, and with it the bloom of youth. But the gain had been substantial. She had fined down well. A thinner face and body, sad eyes and a quiet collected composure gave her a delicate appearance that can only have been attractive to any man looking for a presentable intellectual companion. In fact 1894, now that she had decided to lower some of the barriers to her fellow men, produced a certain embarrassment of riches.

Chapter 5

Pierre

She was like a hot-house plant put out in the spring sunshine after a long winter under glass, and there was more than one young man passing through the Place de la Sorbonne or between the benches of the inorganic chemistry laboratory who stopped to admire her delicacy. One of them, a Monsieur Lamotte, who had watched the shy, simply dressed figure drifting through the streets of the Latin Quarter, mistook the delicacy for fragility. Clearly with a view to giving her some permanent protection, he courted her during the early months of the year in formal fashion, writing stiff and correct letters in a feminine hand, expressing the profundity of his friendship. He recognised the seriousness of her ambitions and encouraged her work. But like all over-ardent young lovers he found it difficult to recognise the signs when the object of his affections began to try to brush him off.

Maria prepared to pack her bags for the long vacation in Poland and told him that he would quickly forget her once she was out of sight. The result, naturally enough, was that she was never out of his mind, and the one-sided affair dragged on. For he was a stout fellow, hoping as he said, 'to win you still by my patient love', though he sorrowfully admitted that, 'circumstances were against me'.[1]

The most significant circumstance was the appearance on the scene of a serious rival. Through the whole of that year the postman was carrying two sets of ardent correspondence to Mademoiselle Sklodowska (now calling herself Marie in the French fashion). The style of the second set could not have been more different from that of the first. Untidy, informal, mature, always thoughtful, sometimes introspective, but never pitying or self-pitying.

She met Pierre Curie at the home of a Polish physicist staying in Paris. As she went into the room and saw him framed by a french

window leading on to a balcony, she noted his physical characteristics well. He was tall with auburn hair cut *en brosse* and wore
a small pointed beard. The large limpid eyes gave him a dreamer's
self-absorbed look. She thought of him as a young man, though
he neither looked nor indeed was young; he was 35 years old. A
rapport between the two of them immediately sprang up and she
summed up the result of that first day's conversation in the formal
fashion he would have avoided: 'He expressed the desire to see
me again and to continue our conversation of that evening on
scientific and social subjects in which he and I were both interested, and on which we seemed to have similar opinions.'[2]

Curie had too many points in his favour for Lamotte to be a
serious contender for the young woman's interest during that
summer. Perhaps Curie was wise enough to realise that his most
serious opposition would come not from a man but from the somewhat defensive and mentally tough young woman herself. He, like
Lamotte, knew that she planned to re-visit Poland and the possibility was that, having completed her degree, she would not return
to France. The first part of her original plan to give herself a basic
university education and then perhaps use it in Poland's national
interest, was now complete. It was the application of the education that was at issue and Curie, like Lamotte, set out to dissuade
her from staying in Poland with what he had to offer. It was quite
considerable.

He was a physicist and highly educated: both these were aims
to which she passionately aspired. Like her he was a passive
idealist and was interested in the social questions that had once so
held her attention but which she had now abandoned for scientific study.

Also like her he was shy and introverted: she always felt more
secure with people of character similar to her own. A friend of
Marie, when she met Pierre Curie for the first time, found his
reserve at first intimidating, but noticed it hid a simple desire to
please.[3] What expressive dash he had in his character was chiefly
put into his work and his written fluency. But he was not so shy
as to prevent him persuading Marie to let him climb the six floors
to her attic, sit on her hard wooden chair, and talk of his work and

his ideals. He had in mind, she soon learned, a single serious role for himself, entirely devoted to science and the rewards its purity of discovery had to offer. The simplicity of it all appealed to her and he began to influence her thinking. Before that summer was out he was recommending a text on mechanics and a treatise on analysis as well as offering her a copy of Zola's *Lourdes*; he gently flattered her by telling her that in it she would find opinions on religion that would coincide with her own.

Religion had never been part of his education or make up even in childhood. He denied finding any attraction in the idea of fatalism, yet quite out of his rational character, he had quite an interest in superstition and the supernatural. One spring day, soon after they had met, he took her to a mid-Lent country fair. They moved through the thick crowd of blue-jacketed workers, straw-hatted beaux, basket-laden perspiring wives, and parasoled girls. He turned from her for a few seconds, and then looked back down at her. She was gone: swept on and away by the crowd. It took him several minutes to find her again. The memory of the incident worried him and he was later to remind her of it: 'It seems to me that our relationship will suddenly be interrupted like this without either one of us wishing it. I am not a fatalist but this will probably be a consequence of our characters. I shall never know how to act at the right moment.'⁴ It was a strange remark to make at this stage of their acquaintance.

Soon after their first meeting too, he published, in April 1894, a paper describing his latest work: it was one in an already distinguished line in physical studies. To the young woman student for whom publication of experimental results must have seemed the acme of achievement, Curie's distinction in having work printed in the proceedings of the Académie des Sciences, must have been impressive. He scribbled on top of one of the off-prints his dedication: 'To Mademoiselle Sklodowska, with the respect and friendship of the author, P. Curie.' Its title was, 'On symmetry in physical phenomena. Symmetry in an electric field and in a magnetic field.' It was not exactly what every girl might expect from a passionate admirer; but Curie in this case had judged her well.

She was interested deeply in what he did, and she was beginning to be equally interested in what he was. He was the son of a humanist doctor, and had moved easily and painlessly into scientific subjects. His father had a firm free-thinking philosophy, and did not subject either of his two sons to a regular school curriculum.

Pierre had a quick grasp of mathematical concepts and he discovered the beauty of the subject in the formative years of his basic education. He had in particular an unusual and easy comprehension of spatial phenomena: of how nature arranges three-dimensional objects and events – in flowers, and sea-shells, and crystals – and he learnt how to apply a mathematical understanding to them. This conceptual sense which made it possible for him to exercise and to express complex situations in simple rational terms could only have been developed in a man with highly developed contemplative abilities. These he had in abundance; his friends described him more simply as a dreamer. He himself recognised the necessity of being so if he was to achieve all he believed he could.

We must eat, drink, sleep, be idle, love, touch the sweetest things of life and yet not succumb to them. It is necessary that, in doing all this, the higher thoughts to which one is dedicated remain dominant and continue their unmoved course in our poor heads. It is necessary to make a dream of life, and to make a dream a reality[5].

It was the dream he would convince Marie Sklodowska they could truly live together.

But the other life that had been a dream-like success because of its deep emotional content, was that spent with his elder brother Jacques. The two boys had responded in entirely different fashions to their authoritarian father. Pierre, the quiet introvert, absorbed the parental discipline with ease and developed a strong attachment for both his parents. Jacques, an extrovert like the father, had had more problems. The personalities clashed, sometimes unpleasantly. Later Pierre told Marie of the family disputes: 'Mother is very much afraid of Jacques quarrelling with Father: they are both violent.'[6] Marie Sklodowska never found the same shortcomings in the father; their characters were complimentary, and they were always to get on well.

Jacques had turned to Pierre for the satisfying blood relationship his father did not give. Jacques was more ascetic than Pierre but in the end more easily seduced from the 'priest's existence' of laboratory research which so attracted Pierre. As boys the brothers had been joined together in sympathy of thought and action that in his 35 years Pierre Curie had not met again. As he had told Marie Sklodowska, he frequently looked back to the days before Jacques had gone to teach in Provence, when they did *everything* together, the times they had the same opinions on most things, and the situations in which their thoughts were so in unison that 'it was not necessary to speak to understand'.

Pierre was 21 and Jacques 24 when they began to work together as physicists. Their first research followed an original observation that dates back to pre-history: that some types of crystals lying in a fire will attract particles of wood and ash to their surfaces. Tourmaline was one of the crystals to behave in this way and the property of its different faces to acquire different electric charges when heated to different temperatures was studied in nineteenth-century France, as well as in other countries. This phenomenon, the generation of these small amounts of electricity, is known as *pyroelectricity*. The Curie brothers, by a consideration of the symmetry with which the matter in crystals is arranged, reasoned that if a crystal is deformed by mechanical stress, such as by the application of pressure, opposite faces of the crystal should acquire opposite charges. What they were suggesting was that it should be possible, using the right crystal, to turn mechanical energy into electrical energy.

They had soon devised an experiment to put their theory to the test and in 1880 had published their first paper together on the phenomenon of 'polar electricity' produced by pressure.[7] Later it was to get the name *piezoelectricity* (from the Greek, 'to press'). In the next two years they published seven papers together, including a study of the conditions and laws under which their discovery operated.

They were also able to show that the opposite effect is true: that is, that if an electric charge is applied to a crystal then the crystal should be deformed. They realised they now had a direct way of measuring very small quantities of electricity. They were both exceptionally clever with their hands, had the right kind of delicate mechanical skills to be good instrument makers, found a way of amplifying the small deformation of a quartz crystal, and soon had their instrument: an electrometer. They called it their *quartz piezo-electrique*. This method of measuring small electric currents – a refined combination of engineering and scientific skills – was to remain for several years a solution looking for a problem. Then it was Marie Curie's problem that it solved.

After his beloved Jacques left to marry and to take up a university appointment at the other end of France in Montpellier, Pierre found himself a job as Laboratory Chief at the School of Industrial Physics and Chemistry. He had been on the same rung of the teaching ladder for ten years when Marie Skłodowska met him. Much of his time there had been spent on the work he loved best, that which most easily suited his solitary, introspective nature, and made most fruitful use of his conceptual abilities.

He had begun a theoretical study of symmetry; it was the most abstract of his work derived from his love of mathematics and his observant eye for nature and it was that which gave him greatest satisfaction. Throughout his life he loved the countryside and things in it. He enjoyed looking at a frog, a spider's web, a human hand, and observing the consistency of their regularities and irregularities. He followed in a long tradition of men who have studied naturally occurring objects: objects whose symmetry was apparently as simple as a four-petal flower, or apparently as complex, but just as beautiful as the skeleton of a radiolarian, the single-celled sea creature. These observations led other men to invent and draw complicated symmetries for their own amusement and delight to rival those they saw in nature; the mediaeval Moorish mosaics of the Alhambra are among the best examples of the art taken to high perfection in two dimensions. The next stage of sensual reward men could derive from these patterns was to analyse them mathematically, then further to analyse three-dimensional structures such as those of atoms in the lattices of simple crystals.

It was his direct sympathy with this search for beauty and order that led Curie to this kind of contemplative study and to his first work on crystal symmetry; this in turn led him too to a general principle of symmetry, which he worked on over three years. He saw in a much wider sense how the general principles could be applied to physics as a whole. The work which he published between 1883 and 1885 foresaw many of the applications of symmetry on which much modern physics depends.

By 1891 he had arrived at the subject which he eventually felt held enough practical interest and sufficient theoretical potential to turn into a doctoral thesis. This was an investigation of the magnetic properties of different substances at different temperatures. It was pioneering work, which began a great French tradition in the subject. It led, via a student of his called Paul Langevin, to the Nobel Prize for Louis Néel in 1970 for his work on anti-ferromagnetism.

Pierre Curie's work had widespread application even in his lifetime. And although his status in the academic world during most of his life was humble, the fame of this underpaid, over-worked teacher in a fairly obscure Paris school spread far beyond the boundaries of France. Lord Kelvin, the Scot whose singular and sometimes eccentric approach to scientific and engineering problems had given him a prodigious world-wide reputation, noticed what the young Curie brothers had done and took an interest in Pierre's work. At that time Curie could not have hoped for more eminent scientific patronage. Kelvin, then the doyen of British physics, would write him in English in a scrawly hand, as typically bold and disorganised as the man, averaging three words to the line on note-paper surrounded by a thick black mourning edge; with exceptional courtesy the ancient peer would ask for permission to visit the young physicist's laboratory to look at what was going on there. A few years later he would persuade Pierre to have one of the electrometers built, packed and sent for his own use.

Kelvin was only the first of many to see the possible applications of piezoelectricity. Crystal frequency control in broadcasting was a technical mushroom. During World War II the United States alone used something close to 50,000,000 quartz crystal elements. In solid state physics now the hunt for new piezoelectric materials continues in an attempt to satisfy twentieth-century technology's demands for smaller and smaller electronic circuit components.

But Pierre Curie's attitude to the applications of his work was, to say the least, ambivalent. In 1894 he had already set his ideals: purity and the disinterestedness of the scientist. In idealist terms to inspire Marie Sklodowska, he had talked to her of his dreams in her garret bedroom, and he had written her letters confidently predicting that these dreams could be turned to reality and happiness for them both. Yet at the same time he had written up, in a half-hearted fashion, a few patent specifications on devices he had designed such as an aperiodic balance.

In 1888 he had ceded the patent for his precision balance to the Central Chemical Products Company at a 10% royalty for its exploitation and for other benefits. The transaction gave him little pleasure, at least none that he recorded and as it turned out, precious little income.

But in 1894 nothing was further from the mind of Marie Sklodowska than possible applications, then or in the future, of the obviously impressive work of this gentle physicist. Applications were vulgar: she saw Pierre as scientifically refined. As a physicist the credentials of scientific creativity he possessed easily satisfied her scrutiny. However, at that moment she had something else on her mind: her own future.

Chapter 6

A Sense of Values

When she set off for Poland at the end of the academic term neither of her two suitors knew whether she would return. Lamotte knew that she had tried to write him out of her life. Curie knew, however, that although her sentiments for Poland were still strong, her ties with her father and family were no longer such that they could not be broken by the attractions of a full scientific future. Lamotte set about writing his acceptance of fate in a fine formal hand. Curie set about winning Marie back with all his literary skill.

Curie began his letter with no form of address beyond the date, August 10th, 1894. He knew that she resented the over-familiarity of 'Marie', and he rejected the formality of 'Mademoiselle' which Lamotte was simultaneously using.

We have promised ourself (it's true isn't it?) to have at least a great friendship, one for the other. If only you won't change your mind! No promises are binding and these are the things you can't command. It would be a wonderful thing, however, and this I wouldn't dare hope for, to pass our lives close to each other hypnotised in our dreams; your patriotic dream, our humanitarian dream, and our scientific dream.

Of all these dreams it's the last alone that I believe to be legitimate. I mean by that, that we are powerless to change the social state, and even if not, we should not know what to do; in taking action of any sort we could never be sure that we were doing more harm than good by slowing down some inevitable evolution. On the contrary, from the scientific point of view we could hope to do something; the ground is more solid here and all discoveries, no matter how small, remain once they have been acquired. . . .

. . . It is agreed that we shall be great friends, but if you leave

France within a year it would really be too platonic a friendship: that of two creatures who would never see each other again. Wouldn't it be better for you to stay with me? I know that this question annoys you, and I won't speak of it again: also I feel thoroughly unworthy of you from all points of view.[1]

There is no doubt that Marie's annoyance was based on the Victorian sexual code, deeply ingrained in her by her upbringing. The carryings-on of left-bank Paris were too advanced for her to adopt at 26 years of age; for when Curie asked her to stay with him, that is precisely what he meant. He would return to the subject later. A properly brought up young lady in the confined society of Poland at the time could be expected to be thoroughly shocked at such an expression of free-thinking – and she was. Marie Sklodowska gave a proper response.

Curie ended his letter by dropping the broadest hint that he would be willing to travel to Fribourg, where she was to stay with the physicist friends who had introduced them, and there meet her 'by chance'. Her reply was non-committal. Four days later he was writing again, undecided whether he was right or wrong to have thrown up the chance of a few days by her side: 'Wouldn't it perhaps have doubled the friendship we have and given us the added strength not to forget one another in these two and a half months that separate us?'

He recognised what enormous importance she attached to her newly discovered independence.

I don't know why I've taken it into my head to keep you in France, and to exile you from your country and your friends without having anything to offer you in exchange for the sacrifice.

I find that you are a little pretentious when you say that you are perfectly free. We are all of us more or less slaves of our affections, slaves of the prejudices of those we love. We also have to earn our living and because of that become cogs in a machine, etc.

The most painful things are the concessions we have to make to the prejudices of the society around us where, more or less often, we make them according to our weakness or strength. If we don't make enough of them we are crushed; if we make too many we become vile and disgusted with ourselves. Here I am, far from the principles I used to have 10 years ago. I believed then that I had to do everything in excess and never make a single concession to the environment. I believed I had to exaggerate defects as well as good qualities. I only wore blue shirts like workmen etc.

In the end you see I have become very old and I am very feeble.[2]

In early September he was writing from Marseilles, this time in a slight panic, since her last letter had led him to believe that she really meant it when she said she would not return to Paris. He told her of a trip he had just made in the Auvergne with his brother Jacques. At times, he said, it had seemed like the old days when they had once lived together. But beautiful as this recollection of times past was, he recognised it as an illusion and saw that their once perfect communion could never return. By implication of course, a new communion could fill the void: but that he left unsaid.

None the less he well knew that he had competition for her favours. To prevent her thinking that she was the only woman seriously to have twisted his heart-strings, he told her a precautionary tale from his past:

You have an astonishing way of understanding egoism. When I was 20 a terrible thing happened: in terrible circumstances I lost a girl I had known since childhood who I loved very much; I lack the courage to tell you all about it. I was very much to blame; I have had and I always will have great remorse about it all. I went through days and nights with a fixed idea. I experienced a kind of delight in torturing myself. Then I vowed in good faith to lead the existence of a priest and moreover I promised myself only to interest myself in things, and to think no more either of myself or of human beings. I have often asked myself whether this withdrawal from life wasn't simply a device which I used against myself to give me the right to forget.[3]

There was an apparently casual postscript to this letter. She had not replied to his previous one. Perhaps it had not arrived. Or was it perhaps that it might have seemed too forward? 'There was not much in particular in it', he claimed – but nevertheless he repeated the important question which it contained: 'I asked you if you would like to rent an apartment with me in Rue Mouffetard; it has windows looking on to gardens. The apartment can be divided into two independent parts'!

By September 17th he had heard that she had decided to return to Paris. He was, of course, delighted and even before she arrived began to look for ways of keeping her there permanently. He told her she could easily get a job as a teacher in a *lycée* or an *école normale* – 'if you were to become French'.

He showed her photograph to his brother who gave a curt but accurate assessment of her character. 'She has a decided air about her,' said Jacques: '*even stubborn.*'

Even though Marie was not thoroughly shocked by the suggestion that they live, if not in sin, then next door to it, she was by no means ready yet to sacrifice her independence. When she returned in October Curie's Rue Mouffetard idea was dropped. Her sister, Bronia, was now practising medicine and had taken a surgery in Rue de Chateaudun. Marie was able to have it for her own use out of surgery hours. She meantime took up with more seriousness the experimental side of physics at one of the Sorbonne's laboratories, so that she could look with care for a subject that would make a suitable doctoral thesis.

At last Pierre Curie persuaded her to visit his parents. He was proud of them. He took her to their home in Sceaux, an attractive little town, whose inhabitants had once served a fine Louis XIV chateau and its magnificent park, and which was now a southern suburb of Paris. Dr Eugène Curie's house, itself plant-covered, stood in a bower of a garden in the Rue des Sablons; later the street would be renamed after his son. On Sundays friends and neighbours visited their doctor to play bowls and chess. The serene atmosphere attracted the Polish girl. Pierre, the favourite of the two sons, had told her that his parents were 'exquisite'.[4] Happily, she agreed. Between the authoritarian old man and herself there sprang up an excellent understanding. Later when she desperately needed it it was to be of great importance. She so liked and admired him that she awarded his work as a doctor her most cautious and revered adjective: 'disinterested'.

Soon Pierre was writing her notes from Sceaux as he worriedly and tenderly watched his mother during a fever. His attitude to Marie Sklodowska too was becoming increasingly tender. He was now daily more and more committed to her, and told her so. The choice was with her. Once as a young man he had written:

Women of genius are rare. And when, pushed by some mystic love, we wish to enter into a life opposed to nature, when we give all our thoughts to some work which removes us from those immediately about us, it is with women that 'we have to struggle, and the struggle is nearly always an unequal one. For in the name of life and of nature they seek to lead us back.[5]

She could have no doubt that he had given up the unequal struggle when she was invited by him to the Sorbonne to be one of the audience, which would include his parents, at the examination of his doctoral thesis on his work on magnetism. The three professors who carried out the oral spoke throughout as physicists to a physicist of standing. Curie's responses were shy, clear and simple. Marie Sklodowska was impressed indeed. 'It seemed to me that the little room that day sheltered the exaltation of human thought.'[6]

His sense of values was hers: that was clear enough. Disinterestedness was paramount. He was scientifically successful. He published frequently, but not compulsively, and made plain to her that he had no interest in having first claim on scientific priority. By comparison with today's viciously competitive scientific attitudes, Pierre Curie's was that of a rank amateur.

But with these attitudes what of his prospects? In an academic sense they were dim. He wanted a professorship and he badly needed one which would give him facilities for his work. However, he found the process of competition both distasteful and embarrassing. As early in their relationship as September, 1894, he was writing to tell Marie that friends had warned him that one of the School's professors was planning to resign in the first few days of October: 'But I didn't believe a word of it and I'm sorry to have spoken to you about it. I also believe that nothing is more corrupting to the spirit than to let oneself fall into preoccupations of this sort and to listen to all the gossip people come to tell you.'[7]

He also rejected the thought of academic honours: in particular the traditional French system of touting for honours for oneself. Even when they were offered untarnished he rejected them and with them the chance of better pay and an easier future. When the School of Physics and Chemistry's director, Schützenberger, wanted to propose him for the *Palmes académiques*, his refusal of the offer verged on the priggish: 'I hope that you will be good enough to avoid taking a step that will make me appear a little ridiculous in the eyes of many people.'[8]

Curie had little need of material things, and the self-denying ordinances of Marie Sklodowska coincided in this characteristic. With an income of 300 francs a month, workmen's pay in those days, there was in any case little chance for indulgence. Privately this was of no concern to him, but professionally it was crippling. There seems little doubt that there were self-sown seeds of resentment against his superiors. His colleagues and students found it a fine thing that he worked in a corridor of the School when his rank provided no proper laboratory accommodation and equipment. But this can only have held back the work on his thesis which he had begun in 1891. Curie was a practical man when he had to manipulate apparatus, but not when he had to manoeuvre the practical situations of life.

However, in January 1895, whether to provide cash for facilities for his work, or because he had marriage firmly in view, he decided to compromise the purity of his scientific ideals. He agreed to act as technical adviser to a Parisian optical firm, at a fee of 100 francs a month; in addition he stood to make 20% royalty on the firm's exploitation of a photographic objective lens he had devised.[9] But these amounts were too small to make much difference to his standard of living.

The best that could be said of his career was that, after 12 years at the School of Physics and Chemistry, he had held a relatively junior post successfully but with no indication of any likely improvement in his lot. If Marie Sklodowska had been in the least concerned about his prospects she would have assessed him as a bad bet. But she was not concerned. He was, among other things, a gentle and good man, and she decided she would marry him.

But she still had one or two problems to deal with. The persistent Lamotte had stayed in the hunt. Even a year after her attempts to head him off he was still, in July of 1895, penning his sad sentences, headed 'Mademoiselle' and setting them out with the neatness and order of a business letter. When, after trying more gentle methods, she told him the brutal truth and gave what even he had to recognise as the *coup de grâce*, he took it as a 'cruel surprise'. Unhappy constant lover, he had to resign himself to a future without her. 'As the poet said,' he told her, ' "I came too late into a world too old" '![10]

She sent her news to Warsaw. The family responded with blessings to her and to Curie. Sklodowski and Marie's sister Helena set off for Paris.

They were married, he the agnostic, she the lapsed Catholic, in a simple civil ceremony in Sceaux Town Hall. She, practical to the very steps of the symbolic altar, wore a plain dark dress given by a relation that would later be useful to wear to the laboratory and not show dirt. A few days earlier she had written to a school-friend telling her she was to change her name. 'When you receive this letter,' she said, 'write to me: Madame Curie, School of Physics and Chemistry, 42 Rue Lhomond.'[11]

Chapter 7

Discovery

When in 1887 John Boyd Dunlop put his first pneumatic rubber tyre round the rim of a bicycle wheel he assured a social revolution as a result of a technological innovation. The bicycle, though scarcely noticed at the Paris Exhibition of 1889, never looked back. Eastern and Western civilisations, the French in particular, pounced on it. Eulogistically the bicycle was called 'the little mechanical fairy that multiplied the powers of man': and so it did. This truly remarkable piece of engineering altered the communication systems of whole nations, and brought within the range of relatively poor people destinations that had once seemed hopelessly distant. 'The beauty of the bicycle,' said one French nineteenth-century figure 'resides in its sincerity. It conceals nothing. All its workings are open and visible.'[1]

A relative provided a wedding gift of money for the Curies to buy a pair of bicycles, and instantly the pair of lovers fell in love with their new pieces of technology.

Whereas the horse had been ridden by women in such a way as to limit its use – side saddle – the bicycle, even from the start, was not allowed to discriminate between the sexes. A clouded view of women on wheels however was still being taken by some ladies of sharp tongue: 'Bicycling women in breeches. As if there aren't enough calves on view any day in the streets of Paris. I consider that knee-breeches are worse than immodest: they are ridiculous.'[2] Fashionable considerations influenced the new Madame Curie not in the least; in an entirely practical split-skirt straddling the substantial cross-bar, and with black straw hat firmly in place, she headed with her husband for the open road of the honeymoon.

During the next two years the freedom to travel given to them by their bicycles gave Marie Curie some of her clearest memories of happiness. In vacations they would put their machines on a train and aim for the Cevennes, the Auvergne, the Brittany coast, or wherever fancy took them, and stay until they decided that the time had come to return to the work that obsessed them both. On one occasion they walked their bicycles in the gorges of la Truyère listening, late in the evening, to a distant song that came from a small boat making its way downstream; once, when their bicycles frightened a field of cart-horses, they panicked, pushing their machines at poor speed over a ploughed field. And when the days of idyll and adventure in miniature were over, they would walk up the steep paths to the high plateau, and find their way back by early morning moonlight to their lodgings.

Apart from these excursions life in their small new apartment and in their work changed scarcely at all. From being solitary individuals they had become a solitary couple. If there were surprises to be had from the experience of life at close quarters to another being, then in this partnership it would be the man who made the appropriate adjustments. In every relationship she had, and marriage was to be no exception, Marie Curie maintained a position from which she could act as an independent spirit.

During its early years their marriage was a self-contained contented existence which satisfied both their singular but similar needs. Pierre Curie became increasingly dependent on his wife. After two years of marriage the once self-sufficient and introspective bachelor found their brief spells of separation to be painful. When she was on holiday with her father he would write with news of the laboratory and add childish words of affection, or try out a few words of adoration in the written Polish she had taught him. He was clearly as much in love with her as on the first day he had seen the light from the french window falling on her grave face.

Their scientific dream was a simple one and in these idyllic days there was no obstacle to it. He prepared his teaching courses for the School of Physics and Chemistry with great care and in helping him in this preparatory work Marie found that there was much that she could learn from his wide theoretical and practical experience as a physicist. It was solid groundwork for the research she was just beginning. She was given permission to work at the

School so that she would be alongside her husband. But she would have to be responsible for her own financial backing of the research she proposed to do. This was a study of how the magnetic properties of various tempered steels varies with their chemical compositions. She relied on the directors of a number of metallurgical firms to supply her with free samples of steels, as well as on the Professor of the School of Mines, the distinguished physical chemist Henri le Chatelier, for other samples and help with chemical analyses. The subject she was investigating, magnetism, was of course one on which her husband was already a leading authority, so that for this her first exploration into unknown territories of science, she had the left hand firmly held by one of France's leading chemists, and the right by one of France's leading physicists.

Her first paper, completed in the autumn of 1897,[3] was overlong and not particularly original; it was, however, exceptionally thorough and showed that the young woman was as capable as any other worker in the field of many hours of sustained application at a laboratory bench with meticulous attention to her chosen problem's details. If nothing else, she had trained on a kind of assault course for future physico-chemical work. Since she was to approach her next scientific problem as though it were a battle with the forces of nature, the military analogy is not inappropriate.

The life they led between their plain apartment and their small laboratories was repetitive and unchanging: as she described it to her brother, it 'is always the same, monotonous. We see nobody but the Dluskis and my husband's parents in Sceaux'.[4] The Curie parents kept two rooms where Pierre and his wife could stay at any time, and which when they came they used as a place of study in much the same way as they used their rooms in the city.

The first threat to their routine came when Marie found that she was to have a child. From the start she had a difficult pregnancy and deeply resented the sickness that often lasted all day long, and prevented her working. Worse, it coincided with the fatal illness of Pierre's mother who had developed cancer of the breast.

That summer she spent with her father at Port Blanc. Pierre remained at Sceaux, wanting to be off to the sea and to his pregnant 'chère petite enfant cherie', yet also wanting to stay by the bed of his dying mother. 'Mother is so sad when I speak of leaving that I still haven't had the courage to fix the day.'[5]

When at last he did tear himself free it was to take his eight months' pregnant wife on a bicycling trip to Brest. It was an almost wilful act of naïvety by this highly educated couple, and it ended as might have been expected. Unable to continue, Marie was forced to return to Paris. On September 12th she was delivered of a daughter, Irène, by Eugène Curie; and with such familiar synchronisation in family affairs, a few days later his wife, the child's grandmother, died.

If Marie Curie wished to continue with her career, a servant had to be employed, and that brought the difficulties of the master-servant relationship and the dividing of the mother's share of duties. The problems facing the educated working mother with the young child were formidable. There were few enough women laboratory physicists who had continued their careers after graduation but for a young mother to be involved in this way only weeks after her confinement, even in the more liberal atmosphere of France was looked on as extraordinary, if not neglectful.

But Marie Curie was single-minded about her scientific future. At the same time she was preparing her monograph on steels for publication, she began to look for a subject she could study for a doctorate in science. The precedents for this were almost non-existent, even outside France. No woman in Europe had managed to complete a doctorate, though one in Germany, an unmarried girl, Elsa Neumann, was well into a thesis in electrochemistry.

Marie Curie's attitude on feminism, as with everything else, was uncompromising. She never embraced any feminist cause and saw full well that she could only achieve equality by making for herself the conditions under which she could compete with men on equal terms. She must expect no concessions, and be wary of prejudice. It was an advanced attitude. To follow such a path in the years before the turn of the nineteenth century argued great self-confidence and self-sufficiency: Marie Curie had both in good measure.

The way in which she approached this next stage of her career, with absolute refusal to tolerate any thought of deflection, is all the more remarkable when it is remembered that she launched into it physically debilitated after a wretched year of pregnancy and its after effects. It was as though she had a perverse streak that was stimulated by the challenge of adversity.

What now remained was to choose the subject for the thesis. It was to be the most important decision of her scientific life. It would govern not only the rest of her career but the private lives of her husband and herself.

It would not be unreasonable to date the atomic age from November 8th, 1895. On that day an observation had been made in a Bavarian laboratory which ever after altered physicists' views of their subject. Wilhelm Röntgen had taken a pear-shaped cathode ray tube from its rack, part-connected it in a circuit, surrounded it with black cardboard and, having completely darkened the room, passed a high tension discharge across it. All he was concerned with was whether the cardboard was completely shielding the tube. Having satisfied himself that this was so, he was in the act of moving towards the apparatus to continue the experiment when, about a yard from the tube he saw a glimmer of light. He lit a match to see where it was coming from. He found it to be a small card coated with barium platinocyanide, which was luminescing, in spite of the fact that it was completely shielded from the cathode ray tube by a thick sheet of cardboard. He switched off the tube: the barium-coated card stopped glowing. He switched it on, and it glowed again. Röntgen had discovered X-rays.

He gave the rays the name X because this was a physicist's usual symbol for an unknown (and in this case a not understood) factor. But by December 28th, when he made his first report, Röntgen had carried out a systematic and thorough examination of the rays and was able to give an accurate description of most of their basic properties. Four weeks later he gave the first public lecture on his discovery to a crowded auditorium. At one point he asked permission from the distinguished 78-year-old anatomist Albert von Kölliker to photograph his hand. Von Kölliker

agreed; when Röntgen later held up the developed plate showing the old man's bone structure, the audience burst into loud
cheers.[6]

The shout that rang out was world-wide. The phenomenon
was not only spectacular, but the simpler principles behind it were
easily understood by non-scientists, and its applications were
immediately obvious. Within four days of the reports of Röntgen's
experiment in America, X-rays were used to locate a bullet em-
bedded in a human leg. The seemingly limitless and indiscriminate
uses to which the rays could be put were soon exaggerated; their
powers to display what lay behind closed doors and even beneath
layers of Victorian clothing raised some of the earliest doubts of
intrusion by scientific devices into personal privacy.

Running parallel with this almost hysterical lay reaction there
was a quieter, but still feverish reaction in laboratories throughout
the world. Within a year 48 books and over 1,000 articles had been
published on the subject of the new X-rays. Soon arguments
would begin as to whether the rays were waves or particles. Their
extraordinary penetrating power would turn them into a useful
tool to investigate and re-assess the structure of matter. X-rays'
peculiar properties would point the way to the realisation that
atoms were not the inviolate and impregnable ultimate particles
of matter, as dogma had had it for so long. The classical particulate
view of physics was at an end. This was the beginning of the
ferment of new concepts which would disturb the whole basis on
which the physical science of the day rested. A new era was
beginning.

British science in particular was highly excited by the news
from Germany. The Professor of Physics at Finsbury Technical
College, Silvanus P. Thompson, wrote to a friend, 'All the (inventive) world seems to have gone off in two crazes – bicycles
and the X-rays. With the latter I have been badly bitten.'[7]
Cambridge took Röntgen's discovery with great seriousness.
Its far-reaching consequences were quickly appreciated there and
within days of Röntgen publishing his findings his experiments
were being repeated and enlarged on. On January 15th, 1896, a
young graduate physics student from New Zealand, Ernest

Rutherford, wrote home to his fiancée to tell her with what speed
the Cavendish laboratory workers, and in particular his professor,
J. J. Thomson, were responding to the news. 'I have seen all the
photographs that have been got so far. One of a frog is very good.
It outlines the general figure and shows all the bones inside very
distinctly. The Professor of course is trying to find out the real
cause and nature of the waves, and the great object is to find the
theory of the matter before anyone else, for nearly every Professor
in Europe is now on the warpath. . . .'[8]

Rutherford himself was firmly on the warpath; what is more,
he intended to lead any attack he was involved in. Reticence was
not one of his qualities.

In 1897 this would have been the obvious field for Marie Curie
to work in for her doctorate. It was being well worked over, but
with reason; it still promised to be one from which to obtain quick
results. But she rejected it in favour of a subject which at the time
seemed by comparison to have poor potential, and relatively little
importance compared with the X-ray bonanza's promise.

The effect she proposed to study had been observed, as is so
often the case when a broad new front of scientific investigation
is being opened up, by two men working simultaneously and independently in different laboratories. One of these, Silvanus P.
Thompson bequeathed to generations of English working-class,
and other aspirant mathematicians, his text book, *Calculus Made
Easy*, and its hopeful dedication, 'What one fool can do, another
can.' Thompson was not aware when, in his London laboratory,
he put a small quantity of uranium nitrate over a shielded photographic plate and observed its effects that another fool was doing
the same thing in Paris. Thompson's experimental method was to
leave the photographic plate and its aluminium shield with the
uranium salt on top on the window-sill of his laboratory, 'to
receive so much sunlight (several hours as it happened) as pene-
trates in February into a back street in the heart of London'.[9] He
then developed the photographic plate and discovered that it was
blackened at the spot over which the uranium salt had been sitting.
He was more than surprised that uranium could in some way
affect his plate in spite of the thick aluminium protection, and

immediately wrote to the President of the Royal Society, Sir George Stokes, to tell him about the effect, which he later called *hyperphosphorescence*. Three days later on February 29th, 1896, Stokes replied to Thompson telling him that he hoped he would publish this interesting result without delay, 'especially as so many are now working at the X-rays'.[10] In less than a week Stokes was writing again to tell him something he had discovered while browsing through the French scientific press: 'I fear you have already been anticipated. See Becquerel, *Comptes Rendus* for February 24th, p. 420, and some papers in two or three meetings preceding that.'

When Thompson got to the magazine he found he was already too late. Henri Becquerel, thinking no doubt that only a fool would delay getting his results into print – what with the plethora of publications on X-rays – had published his similar findings with great speed.

Like Thompson, Becquerel originally believed that it was the effect of sunlight on the uranium salt crystals that stimulated them into exposing the photographic plate, perhaps by causing them to emit X-rays. Thompson's interest in the phenomenon cooled with the Frenchman's publication. But Becquerel felt there was more yet to be got from these uranium salts.

On February 26th and 27th he had wrapped some photographic plates in black cloth, covered them with a sheet of aluminium, then placed some crystals of potassium uranyl sulphate on top of the aluminium. Since it was a dull day, and since he was particularly interested in seeing the effects of the sun on the crystals, he put plates and crystals in a drawer and closed it. He left it closed when the Friday and Saturday of that week also turned out dull; so did Sunday, when, for some reason that posterity will never know[11] Becquerel decided to take the plates from the drawer, unwrap them and develop them as they were. He was staggered to find they were intensely fogged where the crystals had covered them. The next day (and this might have been the reason that spurred him to work on a Sunday) was the weekly meeting of the Académie des Sciences. There he was able to seal his fame and announce with only twenty-four hours' delay, the discovery that uranium salts emit rays which, like X-rays, penetrate matter.[12] Becquerel had discovered radioactivity.

It was a seminal discovery, though at that meeting nobody recognised it as such, though Becquerel's originality was politely and interestedly acknowledged. During 1896 he published six more papers on the subject, and two the following year. Then even his interest appears to have been dwindling. In other quarters, however, the enthusiasm for the spectacular X-rays was continuing without pause.

At this stage Marie Curie decided to look into uranium rays as a possible field of investigation for her thesis. Becquerel had shown that, even if salts were kept in his closed drawer for weeks, they were still capable of affecting photographic plates. The interesting question was, from where did the uranium compound get the energy that made it capable of darkening photographic emulsions through several thicknesses of protective paper, or even metal? The Curie's looked at the problem. Pierre Curie pointed to the fact that as a scientific investigation this was virgin territory. Marie Curie chose it for her own.[13]

The first problem requiring a solution was where was she to work? She would need a laboratory. The obvious place was the School of Physics and Chemistry. Schützenberger, its director, was a sympathetic man. His slant-hooded eyes hid a great deal of warmth and their twinkle inspired both loyalty and enthusiasm. Those who worked in his establishment called him 'daddy Schütz' and Curie turned easily enough to him for his paternal help. Curie pointed out a small glassed-in room on the ground floor of the School that was being used partly as a store room and partly as a laboratory machine shop. Schützenberger agreed that the sad-eyed, always plainly and darkly dressed wife of his equally grave-faced and silent laboratory chief could occupy it. Under the circumstances he perhaps found it difficult to refuse. Curie had been with him for 14 years, had had little promotion and his sickly wife had just had a child. It was clear that the experiments she was proposing would require a minimum of inexpensive equipment; it must also have seemed clear that the chances of her completing a doctorate were minimal.

The main drawback to the room was that it was damp. Quite apart from the discomfort, this was a serious hindrance to the electrostatic experiments she was proposing to carry out. What she later described as her plan of work was the following: Becquerel had shown that uranium rays, like X-rays, caused air to conduct electricity; she would carry out the first quantitative study of the phenomenon with the ordered thoroughness which gave her such satisfaction, using the piezoelectrique-quartz electrometer to measure the small quantities of electricity conducted by air.

This description has a nice, ordered ring to it. However, an examination of the circumstances under which the experiments were carried out suggest that, if not inaccurate, it is at least an idealised description. Marie Curie was chronically short of funds and equipment, and working in a laboratory under sufferance. Initially at least, she had to design her experiments around the little equipment there that was free and available. Pierre Curie had an electrometer sitting unused in his laboratory which he would be more than happy to see applied. It would therefore be a matter of thrift and prudence to look to the uranium rays for a measurement problem for which they already had the convenient means for a solution.

Whatever the order of events, Jacques and Pierre Curie's piezoelectrique-quartz at last came into its own in the hand of Marie Curie. She set out to investigate whether there were substances other than uranium which could cause air to become a conductor of electricity. From acquaintances in and around the School of Physics and Chemistry she begged and borrowed as many samples of metals, metallic compounds and minerals as she could lay her hands on. The fundamental experiment was easy. She simply put her substance on a metal plate, opposite which was a second metal plate forming a condenser, and used her electrometer to detect whether she could make an electric current pass through the air between the plates. In this way she could quickly test dozens of substances with the thoroughness that for her had already become an obsessional scientific method. Within a very short time she had her first results. She found that thorium and its compounds caused air to conduct electricity, and gave off rays which, as far as she could tell, were like the rays Becquerel had observed from uranium.

It was a little triumph. The discovery was made within days of Marie Curie beginning her experimental work: no research worker starting out on a doctoral thesis could hope for better fortune. Immediately she began another systematic investigation, this time using the electrometer to measure the intensity of the current caused by different compounds of uranium and thorium.

The first result to emerge was that the activity of the uranium compounds depended only on the amount of uranium present. It mattered not in the least whether the uranium salt was wet or dry, whether in lumps or powdered, nor which other elements were present in the salt. This was a highly significant piece of information; how significant, she did not realise at the time, though it became clearer to her in due course.

In scientific terms it is this, and not the other discoveries for which she is much more famous, that is the most important single piece of work carried out by Marie Curie. What she had shown, was that the radiation was not the outcome of some interaction between molecules; it was not the consequence, say, of atoms forming new molecules, or of molecules rearranging themselves in new shapes as in an ordinary chemical reaction when energy as heat or light is given out as a product of the reaction. This radiation energy has a different origin and must come from the atom itself, irrespective of what the atom is joined up with or how it is behaving: radiation must be an atomic property. From this simple discovery twentieth-century science was able to elucidate the structure of the atom, and from it sprang all the practical consequences of a knowledge of atomic structure.

Marie Curie did not stop to ponder this result. There were further immediate and exciting consequences. In measuring the conductivity of air due to substances containing uranium, she included in her systematic studies two uranium minerals, pitchblende and chalcolite. Her electrometer showed that pitchblende was four times as active as uranium itself, and chalcolite twice as active. She reached the conclusion that, if her earlier results relating the amount of uranium to its activity were correct – and they were – then these two minerals must contain small amounts of some other substance far more active than uranium itself.

The idea was her own; no one helped her formulate it, and although she took it to her husband for his opinion she clearly established her ownership of it. She later recorded the fact twice in her biography of her husband to ensure there was no chance whatever of any ambiguity.[14] It seems likely that already at this early stage of her career Marie Curie had realised that her role as physicist would present unusually intractable problems, one of which would be that many scientists would find it difficult to believe that a woman could be capable of the original work in which she was involved. Her response, or over-response, was typical. On all occasions, verbally and in print she spelled out, without any chance of misunderstanding, the work for which she and she alone was responsible. She gave credit to her co-workers, particularly to her husband, when it was due, but never was her ownership of her own thoughts and work left in doubt, even in works of co-authorship. The first word of her first paper on radiation to be published was 'I'. Pointedly and firmly she used it throughout. It was the first public display of her own rigorous independence.

The question of publication was important. Although she had only been working on uranium and thorium for a few weeks she had already in her notebooks columns of figures which she and Pierre Curie knew to be important and scientifically of great interest. Pierre's attitude on publication was admirably pure, but characteristically naïve. He was not in the least interested in a race for priority and preferred to publish his work after long deliberation. If he was beaten by some other physicist who preferred to risk publication and later damnation, then so much the worse. Marie Curie later proudly drew attention to his aloof attitude. It must be assumed therefore that it was she, and not her husband, who took the steps to see that this work got into print as soon as possible.

There were excellent reasons, still fresh in scientific memory, for her doing so. Had Becquerel, two years earlier, not presented his discovery to the Académie des Sciences the day after he made it, credit for the discovery of radioactivity, and even a Nobel Prize, would have gone to Silvanus Thompson. Marie Curie chose the same rapid method of publication. The Académie's sessions were held every Monday and any paper presented there would be in print within ten days and in circulation for the world of physics to read. Since neither Curie nor herself were members of the Académie, her paper,[15] giving a short and admirably simple account of her work, was presented for her on April 12th, 1898, by her one-time professor, Gabriel Lippmann.

Even so it was too late. By a remarkable and heart-breaking chance, just as Thompson was beaten by Becquerel, so too was she beaten in the race to tell of her discovery that thorium gives off rays in the same way as uranium. Unknown to her, a German, Gerhard Schmidt, had published his finding in Berlin two months earlier.[16]

But no one else in the world of physics had yet spotted what she recorded in one sentence of that paper in describing how much greater were the activities of pitchblende and chalcolite compared with uranium itself. She wrote, 'the fact is very remarkable, and leads to the belief that these minerals may contain an element which is much more active than uranium'. The realisation that she might have stumbled across a new *element* raised her to an excitement she had never before experienced. She, the mistress of understatement, later recalled how she felt 'a passionate desire to verify this hypothesis as rapidly as possible'.[17] Better still, it was a passion she could share with her husband. Curie was sure that it was not a spurious effect she had discovered. He was so intrigued that he decided, as a temporary measure, to throw up the work on crystals that was so dear to him and join her. It would, it seemed, be a labour of love. What they were not then to know was that what they were searching for was present in the minerals in such minute quantities, that it would be truly hard physical labour. On April 14th, 1898, ridiculously optimistic, they weighed out a one hundred gram sample of pitchblende and ground it with a pestle and mortar. It was the first step of their long haul. Eventually they would work in tons.

Chapter 8

Fruitful Years

With the same meticulousness that she used in recording the notes, the problems and the laboratory experiments of her student lectures, Marie Curie would write down the measurable events in her family's day-to-day life.

15 April. Irène is showing her seventh tooth down on the left ... for three days now we have bathed her in the river. She cried, but today (4th bath) she stopped crying in the water ...

25 April. We put tapioca in her milk.

5 September. First egg. She eats the liquid but spits out the white.[1]

Whatever it was that had quantifiable content Marie Curie wrote down. The only criterion for a fact to be recorded in one of her tiny notebooks, was that there should be a number that could be attached to it: the 3% profits made on the small investments for Irène; 5f.50c. for a pair of woollen cycling stockings for Pierre; two bicycle tyres, 31f.; laundry 4f.50c.; 'Pierre has kept 51f.' The habit went on throughout her life: details of centimes spent on omnibuses on holiday; the price of three cups of coffee, postage stamps; every single day's account of expenditure for a holiday spent in Brittany; similar details for a trip to Zakopane, with two columns, one for expenditure in francs, another giving the equivalent in crones. Even near death she still kept minute accounts of sums spent on laundry, jam, stamps, electricity and cheese.

This obsession to put down all events no matter what, so long as they were observable and measurable, which appears so banal but touching in her private records, was vital to her success in the scientific problems she had chosen for her research. Rarely from observations either in her work or in her private life did she write down a subjective assessment. Just once, after recording the price of a night in a hotel on holiday at Puy, she allowed herself the comment that the service was 'inadequate'.

But if their research was exciting and fruitful, the same could not be said of the life she and her husband were leading outside the laboratory. Their life *was* their work. The jottings in her note-book show, with the usual exactitude, the late hours she spent at the laboratory bench. This dedication was a conscious decision. A rare visit to the theatre, a bicycle outing, or a weekend after-noon discussion with scientific colleagues were the most relaxa-tion they allowed themselves. Beyond this, life was drab and monotonous, and Marie Curie acknowledged it to be so in the letters to her family. After more than six years in Paris, she made no attempt to hide her loneliness and her homesickness for Poland.

The routine of life had been relatively easily achieved. Eugène Curie, having lost his wife, had taken on the grandfather's tradi-tional role and in his old age had discovered the joys of being a nursemaid. His help was all the more valuable since, throughout her life, Marie Curie was unable to see any virtue whatever in the domestic art. When she was an old woman, a young girl in her laboratory came to tell her that she was to marry soon, Marie Curie told her: 'Myself I never knew how to set about cleaning a kitchen properly. I used to have my pail alongside me, with a cloth, but as soon as I moved it, everything looked as though it needed doing all over again.'[2]

Neither husband nor wife had much need nor care for posses-sions. They spent little, as Marie's fastidious accounts show. They lived a spartan existence, ate simply and dressed to match. Already the thin, dark-clothed pair, gliding as though not wishing to intrude, was a familiar sight in the left-bank streets near the laboratories.

At the top of one page of her notes, early in 1898, Marie Curie neatly recorded the temperature of the apparatus she was working with: 6.25°!!!!!!!!!! The ten exclamation marks showed that the temperature of the room was also six degrees above freezing. Illness troubled them both. For Marie it appeared to date from her pregnancy. It could equally well be dated from the time she took up work on the new rays. She recorded her own illnesses and their progress in the same way that she recorded other events. One, which did not develop further than initial symptoms, was a suspected tubercular lesion of the lung diagnosed by the family doctor soon after the birth of Irène.

Knowing the cause of her mother's death, this must have been a profoundly depressing piece of information. But the unswerving interest the Curies paid to their laboratory was beginning to reward them handsomely. They dissolved the ground pitchblende in acid and separated its different elements by the standard techniques of analytical chemistry then available. Marie Curie took over the role of chemist and taught herself the skills required for the endlessly repetitive and boring functions which this kind of separation requires. Her suspicion that the pitchblende contained a small amount of substance giving off a far greater amount of rays than uranium, grew with each stage of the separation and purification. At last it was clear that she could separate this substance, whatever it was, from all but one element: bismuth.

On June 6th, 1898, the laboratory notebook shows a sudden outburst of excitement that even Marie's self-control could not contain. Until that time the notes had been made mostly with her thin-nibbed pen on squared paper, using the horizontal lines for observations and the vertical columns for figures. An occasional annotation by Pierre in a quick vertical or diagonal scrawl indicated that one or other of the observations had struck him as being particularly interesting. But on this day the notes show that Marie took a solution of bismuth nitrate containing, so she believed, her new element, and added hydrogen sulphide. She then carefully collected the solid that was precipitated and measured its activity. In bold letters at the bottom of the page she wrote and underlined the result: *150 times more active than uranium*.

On the same day Pierre Curie put a tiny sample of the impure bismuth sulphide they had collected into a glass tube and began to heat it gradually. He noticed that the bismuth sulphide stayed in the hotter parts of the tube, whilst a thin black powder was deposited on the glass at 250–300°. He kept on heating the tube, until it finally cracked. But he had found all they needed. He scraped the black powder from the tube and measured its activity.

Eventually they were to produce a sample with an activity 330 times greater than that of uranium. It had been a phenomenal day's work.

By June 27th Marie was precipitating substances about 300 times more active, and recording the triumph in her notebook in even bolder strokes. There was now no doubt. They had discovered a new element. Every time they got rid of a little more bismuth, the new substance showed its presence more dramatically. This was high excitement at a time when psychologically it was most needed. Marie Curie, in the trough of a long period of longing for her homeland, had a name ready and waiting. They wrote in the paper which they quickly prepared for publication, 'If the existence of this new metal is confirmed, we propose to call it *polonium* from the name of the country of origin of one of us.'[3]

It was in this paper that the Curies first used the word *radioactive* to describe the behaviour of uranium-like substances. Silvanus Thompson's concoction for the same phenomenon, hyperphosphorescence, thankfully never entered the English or any other language. But radioactivity had come to stay.

At that time Marie Curie clearly felt polonium to be her great discovery, and for that reason she had reserved for it the name most dear to her. But before she had time to get it into print to demonstrate the passion she felt for her native land something jolted her and Pierre's thoughts into the recognition that there was something beyond polonium to be dug from their mine.

The important work Marie and Pierre Curie did together in the three years beginning in December 1897 was recorded in three small black linen-covered notebooks. These are still preserved. Most of their other notes or papers have been decontaminated, but these books are still considered dangerous to handle – more than three-quarters of a century since they received their first contamination from the fingers of Marie and Pierre.*

* One day as I sat at Marie Curie's desk making notes, two workmen appeared in the Laboratoire Curie to carry out routine radioactive level tests in rooms other than laboratories. After using their Geiger counter on various pieces of furniture in Marie Curie's study they turned it

Marie Curie

In July of 1898 the notes in these books come to a sudden end. No more are added for many weeks. During this period the Curies obviously took out their bicycles and headed for the countryside and their long vacation. But something else of importance must also have distracted them since their notes do not begin again in a new book until November 11th. The likelihood is that, far from wishing to have a leisurely break from work, they had to take a forced rest since both were suffering from inexplicable illnesses and annoying minor malaises. Pierre had pains about his body, which he told his friends were due to rheumatism; both succumbed easily to many minor common ailments; both were quickly tired and had to fight continual lethargy. Another peculiar annoyance was that the ends of Marie's fingers were becoming sore and cracked, as she handled more of their purified substances.

We now know a great deal more about radiation sickness and the awful physical problems that ingestion of radioactive substances can cause. These two were the first involuntary guinea-pigs to suffer the early symptoms.

On November 11th the notebook begins in Marie's typically compulsive orderliness. But it does not last long. The notes begin to be more cursorily and roughly made, and mostly undated. But it is quite clear from the notes of the last weeks of November that they had already discovered (though had not recorded) the highly significant fact that the residual liquid when they had got rid of both bismuth and polonium was still highly radioactive. Simple tests showed that this was due neither to uranium nor polonium that had been left behind. The main impurity in that liquid was the well-known element barium, but that was known not to be radioactive. There must be – and this conclusion they probably came to on their holidays or even before that – not one, but two previously unknown and unsuspected elements in their sample of pitchblende.

Their expectations were exceeded in a shattering fashion, when they had precipitated their new substance from its solution. Re-

onto the chair I was sitting in. Immediately it began clicking in its noisy and upsetting fashion. Politely they asked me to remove myself from the seat so that they could decontaminate it.

dissolving and reprecipitating time and time and time again, they eventually arrived at a substance which had a radioactivity no less than 900 times greater than that of uranium. And the only factor limiting their abilities to refine it still further and get an even more strongly radioactive substance was the fact that their wastage rate due to their losses with their waste products, and due to spillage and breakage in inevitable frustrating accidents, was such that they were running out of material with which to work.

It is in the middle of an undated page, about the beginning of December, 1898, that Pierre Curie scrawled the following:

$$? \begin{cases} \text{thus radium sulphate} \\ \text{more soluble in } H_2SO_4 \\ \text{than barium sulphate} \end{cases}$$

They had found a name for their new element. They had decided to call it *radium*. It was to be the jewel in Marie Curie's crown.

Ironically, polonium, the name she had especially kept for what she hoped would be this pearl, had neither the instant importance nor the fame of the later discovery, and popularly she was to be called not the Polish scientist, as she might have wished, but the French radium woman.

Radium's existence had therefore been suspected in advance of the news of polonium being published. But before the announcement of the birth of the latest new metal could be made to the world, the Curies had to attempt to prove that it was what they believed it to be: an element. The instrument to be used in this proof was one of the most remarkable and versatile inventions of the nineteenth century: the spectroscope.

The skilled operator of the spectroscope for the Curies was a man to whom Marie was already in debt for the loan of samples of materials on which she could base her early work: Eugène Demarçay. He had already tried to help the Curies by attempting, but failing, to find a new spectral line for polonium. Remarkably, considering that his immense contribution to this work depended a good deal on the accuracy of his sight through the eyepiece of his spectroscope, Demarçay had lost one eye in a laboratory explosion.

Demarçay now took the tiny sample of substance the Curies

gave him, dissolved it in acidified water and painted the solution on electrodes, across which he could pass an electric spark. With considerable skill he succeeded in photographing the spark spectrum of the substance. He found on this photograph a spectral line which was due neither to barium nor to any other known substance. Better still, each time the Curies further purified the solid, the spectral line became more intense.

Demarçay's devotion to the Curies' cause exposed him to the same dangers as the Curies themselves. On one occasion he enthusiastically told Marie Curie that her latest radium sample had made the air in his laboratory so radioactive that he had had to take his electroscope out of the room and make his measurements in another less contaminated room. 'It's just like being in prison,' he gaily told her.[4]

Demarçay's work was to confirm the existence of radium.[5] It was all the Curies needed to be able to publish with confidence; theirs and Demarçay's work was in print by December 26th, 1898.[6]

Demarçay intensely admired the work of Pierre Curie. As it happened he had only a few years to live, and he left to Curie in his will his laboratory apparatus, including his beloved spectrograph.

But there was yet a fourth scientist, who, like Demarçay, was in and out of the Curies' laboratory during this period, and whose name is associated with the discovery of radium. It is a name which subsequent publicity and glamorised accounts, however, have almost completely dismissed. Gustave Bémont was a devoted worker in what he saw to be the service of science, which he worshipped. His temple was a dark laboratory in the School of Physics and Chemistry in the Rue Lhomond, which he occupied for 45 years. He had an unspectacular devotion to his work: his only self-indulgence was to take himself off to Aix-les-Baines for the cure every year. He was so devoted to his subject and so inseparable from his laboratory and its contents that his students nicknamed him 'Bichro', because the colour of his red beard was identical to that of the sodium bichromate on his shelf.

Bémont's handwriting first appears in the Curies' notebooks on May 5th, 1898, significantly earlier than the realisation of the possibility of the existence of a substance such as radium, and his influence on the work in progress is recorded until the day that the word for the new element was coined. That Bémont contributed to the great discovery is without question; his contribution was important enough for the Curies to include him as one of their co-authors on the publication announcing the discovery of radium. Just how important or how indispensable this contribution was will never be known.

But the brief mention on top of this short scientific paper was not enough for posterity to remember Gustave Bémont by. He shared none of the Curies' honour and none of their glories. By the same token he shared none of their sufferings. He became the forgotten man of radioactivity.

The spokes in the wheel that worked the Curie laboratory were never at any time more than a tiny group of peculiarly reticent co-workers, such as Bémont, and reverently devoted laboratory assistants such as Petit, the white-haired Uncle Tom-like figure whom Pierre Curie had brought with him from the Sorbonne years before and who shared his workload for many years. But the hub of this wheel were the Curies themselves, and its hard driving force was indisputably Marie Curie.

The picture given by Eve Curie of her mother in her later years[7] is of a frail woman, of a meek and retiring nature. If these were the characteristics Marie Curie demonstrated to the closed family circle to which she restricted herself in her later years, it was not the behaviour that impressed itself on some of those who visited the laboratory in the School of Physics in the years at the turn of the century. They found a composed little woman it was true: but hers was clearly composure with a cutting edge. In every discussion her tough intellect was evident. One chemist who visited her noted[8] that in laboratory conversations in which she was involved it was she and not the men who led the discussions. This same chemist, George Jaffé, noticed that it was the amiable and self-deprecating Pierre who introduced the ingenuity into the scientific concepts which were now fascinating them, and the powerful temperament and persistence of Marie that maintained their momentum.

And above all this – and Jaffé noted it well – the pair of them carried with their simplicity of manner, of dress and of laboratory style, an immense air of superiority, commanding respect from those who worked for them, and awe from those who worked with them. Some outsiders found it attractive: others were repelled by it – particularly in the woman.

But all respected her dogged energy. And it was at this point, convinced of the reality of radium, that she most needed that energy. She had given birth to one child and she cherished it. Nevertheless, as she confided to one of her young woman pupils, radioactivity was also the child to which she had given birth, to whose education she intended to contribute with all the power she possessed, and to which she was prepared to devote the whole of her working life.

No human child was to get more devotion. The first step in its education was to try to separate radium into its pure form, and to do the same for polonium. It had become dauntingly evident to the Curies that the cupful of pitchblende that, a few months earlier, they had weighed out into their mortar and so carefully ground up with their pestle, contained such tiny quantities of their new elements as to be useless as a source. They needed not a cupful but a hillside. To work that hillside, no matter how or where they could find it, would cost money, and it would require space, and hard physical labour.

The source of energy for the labour could be easily decided on. That would be Marie Curie's. They had already agreed that she would specialise in the role of chemist with her main task that of separating the new metals. Pierre Curie, in his accustomed role of physicist, would study the physical properties of the materials during the various stages of the chemical separations. This easy decision was tragically to affect their health and their subsequent lives together.

The problem of finding the hillside of material was not so easy. Pierre Curie began a systematic search of published scientific literature for hints of the existence of partly refined ores which might shorten the task ahead. He wrote letters to Norwegian shippers, Hatton Garden manufacturing chemists, Bar-sur-Seine dealers and any other agents he could think of, in places as far apart as America, Portugal and the West of England. One London Regent Street dealer offered him 25 pieces of uranite, 'size about 1½ inches, fairly covered with crystals, one and sixpence each . . .'[9] With generosity and sympathy one member of the US Geological Survey packed off 500g of uranite via the Smithsonian Institute, free of charge. But these were the merest thimblefuls compared with what was really needed.

The chief European source of pitchblende, an expensive ore, was the St Joachimsthal mine in Bohemia, then part of the Austrian Empire and worked with considerable profit by the Austrian government for its uranium. The Curies realised that, once the recoverable uranium had been extracted, the residue would be discarded as useless and, as a waste product, would even be something of a nuisance to the mine. Just as important, the massive first stage in the recovery of radium – the removal of the bulk of uranium – would already have been carried out, saving them months of work.

A professor at the University of Vienna, Eduard Suess, first helped the Curies get hold of Joachimsthal pitchblende samples. These told them that this material had most of the qualities they needed. Other enquiries told them what they already suspected: that the pitchblende residues were being tipped in a pine forest near the uranium plant. They now had to set about getting hold of large quantities of this material at a price they could afford. Eventually, through the Vienna Academy of Science, they succeeded in getting the Austrian Government to intercede with the Joachimsthal mine authorities on their behalf.

It was in pleading their case that Marie Curie first put on paper her commitment to an entanglement of her 'pure' science with an industry that might see fit to apply it. She asked for an intervention on their behalf, making a strong point of the fact that '*the aim of their research is purely scientific*', (she underlined the words), 'and that this research will benefit the Joachimsthal factory, who could sell or exploit the otherwise valueless residues'.[10]

They were soon able to negotiate to buy reasonably cheaply with their own funds several tons of the material, which the

Bohemians were doubtless delighted to see removed at a small profit from their dumping ground.

The heavy sacks deposited in the yard of the School of Physics in the early months of 1899 were a source of undisguised and long-remembered pleasure by the intense woman who went out of the laboratory to receive them. And the pleasure was doubled when she slit one open, ran her fingers through the mixture of brown dust and pine needles, scooped out a sample in her hand and took it to the electrometer in the laboratory. It told her what she had already guessed, but what no Bohemian mine manager could suspect. His waste product was more radioactive than the pitchblende he had started out with.

Still to be solved was the problem of where to work with several tons of material. The store room that had led them to this stage of their work was clearly no longer adequate. Ideally they needed the facilities of a small factory. Yet again the Director of the School of Physics found himself faced with the pale, darkly-clothed pair. It was no longer the tolerant hooded eyes of 'daddy Schütz' they had to look into to make their request. Schützenberger's successor, Gariel, was a man whose administrative abilities were insufficient to keep him in his post for much more than a year. This, however, was long enough for him to have a few brushes with Pierre Curie; they had very different ideas about the way in which the research in the School should be run. In facing the new man, Curie was no doubt as reticent and hang-dog as in every request he made to his own advantage, and his wife was the quietly irresistible force that made it inevitable that Gariel should at least do something in response to their request. Gariel, however, made little more than a token gesture. In the yard of the School stood an abandoned shed once used by the School of Medicine as a dissecting room. It would serve for their analytical work and for the less bulky stages of the separation process. The yard itself would have to serve for the heavy work. Marie Curie later described the place she was to occupy for by far the greater number of waking hours of the next four years:

Its glass roof did not afford complete shelter against rain; the heat was suffocating in summer, and the bitter cold of winter was only a little lessened by the iron stove, except in its immediate vicinity. There was no question of obtaining the needed proper apparatus in common use by chemists. We simply had some old pine-wood tables with furnaces and gas burners. We had to use the adjoining yard for those of our chemical operations that involved producing irritating gases; even then the gas often filled our shed.[11]

Many scientific ventures during the nineteenth century were undercapitalised and most laboratory bench workers struggled in conditions which today would be unacceptable. The legend of the impossibility of the situation in which the Curies worked has grown with the years. Marie Curie plainly felt a great bitterness at having to work in inadequate conditions, without proper equipment. The fact that she also plainly recorded this bitterness, helped the legend along. But the bitterness was not without some justification; the conditions were undoubtedly primitive, even for those days. The great German chemist, Wilhelm Ostwald, one of the first to recognise the significance of the Curies' research travelled from Berlin to see how they worked:

At my urgent request the Curie laboratory, in which radium was discovered a short time ago, was shown to me. The Curies themselves were away travelling. It was a cross between a stable and a potato-cellar, and, if I had not seen the worktable with the chemical apparatus, I would have thought it a practical joke.[12]

But the first stage in the new regime needed no sophisticated apparatus. From the several tons of material they had collected from St Joachimsthal, Marie Curie selected about 20 kilograms, enough to fill the largest cast-iron containers she was strong enough to handle, sifted out the pine cones and more obvious lumps of impurity, and then began on the first of the processes she was to have to repeat over and over again. Each batch of material was ground, dissolved, filtered, precipitated, collected, redissolved, crystallised, recrystallised. . . . When the material she was hunting for had been confined into a sufficiently small bulk, she could start again with another 20 kilogram load and move through the same series of events.

Summer months were the easiest. Then she could heat the cauldrons in the open yard and hope the wind would carry off the fumes. The shed itself had neither fume cupboards nor fume hoods, so that when she was forced indoors by cold or rain, the exercise had to be carried on with as many open windows as possible within the limits of an acceptable working temperature. At that time they had no idea of the dangerous nature of the materials they were looking for, though they knew full well the poisonous characteristics of the common gases, such as hydrogen sulphide, which the different stages of the purification forced them to use.

The work was utterly exhausting for a woman. One of the very few friends who came to visit them in their consciously secluded work area was a young physicist, Georges Urbain. He ever after felt himself privileged because he had succeeded in seeing 'with my own eyes the birth of radium . . . I saw Madame Curie work like a man at the difficult treatments of great quantities of pitchblende.'[13] Not only did she have to move the heavy containers required in the first stages of separation, she had to transfer their contents from one to the other and, using an iron bar almost as big as herself, spend the whole of a working day stirring the heating and fuming liquids. She was proud of what she did. 'I would be broken with fatigue at the day's end,' she wrote.[14]

By contrast, when the bulk solutions had been reduced to only a few hundred ccs. of liquid, the experimental minutiae and the care required in the technique presented frustrations of an entirely different kind. The shed's pine tables would be spread with small porcelain crystallising bowls from which no amount of delicate protection was capable of excluding the airborne dust, coal and iron particles drifting in from the yard. Any laboratory accident or act of carelessness could bring to grief in a pool on the floor the concentrated product of weeks and even months of patient, dedicated work. There were several small tragedies which Marie reported in her letters to Poland.

But for all the self-denial and the conscious exclusion of outsiders from this scientific world it produced, for Marie Curie at least, periods of intensely-felt pleasure. Twenty years later she described the time spent in 'this miserable shed' as the 'best and happiest years of our life . . . I shall never be able to express the joy of the untroubled quietness of this atmosphere of research and the excitement of actual progress with the confident hope of still better results.'[15]

Jaffé had observed how the few who entered the work-area's precincts had the makings of a deliberately élitist little group such as might attend the processes and the trappings of a closed order. Other friends saw similar manifestations of the same attitudes. A friend who knew her well described Marie Curie's attitude to her work as being that of one belonging to a priesthood.[16]

She kept a strict discipline, even a ritual, for her work. She established laboratory customs which she herself rigorously observed and which therefore she expected others to observe. Each night she saw to it that the laboratory assistant left the bench-tops clean, and if he had not done so, she cleaned them herself. She had a horror of noise and preferred others, even her children when they were old enough, like herself never to raise their voices either in joy or in anger. Already she had acquired the qualities which could make her into a martinet when the need arose.

The atmosphere she preserved for her laboratory was a vital ingredient in the satisfaction which her life in it gave her at that time. But clearly its most important constituent was the indefinable sense of achievement which the results of their work were giving her. She and her husband were treading a new path on which no other scientific workers had yet left their footprints. She was taking part in a piece of scientific creativity, and if there was no Creator Himself then there was still a vital role to be played by the priests of the scientific establishment. No other activity in which she had indulged had ever begun to equal it.

There were tangible as well as intellectual rewards to be had. She later recorded how they enjoyed them. As their refined solutions and crystalline solids became more and more rich in radioactive product they could watch it signal its presence with their own eyes. At night they would occasionally return to their workroom, stand in the centre of its cold, hard bituminous floor, and look around at the bottles of liquids and capsules of crystals. As their eyes became accustomed to the dark they would begin to see the feebly luminous silhouettes of the containers glowing from the tables and makeshift shelves. They stood together and watched, and felt themselves to have reached great heights. And this simple act of actually looking together at what they had made raised their own relationship to a height it had never reached before. Marie, rarely given to hyperbole or to betraying her innermost feelings, described the moments when they stood together in that shed as those which 'stirred us with ever new emotion and enchantment'.[17]

But the height they had reached was precious close to the top of their mountain.

Chapter 9

Competition

At the turn of the century they had been married over four years. Irène was two, being looked after by a servant and by Pierre's father. The old man had moved in with them into a rented house in the Boulevard Kellermann, so that everybody could benefit from his and the child's companionship. The pair mutually satisfied the emotional gaps left by a frequently absent mother on the one side, and a permanently departed wife on the other.

Marie was passionately involved in her work. Pierre had laid aside his work on symmetry into which he had poured the most part of his intellectual passion, because he recognised the importance of what they were now doing together. It was not, however, his first scientific love; he planned to return to symmetry and its problems after this temporary excitement was over. But apart from the upheaval in his once placid scientific way of life, he had problems. His ambivalent attitude to his career within the scientific establishment gave him trouble. And this period, which in retrospect appears so fruitful, was one when he was increasingly subject to bitterness and lack of self-confidence.

The conflict lay between the concern for the abilities which he knew he possessed, and the limitations his own character imposed on their development. Not that his character was dislikeable. Quite the contrary: in his quiet way he was everybody's friend. J. J. Thomson, when Curie made his first visit to Cambridge, described him as 'the most modest of men, ascribing everything to his wife', with 'a most attractive simplicity of manner'.[1] And yet when the scientific hierarchy was in question, or where he was involved with it, he had a prickly, indecisive attitude. The result was that the funds and equipment which he needed to stretch his abilities never came, because he never had the academic status, which would have given him these facilities.

The death of Schützenberger, whom he had loyally served for a dozen years, should have been the moment for a reshuffling of posts, and which could have given him a more senior status at the School of Physics and Chemistry. But his brushes with Schützenberger's successor, Gariel, heightened his dissatisfaction. Gariel immediately instituted rules that made Curie's hackles rise. First, all the teaching staff of the School had to get authorisation from him before allowing anyone to work in the laboratories; secondly, no one was allowed to enter the School without his authorisation. Curie wrote at once to his wife, on holiday at Port Blanc, telling her how he had received the new standing orders. 'I wrote him a very polite letter, but one in which I told him exactly what I thought. I asked him to renew the authorisation Schützenberger gave you to work here; then I asked him for an authorisation for Jacques to come here when he is in Paris. Finally, I asked that I should be able to welcome here whoever comes to visit me without the authorisation of anybody.'[2]

Considering that among the chosen few who felt free to wander in and out of the Curie laboratory were some of the most distinguished of Europe's scientists, including Lord Kelvin, it is scarcely surprising that Curie should have felt piqued. But his manner of drawing Gariel's attention to the fact cannot have furthered the prospects for the promotion he now so desperately needed. Without it he had neither the freedom to work as he and his wife wanted, nor the resources for a household of five to live without worry. He was in any case, with his diffident manner, total lack of interest in claims of scientific priority and dislike of the hierarchical system, what one friend called a 'miserably poor candidate' for academic posts.[3]

As promotion chances passed, his bitterness increased. Marie continued to bear signs of the same bitterness on his behalf long after his death. They felt that part of his problem was due to his being tuned out of the old-boy net. He was a graduate of neither the École Normale nor the École Polytechnique. He felt that mere membership of one of the élite Grandes Écoles would have given him all that was missing on his application form for posts at the University of Paris. Its absence, he believed, meant that his achievement, which should have counted for everything, instead counted for nothing.

Early in 1898 the Chair of Physical Chemistry became vacant at the Sorbonne, and Curie asked for it. He was refused. In 1900, when his work on crystallography, piezoelectricity, symmetry and magnetism were widely known, and the radium and polonium discoveries not in serious doubt, he had to suffer the offer of the lowly post of Assistant Professor (*répétiteur*) at the Polytechnique.

The Brain Drain, often thought to have had its birth in the 1960s with tempting American offers to under-paid European scientists in ill-equipped laboratories, has in fact its origins in the distant past. In 1900 Pierre and Marie Curie were in an ideal state to be syphoned-off by an opportunist foreign university physics department. The Brain Drain technique of the Americans, as it happens, was no more and no less aggressive than that of the Swiss 60 years earlier. In this case the University of Geneva approached Curie; its dean came to Paris in July of 1900 to wave before the couple 'a salary larger than the average one', a physics laboratory to be designed to their own specifications, and an official position in the laboratory for Marie Curie. Bowled over by the charm of the dean, and in the first flush of euphoria, Curie wrote off to a Swiss friend that he had accepted the post. He and his wife were whisked to Geneva, no doubt wined and dined in a manner best suited to an academic establishment, and the advantages of their prospective institution duly pointed out to them.

Marie Curie records[4] that it was Pierre Curie's wish to see their work on radioactivity come to fruition that in the end decided him against accepting the Geneva offer. Without doubt, any interruption at this point in their researches would have delayed her by months, if not years in her task. However, as they deliberated the advantages and disadvantages of a new life, a vacant Chair of Physics was found at the Sorbonne as a possible counter to the Swiss offer. Henri Poincaré, the most brilliant French mathematician of his age, who was to anticipate many of the ideas and results of Einstein's special theory of relativity, and who was well-versed in contemporary physical advances, had seen both the value of the Curies' work and the possible benefits to France of keeping the couple there. At his instigation the old-boy net was called in to precipitate activity. Curie was asked to apply, and was duly appointed. At the same time his wife was offered a part-time post teaching physics at a girl's Normal School at Sèvres.

The posts were designed to ease the couple's financial burdens, and so they did. But if they were conceived with any thought of easing their scientific research, they were a signal failure. Pierre's physics, chemistry and natural history course at the Sorbonne doubled the teaching load he already had at the School of Physics, and Marie suffered the time-consuming routine of preparing and mounting laboratory courses for eager young ladies. Neither of their appointments brought them any additional laboratory facilities, and the single plum attached to Curie's new Chair was the use of a small room in the Sorbonne annexe in Rue Cuvier.

The net result of this flurry of academic activity on their behalf therefore, was an easing of some of their financial burdens, with a severe limitation on what was now their most precious commodity: time. It was precious because they were genuinely enamoured of their work and its scientific potential and so, when the going looked so good, loathed to spend time away from the shed in the Rue Lhomond. And it was precious because there were plain signs that there were others, particularly in Germany and Britain, who had also seen the potential of radioactivity, and were running fast in the same direction. Pierre Curie was not particularly interested in competing in the hurly-burly of the race: he suspected its corrupting effects. Nevertheless, he was most conscious of its existence and his attitude was jingoistic rather than participatory. 'Elster and Geitel', he wrote to a physicist friend, 'are certainly those who have worked best on the question of uranium rays (in a foreign country!!)'.[5]

But the most vigorous competitor of all was farthest from Paris: the young colonial boy Ernest Rutherford. In 1898 he had taken himself from Cambridge to Canada and with his plain New Zealand farmer's approach was hugely enjoying this gallop to be first to extract useful information from the extraordinary discovery of the Parisians. In his mind there was not the shadow of a doubt of the existence of a competition, and that he had a significant place in it. He wrote to his mother from Montreal on January 5th, 1902, 'I am now busy writing up papers for publication and doing fresh work. I have to keep going, as there are always people on my track. I have to publish my present work as rapidly as possible in order to keep in the race. The·best sprinters in this road of investigation are Becquerel and the Curies in Paris, who have done a great deal of very important work in the subject of radioactive bodies during the last few years.'[6]

Marie Curie had no doubt of the importance of establishing radium and polonium unambiguously as elements, and for this reason she was pushing on single-mindedly with the monotonous task of chemical separation and purification. It had become clear to her that radium, besides being the more active of the two elements she was hunting, would also be the more easily extracted in the pure form and she was concentrating all her efforts on it. Even as early as 1899 it had been obvious to Pierre Curie and herself that the work which she was now doing, was really that of a factory-hand, and that the whole operation of purification could be more efficiently organised in a factory. When the Central Society of Chemical Products, a firm Curie had been involved with in the manufacture of some of his apparatus, offered facilities for a trial of an industrial scale operation of radium separation, they grabbed the chance. With characteristic naïvety they interpreted the industrial firm's generosity as a selfless gesture.

Another young physicist, André Debierne, took over direction of the process. Like so many of those attracted by the Curies in this period, he too was of the Pierre Curie type: shy and reticent. He was very able, but often moody and inarticulate, seeking out the Curies for friendship as well as for their scientific abilities. Debierne was never to leave the shadow of the Curies. He published several papers in co-operation with both of them, discovered a third new radioactive element, actinium, and was instrumental in the success of the experiments which Marie Curie was now bringing towards their final phase.

But there was another drain on the Curies' time. Increasingly their annoying and apparently trivial ailments were beginning to keep them from their work. Marie had partly grown out of her hypochondria and was confused and annoyed by the symptoms she saw in both of them. The constant problem of fatigue was bothering them more and more. She attributed Curie's weariness to the fact that he now had continually to trek back and forth between his Sorbonne teaching laboratories and their shed in the School of Physics. Also he was suffering badly now from what had been diagnosed as rheumatism.

In March, 1899, she had written to brother Jozef to give news of Irène's progress, and of the lack of progress of her doctorate because the work on the new elements was taking up so much of her time. She added[7] that their health was good, though it needed no great effort of reading between the lines to doubt it. Pierre, she went on, was on a diet of milk, eggs and vegetables, and had had to forego meat and red wine, and drink large quantities of water; the ascribed a recent improvement in his rheumatism to this regime. She told Jozef that she herself was very well, but went on to reveal that she had been in the hands of doctors for examination of her suspect lungs and for sputum analyses. But the intense interest of their work during this period carried them over the bad patches. It was a time of phenomenal productivity which neither of them were again ever to equal. Pierre Curie's special skills as a practical physicist were now particularly useful and he was emerging from their seam of gold with some nuggets. The three years beginning in 1900 saw their publications at a peak. In that year Pierre Curie's name was on five published papers and Marie Curie's on three; in 1901 his was on six, and in 1902 his on four and hers on one. Marie published either in her own name or in collaboration with Pierre; Curie himself invariably did work with a collaborator: either his wife or another physicist such as André Debierne or Georges Sagnac. All the work they did now was related to radioactivity, aimed at increasing knowledge of the new metals and their rays.

The competitive field was growing daily. Becquerel himself, after an initial loss of interest in the phenomenon he first discovered, was now back with it. And whereas it was Lippmann who had presented the Curies' earliest radioactivity papers to the Académie des Sciences, it was Becquerel who in 1899 began to do this for them.

In Germany two chemical firms had succeeded in making marketable amounts of impure radioactive elements.[8] The director of one of these companies, Friedrich Giesel (his firm manufactured quinine), was generous with his samples of radioactive materials to fellow research workers. The Curies too were generous with the solutions they had so laboriously prepared, and Becquerel and Rutherford were among those who benefitted from their gifts. This generosity was what was then regarded as the true scientific spirit of the age.

The ready availability of materials with which to work meant that within two years of its discovery impure radium could be begged, borrowed or bought throughout most of Europe and was certainly being worked on in North America. Duplication of research was therefore inevitable. So that, as Marie Curie worked away persistently on the final stages of purification on the make-shift laboratory's wooden benches, and as her husband worked away equally persistently on another bench exploring the exact nature of the radium rays, both knew that it was quite possible that what they were doing was being done in some better equipped laboratory somewhere else. For all they knew, the results of that work might be on its way to the printers and could appear within weeks in some foreign scientific publication.

This was exactly the case with Pierre Curie. Several other physicists had, like him, decided to try to identify the constituents of radium rays and, like him, were trying out the effects of passing the rays through magnetic fields and watching how a magnet could deflect certain of the rays; they were seeing how these deflected rays ionised certain gases and watching their effects on different substances and on chemical reactions. It was an open subject now and, as with X-rays, everybody who was able was milking it and quickly getting their results into print.

But Marie Curie as it turned out was without competitors. The reasons are not difficult to see. First, the task she had set herself was difficult and tedious in the extreme; second, few people rated it sufficiently important to deserve such devotion, hard labour and time.

Marie Curie was obsessed at that time with the idea that the scientific world in general was sceptical that what she claimed to be completely new elements, previously unknown to mankind, were in fact elements at all. She was looking for what she later called, 'the kind of evidence which chemical science demands, that radium is a true element'.[9] It is true that there were sceptics, but in a sense she was tilting at a windmill she had built herself. Isolated as she was from all but a select band of visitors to her laboratory, she was unaware that those who really mattered in the international scientific community had never doubted the reality of radium and were as confident as she of its importance in the history of science.

But nothing could have shifted her from her path once she had clearly decided on it. She had first begun the purification process in 1898. In the first months she had extracted from her pitchblende hundreds, if not thousands of gallons of liquor and patiently reduced it literally to thimbleful quantities of radium solution. There were times when she believed she had reached journey's end, only to have to admit that she was mistaken. On July 23rd, 1900, she had written in premature triumph in her notebook '*pure radium* in this capsule'. Even if there was pure radium chloride in that tube, it was in too small a quantity for its atomic weight to be measured; and without this figure, she was still an age away from achieving the object of her exercise.

A few days later the notebook shows she measured the atomic weight of another sample of radium as 174. She knew the result was no good. The figure was much too low a value to make it worth considering. She did a quick calculation on the next page and then in disgust with herself, and beginning to despair, wrote at the bottom of the page, '*it's impossible*, the product can't have been converted into its chloride'. Her attempts at purification had failed and if she was to get anywhere at all she would have to start the whole procedure all over again.

She did. There is now a gap of two years in that notebook, indicating sometimes perhaps continuing lethargy, and sometimes despondency. The next recorded date is March 28th, 1902. She had taken her latest sample of radium chloride to Eugène Demarçay. It weighed slightly more than one-tenth of a gram, and the powerful radiations it was emitting caused his delicate electrical apparatus to go haywire. But he confirmed that the amount of barium it contained was now negligible. That day Marie Curie assessed and wrote down the first figures she had written in that notebook during those two years: $Ra = 225.93$. This short equation was the statement of what she had taken four years to achieve. Having conceived, given birth to, and christened her child, now she knew that she had purified and confirmed it.

Chapter 10

All the Rage

It was now radium's turn to become the rage. Journalists whose copy a few years before had blazoned the mystery and the wonders of the new X-rays in the first of the popular, and often enough, inaccurate pieces of science journalism, now looked to this new element for some extra excitement to add to their futuristically inclined columns. The Curies had yet to experience the knocks on their laboratory door and self-confident young men with short-hand notebooks. Other scientists, however, had already experienced the technique of 'the interview' and its consequences. Further west, where journalistic methods were even less refined, Ernest Rutherford, whose work in Canada on radioactivity was moving on apace, was to find himself besieged with reporters; he only put an end to a series of heavily embroidered stories when he forbad them the sacred precincts of his laboratory.

But in the world of physics too the excitement was high. Optimism and activity surged beyond reason, as it had with Röntgen's first announcement of X-rays. In England Sir Robert Ball, with suspiciously religious overtones, described radium as 'not a mystery, but a miracle'. The folklore grew even among physicists. One eminent professor, warned by his doctor that he had not long to live, is reported to have replied, 'I can't die yet, I want to know more about radium!' He is also reported to have recovered.[1]

The glimmerings of what new avenues of discovery this element might reveal because of its singular properties were bright indeed. Pierre Curie's enthusiasm was boyish. He was fond of pointing out the staggering fact that radium was now shown to be no less than a million times more radioactive than uranium. Curie had no doubts about the avenues of discovery along which their new work would lead. One evening, sitting at the dinner table with a few guests, when the light was fading, he produced from his waistcoat pocket a tube of radium salt. It gave out its blue, mysterious glow over the table, and he turned to the young maid who was serving the meal and said, 'This is the light of the future!' But his wife had the habit of reproaching him with a quiet but firm 'Oh! Pierre!' when he made such out of character predictions.[2]

Nevertheless, it was *her* persistence that had raised the name and fame of this insignificantly small amount of radium to the point such that much of the scientific world was singing its praises and its potential. It was four years since they had together discovered radium. Since that time Marie Curie had worked under extreme conditions to get at what she wanted. It was not so much what she had done, but the way she had done it – in an old shed in the back yard of a Paris school, a woman with a small child, working a man's role and a workman's hours – that was just beginning to catch the imagination of the rest of Europe.

The truth of the matter is that radium and polonium, with the Curies' suggestion that radioactivity is atomic in character, were their greatest discoveries. The purification of radium chloride and the determination of the atomic weight of radium were, in scientific terms, routine tasks and of secondary importance. But Marie Curie had carried them out against such odds that her achievement had the makings of a legend. The little blue light shining from the glass tube was seen as a great lamp of achievement shining out to lead others on in the field of radioactive research.

But the legend was not seriously to influence them for some time yet. They could still continue with their reclusive pattern of life. The slowly pedalling grey-cloaked figures, cycling home on their bicycles in a dignified fashion, had become personalities worth noting by visitors to the *Quartier Latin*. And the little house in the Boulevard Kellermann where they lived with Eugène Curie was becoming well-known to those familiar with their work. Beyond that, and the fact that they were occasionally invited to functions and to salons run by ladies in whom they had no interest and with whom they had nothing in common, life continued for a little while in its unvaried fashion.

The house, 108 Boulevard Kellermann, is no longer standing. A small plaque set into a wall records the years the Curies spent there. Behind the wall now stand a few rusting motor cars. But number 106, where their friends the Perrins came to live alongside them, still stands and gives some idea of the quiet idyll to which they could return after a day in the laboratory. It is a pretty little place hiding behind a sycamore and a bower of lilac, ivy and ferns: though today it stands self-consciously overshadowed by a reinforced concrete tower block of apartments.

Weekends spent in the garden of number 108 were peaceful, disturbed only by the acceptable group of friends they had got to know well through their work. Jean Perrin, already distinguished for his work on the nature of cathode rays, was a regular visitor. A large halo of hair surrounding his angelic face, he would appear as often as not with a bunch of flowers to remind Marie Curie that she deserved not only the respect she was now beginning to expect as a scientist, but that also due to a woman. On Sunday afternoons a small clan of physicists would gather from the School of Physics or from the Sorbonne – André Debierne, Georges Sagnac, Aimé Cotton, Perrin and others – and listen to Curie, now very much the senior and most distinguished among them, and to his reactions to their ideas. It was an élite and satisfying milieu which many of those beginning to work in this new and booming field of physics found to their liking. Several of Curie's ex-students joined the group. Paul Langevin, good-looking, dapperly dressed, hair cut *en-brosse*, waxed moustaches and a bosom friend of Jean Perrin, was one of these. He was to move his young family to a place nearby so that he could be nearer the Curies.

Only occasionally did the Curies let themselves be drawn into groups with wider interests. There was one salon, for example, that centred on a pretty and talkative young woman, Marguerite Borel, the wife of a distinguished mathematician, Émile Borel, who herself had literary aspirations, writing under the pen-name of Camille Marbo. Marguerite was to become a close and astute observer of the Curies, their friends, and their way of life. The Borels were a worldly couple, and gathered about them artists, writers and politicians as well as scientists and mathematicians. Their social circle was one for which the Curies had no affection whatever, even despising it. On the few occasions the Curies put in an appearance they would glide in with what Camille called 'conspicuous inobtrusiveness', and find some protected corner of the room where they could watch and listen. Only when scientific subjects were raised would Marie Curie enter the conversation. Quite suddenly she would give her point of view, with firmness and confidence, then return to her introverted contemplation. This style intimidated the young, flirtatious Marguerite Borel, who herself took an undisguised enjoyment in the social chit-chat between the men and the women.

But it was also a world which brought Marie Curie into contact with a few people whom she could admire for what they did, and not for what they were. Rodin was one of these: small of stature, large of head, he showed a magnificent indifference to what others thought of his art.

Pierre Curie, who showed great disdain for competitive science, was nevertheless ambivalent to others' opinion of his science. His instincts were entirely opposed to seeking honours, yet he had a knack of putting himself in positions which invited humiliation. In May 1902 he agreed to have his name put forward as a candidate for election to the Académie des Sciences. The system of election was as chastening to the candidate and as outmoded then as it is today.

Since 1635 the Académie Française had assiduously followed its role of guarding and purifying that essence of civilisation, the French language. The Académie des Sciences had subsequently assumed the same lofty responsibility for French science; it was a strictly professional foundation, far less amateur in concept than the Royal Society of London. Pierre Curie, after he had been proposed for membership, had to follow the traditional method of trying to gain a seat in the Académie des Sciences. He had to visit each existing member in turn and tout for his vote. His opponent for the seat had to follow the same routine. It would be difficult to devise a system more demoralising to a man so sensitive. His candidature failed by 20 votes against 32.

Curie was in good company. Zola's candidature for the Académie Française failed several times. Curie told his friend Georges Gouy not to 'believe that I am sensibly affected by these things'. But he clearly was bitterly hurt.

A year later the Dean of the Sorbonne Faculty of Science, Paul Appell, Marguerite Borel's father, wrote Curie, begging to let him be put on the list Appell was compiling for the appropriate Minister for recommendation for the Legion of Honour. 'I ask it of you,' Appell wrote, *'as a service to the faculty.'*[3] Although nothing further would have been required of him on this occasion, Curie refused the offer haughtily.

But although official recognition for his work – and by implication, his wife's – was withheld, unofficially the shed in the Rue Lhomond was well marked on the scientific map of Europe. The trail to the Curies' doorstep brought within their sphere distinguished chemists and physicists who came to see how closely the legendary conditions under which the Curies had worked corresponded with reality. Lord Kelvin, longer in white beard, but seemingly impervious to age, continued his benevolent patronage, and his embossed visiting card was frequently carried by the lab-boy through the shed door and placed reverentially on the laboratory bench in front of Madame Curie. The Old Testament figure inspired confidence in many others besides the Curies. Ernest Rutherford's mother once wrote to her son: 'You cannot fail to know how glad and thankful I feel that God has blessed and crowned your genius and efforts with success. That you may rise to greater heights of fame and live near to God like Lord Kelvin is my earnest wish and prayer . . .'[4]

But Ernest was a shade more sceptical of Kelvin's godliness than his earnest mother. Kelvin was old, and his contribution to nineteenth-century physics had been magnificent, but his attitudes to some of the implications of the new radioactivity were to say the least reactionary. The energetic young Rutherford, so often in opposition to Kelvin's ideas, was at this time just beginning to see the really revolutionary implications of the work which he, the Curies, Becquerel, J. J. Thomson and others had thrust in front of the new century's physicists. This work was to alter every scientist's concept, inherited from the Greeks, of the atom as the smallest, ultimate particle of matter. Lord Kelvin, long after most others had accepted the inevitable, was still insisting at a British Association meeting in 1906, on the indestructibility of atoms. Rutherford, never one to mince his words, had earlier written to his wife, 'Lord Kelvin has talked radium most of the day and I admire his confidence in talking about a subject of which he has taken the trouble to learn so little.'[5]

Marie and Pierre Curie had been playing their full parts, at first not fully conscious of the truly revolutionary nature of the implications of some of their work, in trying to find out more about the nature of the new rays. They were observing how these rays caused air to conduct electric charges, their effects on photographic plates, whether they could be reflected and refracted as are rays of light, and in particular wondering what could be the source of the radiations that their new substances gave off in apparently never-ceasing streams.

The great surge of interest in this kind of work throughout the whole of Europe had arisen because the Curies had thrown into the scientific arena their immensely powerful radioactive sources, the likes of which had never been experienced before. It was their generosity in giving Becquerel samples of Marie's hard-won material that encouraged him to join the race in France to discover more. In Germany Julius Elster, and Hans Geitel and in Austria Stefan Meyer were also hard at work. In the space of a few weeks, late in 1899, these workers in a sudden burst of simultaneous discovery in their three different countries, found that if the rays were passed through a magnetic field they were deflected: the rays curved, just as a current of electricity would if it were flowing out of the radium. Pierre Curie too was at work on the magnetic deflection of the rays. He came to the conclusion that there were two kinds of radiation given out by radium. One set of rays seemed to disappear after travelling for a few centimetres through air and to be unaffected by his magnet. The other rays he found to be bent. Then, shortly afterwards, he and Marie together found that the rays that could be bent were electrically negatively charged. It was as though a current of negative electricity was flowing out of the radium.[6]

Thousands of miles away in Canada Ernest Rutherford, because of the slowness of transatlantic mail weeks out of touch with the race in which he was so joyfully competing, was gathering together the mass of confusing information into the beginnings of a cohesive theory. Already at the beginning of 1899 he had published a brilliant paper dealing with radiation given out by uranium, had shown that there existed quite distinguishable types of rays and had demonstrated the effects of putting thin sheets of metal foil in their paths. One set, which he had named *alpha* rays, he found were halted by the foil, and even by thin cardboard. '*My* alpha rays' he called them. He even took a delight in asking his students to test the sensitiveness of their fingers by having them hold their hands over radioactive sources to see whether they could 'feel' his alpha rays! The second set, which he called *beta* rays, he found would penetrate quite large thicknesses of certain metals and were very similar to some X-rays.[7]

Later, another Frenchman, Paul Villard, showed that radioactive substances gave out yet a third set of penetrating radiations, which were later called *gamma* rays. Those few scientists who were at the heart of radioactive work were now beginning to see that these discoveries were plainly showing the virginity of the atom was a myth. Marie Curie's radium, to all intents and purposes, had told all. A young British chemist, Frederick Soddy, then just starting on the subject, later wrote of what the metal's discovery had meant to science: 'This one element has clothed with its own dignity the whole empire of common matter. The ultra-material potentialities of radium are the common possession of all that world to which, in our ignorance, we used to refer to as mere inanimate matter. This is the weightiest lesson the existence of radium has taught us.'[8]

Matter was far from inanimate. Its animate behaviour was still raising more problems than it seemed could possibly be solved. One of the Curies' earliest observations, for example, was that radium of its own accord gave out heat, and in quite sufficiently large amounts to be measured by simple laboratory techniques. Pierre Curie showed that the equivalent of 1 gram of radium gives out about 100 calories of heat an hour – a little powerhouse. But where did all this energy come from? Curie himself was at first convinced that the, until then, invariant law of physics, the law of conservation of energy (which states that energy can neither be created nor destroyed), was being broken. Marie Curie herself went into print with two possible explanations.[9] In one she supposed that her radioactive substances were borrowing their energy from some external source and releasing it. Was it possible that there were some still unknown radiation permeating the whole of space which her radium was capturing and then releasing? (Lord Kelvin even went so far as to suggest that radium was getting its energy by absorbing mysterious 'ethereal waves'!)

In the other she pondered over the possibility of whether radium drew on itself for its energy. Were there tiny particles in the substance which were agitating themselves in a violent fashion and then being thrown out as radiation? If this was the case, then any loss in weight would only be measurable after millions of years, since so far she had been able to find no loss of weight with time whatever.

Another remarkable phenomenon discovered by the Curies was that when they took one of their strong sources of radiation, either a radium or polonium salt in powder form, and put it on their laboratory bench near a metal plate, although there was apparently no contact whatever between the two, the metal plate itself became radioactive. Even after several hours their electrometer showed that the metal plate had retained some of its radioactivity. They called the effect *induced radioactivity*; it was this phenomenon that had so confused and hindered Demarçay in the spectroscopic work he had been doing for the Curies.

Rutherford in Montreal was poring over this sort of information each time a bundle of journals reached him so slowly by the steamers that came up the St Lawrence river. He now began to piece it together into a more meaningful theory of radioactivity. He had found that by blowing air across some samples of thorium he could collect a gas which, like thorium itself, was radioactive.

He called it thorium emanation, or thoron; its radioactivity, he discovered, diminished exponentially with time. In Germany a chemist called Ernst Dorn showed that a similar effect happened with radium. It too gave off an emanation, later called radon, which also was radioactive. It turned out that any substances which came into contact with these emanations themselves became radioactive. These were gases which drifted in the air of any laboratory where strong radioactive sources were being used and, needless to say, were breathed in and out by workers such as the Curies who were handling the most powerful radioactive materials.

At this time the young Frederick Soddy joined Rutherford in Canada. It was a scientifically timely match of an ideal pair: the combination of physicist and chemist, just as had been Marie and Pierre Curie's marriage. Pierre Curie was a skilled theoretician and a brilliant instrument maker, and so too Rutherford had a unique physicist's mind and a wonderful facility for improvising delicate electrical instruments from simple bits of wire and glass. Soddy had had a thorough grounding as a chemist at Oxford and his skill in handling materials matched that of the doggedly self-taught Marie. Again this combination of the two disciplines was to produce magnificent results.

Rutherford had succeeded in separating from thorium a new substance which, once removed, appeared to take with it all the radioactivity of thorium. He called it thorium X. But he noticed that with time the radioactivity of the remaining thorium returned. This observation led to the most important contribution to the history of radioactivity since Marie Curie's separation of radium. In brief, what Rutherford and Soddy showed was that thorium, uranium and other radioactive elements, by giving out either alpha or beta rays, were breaking themselves down into a series of intermediate, completely new elements. Thorium, for example, slowly formed thorium X which then behaved in a characteristic radioactive fashion. Each of these intermediate elements broke down at a definite rate in such a way that half of any quantity had disappeared in a fixed period of time. Rutherford called this the *half-life* of the radioactive substance.

Soddy later described the great thrill of the moment of discovery, on the day that he and Rutherford realised that they had the answer to what radioactivity was all about: their sudden realisation that the atom was spontaneously disintegrating. 'I was overwhelmed with something greater than joy – I cannot very well express it – a kind of exaltation, intermingled with a certain feeling of pride that I had been chosen from all chemists of all ages to discover natural transmutation.' As he looked up at Rutherford across the laboratory bench he blurted out, 'Rutherford, this is transmutation: the thorium is disintegrating . . .' 'For Mike's sake, Soddy,' Rutherford shouted back, 'don't call it *transmutation*. They'll have our heads off as alchemists. You know what they are.' But not really caring two hoots whether anybody thought him a scientific heretic, or not, he waltzed round the laboratory booming out 'Onward Christian so-ho-hojers', in his usual intonation which, as all his friends were later to notice, was only recognisable by the words and never by the tune.[10]

Rutherford and Soddy developed their theory to show that there were three parent radioactive elements, uranium, thorium, and radium. They drew a chart which showed how each new substance was derived from each parent element by the discharge of an alpha ray, or particle. It was the basis of a substantial theory of radioactivity, though later it was shown that radium was in fact a radioactive product of uranium.

During the same period that Rutherford was spending long hours working into the night, in order to make quite sure that he was first in the race to publish, Marie Curie was spending equally long, late hours on work which was to her of the utmost personal importance. She would arrive back from the laboratory to 108 Boulevard Kellermann, quickly have her evening meal, then give what time she could to the baby Irène. She would bath her, put her to bed, stay, talk and read as the good mother should and wait until the persistent patter of requests to 'Mé' (the name Irène used for her mother until long after she herself was a grown woman), had been quieted by sleep. Then, in the room on the first floor which they used for a study, she would light an oil-lamp, and sitting at the same table as her husband, begin to write.

She was working on her doctoral thesis, gathering together the results of her four years as a mature scientist. Marie Curie was the first female to have engineered for herself a situation in which she could compete in a totally masculine dominated field of science. And she had both the tenacity and determination to win a significant place for herself in that field. Her thesis was a long, comprehensive and careful document reviewing the field of radioactivity up to 1903, of which she could fairly be said to have been the motivating force.

In a hundred or so pages she wrote out in the flat unemotional sentences which have become the unfortunate hall-mark of scientific prose, all the trials to which she had submitted dozens of substances; she listed the positive and now unquestionable conclusions of her polonium and radium work, without a hint of the months of sweat, set-backs and hardships she had had to experience to make these conclusions possible. The sheets she wrote, and then rewrote, reviewed her work on radioactive minerals: the method, now a standard procedure, she had devised to separate her two radioactive elements: the method of purification of radium: the determination of its atomic weight: her attempts to characterise the rays given off by the two elements, and her observations of induced radioactivity.

She had the work complete, printed and ready for submission to the university examiners by June 25th, 1903. It was a day of symbolic achievement. She had never been modest about her own work and she therefore invited the few close friends she had to be present to observe and share it. Jean Perrin and Paul Langevin were to be present in the hall of the Sorbonne where she was to be examined: so was a row of fresh-faced girls from her science class at Sèvres: so too of course were her husband and his father. And from her own side of the family she had invited sister Bronia. It was Bronia who persuaded her to indulge in a new dress for the occasion – black, of course, so that it could be used more fittingly in the laboratory later.

The hall was crowded for the occasion. As celebrities the Curies were becoming of interest to those who had not much more than a passing concern for the real nature of their work. The focus of the crowd's attention, besides the woman in the black dress, was the row of three distinguished examiners who sat at the table facing her. As invariably happens, the affair was conducted in low key with the three professors, Lippmann, Bouty and Moissan, quietly asking questions, and even more quietly being given responses. If they were honest these three men would have had to admit to themselves that Marie Curie's grasp of the subject was greater than that of anybody else in the hall that day, including themselves. And when Lippmann, Marie's one-time professor and now president of the group of three, gave the accolade of Doctor of Physical Science in the University of Paris, adding the distinction of *très honorable*, there can have been none in the audience who, on technical grounds at least, did not feel that the extra blessing was well deserved.

To the polite ripple of applause which ended the session, Marie Curie left the hall as the crowned queen of radioactivity. But by remarkable chance there was present in Paris that day the man who, had he chosen to use the knowledge he had collected over the past few months, could have given Marie Curie a far tougher grilling than any of her examiners. Ernest Rutherford, as-yet-uncrowned king of radioactivity, was in town.

Early in the day he had wandered along to the dowdy Curie laboratory on the off-chance of seeing Marie, only to be told that she was at that moment being examined for her doctorate. The chance that had taken him there was a by now dog-eared postcard sent by Soddy, which had passed through post offices in Notting Hill, Geneva and Paris before reaching Rutherford in France on his tour of the European laboratories. Madame Curie had sent a message hoping that he, Rutherford, would find time to call and see her.

Rutherford took up the invitation within hours of the card reaching him.[11] He had good reason to pay a courtesy call on the Curies. All his work on the deflection of alpha rays in a magnetic field had been a failure until they sent him a sufficiently powerful radioactive source of radium for his work.

But if he missed the ceremony, he was in time for the celebrations, and later that day he met Marie Curie for the first time at a little dinner party arranged by the dapper and brilliant physicist, Paul Langevin. Rutherford and Langevin had known each other well a few years before, as research students under J. J. Thomson, and Langevin qualified for one of the adjectives Rutherford reserved for his bosom pals: 'a thundering good fellow'. To honour Marie Curie Langevin had invited along Pierre, Rutherford and his new, young wife, and Jean Perrin and his wife. It was a distinguished group.

Rutherford immediately took to Marie Curie, and after that first encounter always had a soft spot for her—even when some of his closest friends had developed different sentiments. He liked her no-nonsense way of dressing; he never could stand the new-fangled décolleté the wives of some of his professorial friends were adopting, and had made his views quite clear to his young wife before they married. Clearly, Marie Curie's simplicity appealed to him, just as his enthusiasm seemed honest and worthwhile to her. Once he turned to her and, in a way which she among few others could fully understand, said that radioactivity really and truly was 'a splendid subject to work on'. She was to remember these simple words to the year of her death.[12] She knew that he treated women very much as equals; this must have flattered her. She did not find his bluntness repulsive. He was, at that time, one of the few physicists who was actively encouraging women to pursue scientific careers in his laboratories.

The topics discussed at the dinner table that evening ranged over much that was new in radioactivity, and particularly Rutherford's work. The early work of the Curies had always deeply impressed Rutherford, but on the question of their theories of the nature of radioactivity he was left in no doubt that they were sitting uncomfortably on the fence. Some months earlier, unaware of Soddy and Rutherford's new concept of transmutation, they had even gone so far as to cast doubt on the validity of the work that had first made them famous. They had begun to suspect that polonium, the metal Marie had so proudly named after her own country, was not an element at all.[13] It was to be an embarrassing mistake. Rutherford later expressed himself quite unambiguously on the limits of the Curies' work at the time he joined them for their celebratory dinner. 'M. and Mme Curie have throughout taken a very general view of the phenomena of radioactivity, and have not put forward any definite theory.'[14] Secretly, no doubt the realisation of their limits pleased him.

But the party was a great success. If there were differences of opinion, they were amicable and stimulating. They also were long argued into the late hours. At 11 o'clock they all decided to sit in the garden and enjoy the warm night. Pierre Curie had deliberately kept in reserve a dramatic finale to this satisfying day. When they were all settled, he brought from his pocket a small tube, partly coated with zinc sulphide and containing a solution of radium prepared by Marie. In the darkness, as the tube emerged, the zinc coating suddenly luminesced with a brilliant glow caused by the radium. Each one watched silently, and each one was impressed.[15]

But in the light from the tube Rutherford saw something else. He noticed that Pierre Curie's hands were raw and inflamed. It even seemed painful for Curie to handle the tube.

The next day Pierre Curie sat at his work table to write a letter to Professor James Dewar of the Royal Institution in London, thanking him for the recent hospitality he and Marie had had there. Curie asked that his bad handwriting should be excused. He had to admit that his fingers were now so painful that he could scarcely hold the pen.[16]

Chapter 11

The Prize

Just a week before, on June 19th, 1903, the Curies had been the centre of attraction of the scientific high society of London. That day Pierre had given a Friday Evening Discourse to the Royal Institution. His hands then had been in bad condition. Marie's too were showing signs of cracking and rawness, but were not nearly so badly affected as his. For several days Pierre had had difficulty in dressing himself, and this particular evening required him to struggle into white tie and tails, and she into her one evening dress.

The tradition, the personalities and the attendant paraphernalia of the weekly august occasion of the Royal Institution must have intimidated the reclusive Curies. They were oppressed as they were ushered through the Georgian pillars past a gaping crowd and then swept up a gracious staircase past somewhat more dignified, but still watchful, high-collared and monocled gentlemen. However, they had good reason to be tolerant of Anglo-Saxon tradition. It was the British who, more than any other nation, and certainly more so than the French, had been particularly enthusiastic about the Curies' work and ideas. For if British achievements in, and attitudes to art and music in the last quarter of the nineteenth century were depressingly conservative compared with those of the French, the same could not be said of science.

In such places as the Royal Institution francophiles like Lord Kelvin and James Dewar, Professor at the Institution, were spreading and hotly debating the Curies' gospel. The homage paid that evening to the couple was to help focus on them the attention and recognition of the scientific world outside France. The far-reaching importance of Pierre Curie's work on piezo-electricity, magnetism and symmetry was internationally acknowledged. Radium was already a word well-known outside physics and chemistry laboratories. But its real importance to science had not been fully assessed, though there were several physicists outside France more impressed by its qualities than many inside. Their admirers were now seeing to it that the Curies got the recognition they deserved, even if the style was more glamorous than the recipients would have preferred.

The Royal Institution Friday Evening Discourses were designed to spread an understanding of science to a wide, not necessarily scientifically educated public. Over the years these occasions had acquired the reputation of being amongst the most successful reputable popularisations of science. Quite early in their history they had become so popular that Albemarle Street, where the Institution stood, suffered regular Friday evening blockages of carriages, and became the first one-way street in London.

A large audience in the banked amphitheatre burst into applause when Sir William Crookes led the ill-looking and shy man to the laboratory bench. Facing him, starch-fronted and beflowered, was the *crème-de-la-crème* of British physics: Lord Kelvin, Lord Rayleigh, Sir Oliver Lodge, Professor James Dewar, Professor William Ayrton, Professor Sylvanus P. Thompson. And next to Kelvin, pale and, in comparison with the surrounding finery, very plainly dressed, was Curie's wife. But she was not the only woman present. From the start the Institution actually encouraged women members, provided, as its statutes said, steps were taken 'to preclude the Possibility of any improper Female name being found amongst the Subscribers'.[1] Nevertheless, there is no doubt that Marie Curie would never have been invited there to present the results of her work in her own right. Instead she had no alternative but to listen to her husband alone describe the results of their joint efforts.

However, as a physicist wife of a physicist, she was not so singular a figure amongst the well-groomed set of wives as she had first thought. She discovered that Professor Ayrton's wife, Hertha, the daughter of a Polish jew, could talk her own language: physics – in French if necessary – and was a strong character, quite capable of holding her own in the conversation pieces of this scientific enclave.

Pierre had been well-drilled by Dewar as to how to behave in front of a Friday evening audience! Speak slowly (even if regrettably it has to be in French), speak simply, and throw in as many visual experiments as can be concocted to keep the interest of the members not altogether at one with the deeper implications of the work. Radium gave Curie plenty of opportunity to perform party tricks; he showed its rapid power of affecting wrapped photographic plates, he demonstrated its spontaneous ability to give off heat and, with the house lights dimmed, its impressive luminosity. At some time during this visit he unwittingly left behind a semi-permanent example of radium's persistent radioactive properties. He accidentally spilt some of his wife's precious material: fifty years later its presence was detected in parts of the Institution, in such quantities that certain areas had to be decontaminated by Harwell scientists.

Apart from this minor set-back the evening went well. His lecture was well attuned to the needs of the cognoscenti in the audience and he gave a comprehensive review of his and his wife's latest work on the nature of the emitted rays and on induced radioactivity. He also made the point that he was by no means convinced by Mr Rutherford's hypothesis of the existence of radium emanation.[2]

But, as it was clear to Rutherford a week later, it must have been clear to the audience that night that Curie was far from being a healthy man. And the reason for his feeble appearance was all unknowingly included in a section of his lecture. He discussed at some length the physiological action of radium rays. The first effects of the rays on the human body had been experienced by a German, Walkhoff, who noticed that tubes of radium preparations kept in his pocket or left near the skin produced, after a few days, irritating burns. Friedrich Giesel had also shown that, when he held a closed box containing a radium salt near his closed eye, it produced the sensation of light on the retina.

Curie himself had been quick to follow up these experiments and described in vivid terms to his audience the tests he and Becquerel had carried out on their own bodies.[3] Curie had taken a sample of impure radium salt, wrapped it in a thin sheet of gutta-percha and had strapped it to his arm for 10 hours. After this time the skin looked red, as though burned. After several more days the spot became more sore and a scab eventually developed which had to be dressed. He continued to carry out observations on himself for 52 days, at the end of which time the permanent scar of a grey wound remained. Pierre Curie pulled back his sleeve and showed the mark to his audience.

Becquerel had noticed similar effects on himself after carrying round a tube containing radium in his waistcoat pocket. He had also noticed that when the radium was surrounded by a lead cover it had no harmful effect whatever. There was thus a perfectly good means of protection from the rays – if the radium workers chose to employ it.

But at that time there seemed no reason to take time-wasting precautions to prevent an occasional irritating burn. There were two other members of the audience who had personal experience of the effects. Kelvin had been honoured by the Curies with a gift of a small sample of radium, which he too had kept in his waistcoat pocket, and had suffered the inevitable burnt patch on his chest. The other, sitting next to him, was Marie Curie herself. She had carried round a phial of material for a short time and had still suffered the effects of burnt skin 15 days later. It seemed an acceptable occupational hazard and she was no more concerned about it than her husband. She treated its effects cavalierly. One day when she and Marguerite Borel were staying in the same hotel, the young Marguerite looked at the back of her own hand and pointed out a small violet patch which had suddenly appeared there. The scientist recognised it, rather inconsequentially for Marguerite's liking, for what it was: a radium burn from a small phial Madame Curie kept by her bedside and on which Marguerite had unwittingly put her hand.[4]

Rutherford was as unconcerned with the hazards as were the Curies. Indeed, one experiment involving Friedrich Giesel, who like the Curies had spent many months separating radioactive substances, caused Rutherford some satisfaction. Giesel's breath was so radioactive that it would rapidly discharge an electroscope.[5] The presence of so much radioactive gas in Giesel's lungs neatly confirmed Rutherford's theory of the existence of airborne emanations.

But what caught the public imagination at Pierre Curie's lecture was not so much the possible harmful effects of radium and its rays on living tissues but, as with X-rays, their possible therapeutic value. He mentioned during his talk that night the emotive word *cancer*. Walkhoff had already successfully treated certain cancers with X-rays, and Curie announced to his audience that radium could be used in a similar fashion. Radium, moreover, had definite advantages over other forms of treatment since it could be introduced in a fine tube exactly at the point where it was believed it might be most beneficial.

Already factories were being set up to manufacture radium preparations as therapeutic agents. If there was a future for radium outside pure science, it seemed a hopeful one. If there was a price to be paid, there was still, it seemed, no sign of it other than a few scorched arms and fingers such as the audience in Albemarle Street could see innocently displayed that night by Monsieur and Madame Curie.

They returned to Paris, if not in triumph, at least with the reassurance that they had scored a scientific success. Later that year the Royal Society of London was to award them its coveted Davy Medal. With this honour they could now expect wider international recognition for their work.

But the excitement of the public events of that June were rare and garish incidents in what, for Marie Curie, was still a continuing routine, difficult and drab existence. It was routine because that was how she chose through preference to run her laboratory affairs. It was difficult because health problems were now beginning to dominate their lives. It was drab because they still had no more than adequate means on which to live. The fame which the isolation of radium had given them had opened a few sources of public funds with which they could buy materials for the large scale operations now necessary. By far the largest and most useful of these, however, had not come until 1902, when the Academy of Sciences gave them a subvention of 20,000 francs. With this they had been able to finance the industrial extraction of radium-bearing barium in sufficient quantities for Marie to carry back to the laboratory first to purify, then fractionally crystallise.

As the summer of 1903 wore on each began to worry more about the other's health and both became more concerned about the unsatisfactory nature of their life. Even before their visit to London Pierre Curie had written to James Dewar, with whom he was collaborating on research on the heat emitted by radium, 'Madame Curie is always tired without being exactly ill.'[6] At the same time, Marie Curie was convinced that the source of her husband's problem was the complicated teaching curriculum he had to keep up at the Sorbonne in order to make a living, and the constant travelling to and from the laboratory. The violent pain he was having in different parts of his body was getting worse, and the trembling in his legs was sometimes so bad that he had to stay in bed. Still he called it rheumatism, and still he attributed it to the damp of their shed.

A few months earlier the Chair of Mineralogy at the Sorbonne had become vacant. The subject was not that of their recent fame, but it was one in which Curie's past record and present distinction, having helped open up one of the most promising fields of physics for many years, should have made him a front runner. He put himself forward as candidate and was bluntly rejected. He was bitter at the result and again, his wife shared his disappointment and carried it as an unpleasant memory of the way in which they had been treated by their own academic Establishment.

There were others watching them during this period who saw trouble ahead. One young physicist, Georges Sagnac, was so worried by how they were leading their lives and the physical and mental stresses that were showing on the surface of their marriage that he sat down and wrote a ten-page letter on the subject to Pierre Curie. He made some remarkable observations on their life-style; at first, he started out apologetically, but soon plunged into the plain truths.

23 April 1903. Thursday morning.

. . . I want you to remember that I am your friend, your young friend without doubt, but in the end your friend. That's why I hope you will read what I have to say with patience and care.

Seeing Madame Curie at the Society of Physics I was struck by the alteration to her appearance. I know full well that she has been overdoing things because of her thesis, that she has certainly relaxed since and that she will, once she has presented her thesis be able to rest in peace. But this gives me a chance to point out that she hasn't sufficient reserves of energy to be able to live such a purely intellectual life such as the one you both lead; and what I have to say about her you can also take as applying to yourself.

I should long ago have gone under if I had maltreated my body in the way you both have maltreated yours.

I might just give one example. You eat scarcely anything, either one of you. I've seen more than once when you were kind enough to have me eat with you, that Madame Curie nibbles two slices of sausage, and follows it up with a cup of tea. Just stop and think for a minute. Do you think that *even a robust* constitution wouldn't suffer from such an insufficient diet? . . .[7]

He went on to extol the virtues of regular eating habits, knowing that they snatched many of their meals in the kitchen next to the laboratory in the Rue Lhomond. He was not, of course, aware of how much radioactive material they were ingesting along with their sandwiches.

You ought not to use the indifference or stubbornness with which she opposes you as an excuse. I can also see the following objection: 'She isn't hungry! And she's big enough now to know what she wants to do!'

No, it won't do! *She actually behaves like a CHILD.* I am telling you this with all the conviction of my judgement and friendship.

Then, it's easy to see how she constrains herself into behaving in this stubborn way. You don't give enough time to your meals. You take them at any old hour, and in the evening you eat so late that your stomachs, after the long wait, refuse to function. No doubt some of your research can cause you to eat late in the evening; this is occasionally excusable. *But you have no right* to make a habit of it.

And so it went on, page after page, imploring Curie to lead himself and his wife into a sensible pattern of existence, where physics could occasionally take second place to family life.

Don't you love Irène? It seems to me that I wouldn't prefer the idea of reading a paper by Rutherford, to getting what my body needs, and of looking at such an agreeable little girl. Give her a kiss from me. If she were a bit older she would think like me and she would tell you all this. Think of her a little.

Sagnac went on to say that he hoped that when the conditions changed, as he prescribed, Madame Curie would begin to look less lethargic and that a few of the gayer aspects of her character, now completely absent, might return. But Sagnac's prescription stood little chance in the face of the chemical forces then daily acting on the Curies in their laboratory conditions. The radon they were breathing each minute they spent in their shed, would several years later be shown to be directly responsible for fibrosis of the lungs and other respiratory problems among radium workers. Gamma radiation in quantities their bodies were daily absorbing from unprotected concentrated radio-sources, similarly would later be shown to cause serious damage to bone marrow, and subsequent cancerous blood disorders.

All the worst symptoms were now evident in both the Curies. On December 11th, 1903, Marie wrote to her brother Jozef:

At the beginning of November I had a sort of influenza which left me with a slight cough. I went to see Dr Landrieux, who examined my lungs and found nothing wrong. But on the other hand, he says I am anaemic. ... My husband has been to London to receive the Davy Medal which has been given to us. I did not go with him for fear of fatigue.[8]

Landrieux was no more familiar with radiation sickness symptoms than was any other doctor at this time. There was also one other crushing event in Marie Curie's life which might have had its origins in the exposure to radiation to which she was daily submitted.

Earlier that year she had become pregnant again. She was pleased. It has of course long been recognised that a woman must behave with care during pregnancy if she is to preserve the health of herself and her developing child. Marie Curie, though hypochondriac by nature, never spared herself physically, even in pregnancy. But only in very recent years has the extreme delicacy of the foetus during its first few weeks been recognised. The leukaemias which developed in children whose mothers were X-rayed during early pregnancy in the 1950s are terrible confirmation of this fact.

There was no reason as yet why Marie Curie should suspect that the substances she was working with might be capable of permanently affecting the cells of the human body. Her pregnancy coincided with the time when she was using highly concentrated solutions of radium and polonium, carrying them around her laboratory in plain glass flasks. It is possible, knowing the quantities of materials she was then using, to guess the amount of radiation to which she was exposing herself during a typical week at her bench. This could have been as high as 1 *rem* per week.[9] Expectant mothers working in the radium industry today, because of the known sensitivity of the unborn child to radiation-induced malignancies, are recommended not to expose their bodies to a dose rate greater than 0.03 *rem* per week. There is no doubt therefore that Marie Curie was experiencing doses of radiation many times greater than is wise for a pregnant woman to suffer.

In addition she was working in an inadequately ventilated shed in which open porcelain dishes of crystallising solutions of radioactive salts stood on the shelves. Even the stoppered bottles containing her solutions were a source of danger. Marie Curie had no reason to use anything other than cork or rubber to seal-off her liquids; it was not then realised that radon diffuses to the air through cork and rubber stoppers. The likelihood is that the concentration of radioactive gas in the atmosphere in the shed was several hundred times greater than would be thought safe for radium workers today.

As Sagnac observed, the typical bloom of the pregnant mother was not to be seen on her face. It was to be a summer of pregnancy sickness combined with radiation sickness. But yet she stubbornly believed herself to be fundamentally both fit and strong. She was an ardent believer in physical exercise as a panacea for physical ills.

That August they decided to spend their holidays near the small port of Saint-Trojan. It was Marie's custom to set off with her bicycle for their chosen holiday spot a few days ahead of her family in order to find a suitably cheap lodging which they could use as a centre for their beloved bicycle explorations. Pregnant or not, she decided to stick to her custom and she pedalled round the countryside until she found a room for the three of them. The result, as with the last pregnancy, was that she went unexpectedly into labour. But on this occasion there was no time to return to Paris. She gave premature birth to a baby which was dead within a short time of delivery. There is no direct evidence for the cause of the miscarriage.

She wrote to sister Bronia on August 25th, 1903:

I am in such consternation over this accident that I have not the courage to write to anybody. I had grown so accustomed to the idea of the child that I am absolutely desperate and cannot be consoled. Write to me, I beg of you, if you think I should blame this to general fatigue – for I must admit that I have not spared my strength. I had confidence in my organism, and at present I regret this bitterly, as I have paid dearly for it. The child – a little girl – was in good condition and was living. And I had wanted it so badly![10]

She took several weeks to recover from the severe psychological and physical upheaval. Life as a whole seemed to be turning sour that year.

Bad as 1903 had been, there was to be some consolation at the end of it all. International recognition for their joint work on radioactivity descended suddenly. The honour which signalled that they had bridged the great gap between minor notoriety as the discoverers of radium, and fame, was announced to them and to the world in November in a briefly worded telegram date-marked Stockholm. It told them that they had been awarded the Nobel Prize in physics to be shared with Henri Becquerel for their work in radioactivity.

It was only the third year that the awards had been made. The fact that the views of some of the internationally most distinguished of scientists were solicited to establish who should have them ensured that the attention of the world scientific community was focused on the Curies. The fact that they were accompanied by large amounts of cash gave them an even broader appeal.

They were financed by the fortune Alfred Nobel had reaped from his explosives and armaments industries: 'dynamite money' Strindberg disparagingly called the Prizes.[11] But the Nobel Foundation, by involving the Swedish Royal Academy of Sciences in the physics and chemistry awards, and the Royal Family itself in the award ceremony had invested them with a cachet no others in science have ever equalled.

However, it was the French Minister in Stockholm, Marchand, who stood with Becquerel, and was handed the gold medals by the King of Sweden. The Curies had shrunk from both the journey and the ceremony. Pierre had written to the Swedish Academy, pleading that the timing of the ceremony was such that neither he nor his wife could attend without upsetting their teaching courses. He also added, 'Mme Curie has been ill this summer and is not yet completely recovered.' It was true of course: though he was in no better state than she.

In his presentation speech, the President of the Royal Swedish Academy of Sciences painted the achievements of all three recipients in suitable gilt:

Professor Becquerel: the brilliant discovery of radioactivity shows us human knowledge in triumph, exploring Nature by undeflected rays of genius that pass through the vastness of space. Your victory serves as a shining refutation of the ancient dictum, *ignoramus – ignorabimus*, we do not know and we shall never know. It breeds the hope that scientific toil will succeed in conquering new territories and this is mankind's vital hope.

The great success of Professor and Madame Curie is the best illustration of the old proverb, *coniuncta valent*, union is strength. This makes us look at God's word in an entirely new light: 'It is not good that the man should be alone; I will make him an help meet for him.'

Nor is that all. This learned couple represent a team of differing nationalities, a happy omen for mankind joining forces in the development of science.[12]

The award of the Nobel Prize was to open the most punishing period in the Curies' life. The telegram telling them of their award was the signal for the flood gates of publicity to open, and they were never able to cope with the consequences. Because of the apparently romantic story of their lives and work they became the first scientists to experience popular acclaim and publicity on a vast scale. The effects were devastating. Marie Curie was to write: 'The overturn of our voluntary isolation was a cause of real suffering for us and had all the effect of disaster.'[13]

Already during the past two years they had had annoying interruptions to their work from journalists and from individuals or organisations asking for favours – from public appearances to autographs. But they had not learnt how to deal with what was now to come. Within days of the announcement of the award their laboratory was the hunting ground, not only for the Parisian press, already well marked for the ruthlessness of its early popular journalistic techniques, but also for press representatives of most countries in Europe and America. *Echo de Paris* was soon off the mark with a caricature of Curie's drawn features spread dramatically across two columns. In the accompanying article[14] the journalist admitted that Curie had been so inundated that day that he was willing to give only 15 minutes to be interviewed, as timed by his pocket watch. In spite of the fact that Curie answered all his questions by 'yes' or 'no', he still succeeded in filling a half page with a graphic article that hinted at possible uses of radium as a cure for cancer and blindness.

The day after the award was made, Marie Curie wrote to her brother, 'We are inundated with letters and with visits from photographers and journalists. One would like to dig into the

ground somewhere to find a little peace. We have received a proposal from America to go there and give a series of lectures on our
work. They ask us how much we want. Whatever the terms may
be, we intend to refuse. With much effort we have avoided the
banquets people wanted to organise in our honour.'[15]

The following month Pierre Curie wrote to Georges Gouy, a
physicist friend to whom he was to pour out many of his subsequent troubles:

22 January 1904. My dear Friend,
I have wanted to write to you for a long time; excuse me if I
have not done so. The cause is the stupid life which I lead at
present. You have seen this sudden infatuation for radium,
which has all the advantages of a moment of popularity. We
have been pursued by journalists and photographers from all
countries of the world; they have gone even so far as to report
the conversation between my daughter and her nurse, and to
describe the black-and-white cat that lives with us ... further,
we have had a great many appeals for money ... Finally, the
collectors of autographs, snobs, society people, and even at
times, scientists, have come to see us – in our magnificent and
tranquil quarters in the laboratory – and every evening there
has been a voluminous correspondence to send off. With such
a state of things I feel myself invaded by a kind of stupor. And
yet all this turmoil will not perhaps have been in vain, if it
results in my getting a professorship and a laboratory.[16]

Week after week they were a beleaguered pair both at the Rue
Lhomond laboratory and at home at Boulevard Kellermann.
Always there were people to be dealt with; and when they shut
themselves off from the reporters, the photographers, the publishers, the casual visitors and the rest, there was still a flood of
letters and requests which their consciences forced them to deal
with. They found there was time to lead practically none of the
reclusive laboratory life which had once been their staple existence.
They were in total despair that life might never return to what it
once had been.

Curie reached such a point of frustration and tension that he
threatened to leave their work on radioactivity altogether and

return to the subject which had been his old love: crystal sym-metry. He was in any case never happy with the competitive situation, being forced to rush his work into print if he was not to be beaten by some other worker in Britain or Germany. His wife took it all more in her stride. She, on the other hand, had another cause for concern. In the Spring of 1904, for the second time in twelve months, she found she was pregnant again.

Chapter 12

The Spirit of a Whipped Dog

Fear of childbirth after her last experience, was Marie Curie's major concern that year. But it was only one of her burdens. It was true that the Nobel Prize money, 70,000 francs, had relieved them of their immediate financial difficulties but it brought no relief for the personal problems now bearing down on them. The fight to regain anonymity was already lost. This meant not just that their relationship changed with the world outside the laboratory; it necessarily meant also that their life together must be lived under different circumstances.

Of the two Pierre Curie had less resilience to deal with the new situation. Physically and mentally he was at a low ebb, and worried whether the professorship at the Sorbonne, on which he had set all his hopes, would materialise. It did, though only after he was forced into demanding adequate facilities for research. Liard, the rector of the Academy of Paris, asked the French Parliament to create a new professorship specifically for Curie. It was in being by the beginning of the 1904–1905 academic year. He was to get a laboratory with a small support staff, which could include his wife as laboratory chief; she would receive a salary for the first time in her career. At last they had acceded to the Establishment. As Marie Curie made abundantly plain in the memoirs of her later years, she felt the acknowledgement to be long overdue.

Now they could move out of the shed in the Rue Lhomond which had provided such good journalistic copy, with its leaky roof, draughty windows, and dripping taps. Curie's successor in his old post at the School of Physics and Chemistry, would be the ex-pupil, Paul Langevin, now looked on as a faithful comrade rather than a one-time student.

But during these months and the promise of a new life, Marie

Curie's pregnancy had again been troublesome. She would not give up her research, though she did give up her teaching post at Sèvres as a temporary measure. But by the time her baby was expected at the beginning of December she was again exhausted and suffering.

In times of celebration or of crisis she inevitably turned her face to Poland and to somebody who shared her roots. It was sister Bronia she called for. Bronia once more took the train journey to Paris. When she arrived she found Marie was in painful labour. The child, when it was delivered – a girl – was perfect. It was called Eve. With the birth safely over, their notoriety slightly diminished and the publicity past its peak, they should have been able to look forward with some optimism. Optimism, however, was not a dominant characteristic in either of them. In May, 1905, Eleuthère Mascart, the Director of the Central Meteorological Office, risked reviving some of Pierre Curie's bitterness by suggesting that Curie let himself be nominated a second time for the Académie des Sciences. Assuring him that nomination was a foregone conclusion, Mascart nevertheless added, 'It's *necessary* that you take your courage in both hands and that you make a round of visits to the Academy's members, except you can leave a visiting card with a *corner turned down* when you find nobody at home. Start next week, and in about a fortnight the job will be done.'[1]

Whatever reply Curie gave, probably a justifiable criticism of the stupidity of the procedure, it was tart. The wound of his failure in 1902 was still far from healed. But Mascart persisted. 'My dear Curie, Arrange it any way you like, but before June 20th you will have to make the sacrifice of a final round of calls on the members of the Academy, even if you have to rent a motor car by the day.' He also added his own tart postscript: 'You might also think of the fact that the title of member of the Institute will allow you more easily to give service to others.'[2]

Curie relented and did his rounds, carrying his box of visiting cards and plodding from one man to the next; he made polite and embarrassed conversation over a drink or a cup of tea, and moved on. On a small slip of paper he kept a list, marking with a C the names of those he thought might vote for him, and with an A those he thought might support his opponent, Émile Amagat. Totting up the Cs and the As and the question marks, he knew by June 20th that the result was going to be a close run thing. Interestingly, opposite the name Becquerel, his and his wife's fellow Nobel Laureate, the man to whom they had given their samples of radium, Curie marked his own letter, C; he then crossed it out again. When votes were finally cast Curie, at the second attempt, made his membership by the narrow margin of eight votes. It didn't add to his store of self-confidence. Now that he was a member he had little time for the Academy.

But his election gave Marie Curie considerable satisfaction. Since the birth of Eve the colours of her life had taken on less dreary hues. She began teaching at Sèvres again. On two days each week she would take the steam-tram north from the Louvre; she would get off at an avenue of chestnuts which led to the façade of what had once been Madame de Pompadour's porcelain factory. As she crossed the school threshold a bell would be rung, as was the tradition for the entry of every teacher, and the young Sèvres ladies of the first and second year would gather for their physics class. Marie Curie had already introduced what in its day was a very advanced element into the school curriculum by innovating practical science classes for the girls. Before her arrival they worked from books of physics only: never with their hands.[3]

She went to great pains too to devise what she considered to be correct theory for intelligent girls. There is an evocative example among her papers of a problem in dynamics worked out for her by Pierre. It involves a cyclist freewheeling down a slope and requires her pupils to calculate his speed at the bottom of the slope.

Sèvres at this period provided much more than additional income to the Curie household. It provided a greatly needed break in the atmosphere of siege under which Marie Curie had lived the last couple of years. It took her to a protected and stable atmosphere. It also brought her into close working contact with a different set of colleagues from the one with which she had been familiar for so many years in the little shed. There the quiet and introverted group of three or four men had centred its daily routine on Madame Curie and her husband. Here at the girls' college relationships with co-workers as well as pupils were on a different footing. The attractive and engaging Paul Langevin, also pushed into teaching young ladies because of the need to extend the family exchequer, had joined the teaching staff. He brought a breath of highly intelligent masculine fresh air into the young community. These two days each week represented a period when Marie Curie could refortify herself for the daily grind by being outside the laboratory atmosphere – and in the case of a radium laboratory at the turn of the century, this was an atmosphere in a literal as well as a metaphorical sense. For two days each week it freed her from the effects of radon.

Also at this time she began to relax a few of the barriers she had put up over the past months. Once more a few élite guests were invited to Boulevard Kellermann. There were some surprising additions to the previous number of friends. One was the Folies-Bergère star performer, Loïe Fuller. Loïe, by way of burlesque and Buffalo Bill's Wild West Show, had progressed to the bright and bare lights of the Folies with spectacular illumination effects as her speciality. Paris had gone into raptures about her serpentine dance: 'out of this whirl of flowing vaporous light, a woman's bust emerges, the arms and shoulders gleaming delicately white among the petals of a giant violet'.[4]

A girl with simple, if ample, charm, attractive off stage as well as on, she succeeded during her long career in picking up a wide circle of surprisingly contrasting friends. They included Toulouse-Lautrec, Rodin and the Queen of Rumania. Agog as the rest of the world at the reported wonders of radium, Loïe had thought up the possibility of a phosphorescent costume using radium as a light source. She had no hesitation in writing to the Curies to suggest the idea. The Curies, with grave courtesy, replied to her enquiry as they did to every time-consuming crank proposal. The result of the exchange of letters was that an unlikely friendship sprang up among the trio, and Loïe was eventually admitted past the barred doors of 108 Boulevard Kellermann, to give a special electrically illuminated dance for the pair of scientists, and their family. They returned the honour by visiting her at her home.

Daily life began to approach something near normalcy once more: the hard routine of teaching, research, travelling, housework and devoting at least some hours to the children. The two small girls were already beginning to show their differences in character: the younger was dark and her attractive qualities were extrovert even as a baby; the elder was fairer, more introspective, with the quiet contemplative behaviour of her father. Marie Curie succeeded in leading one of the most difficult periods of her life – it was by far her most creative period – when she had either a babe-in-arms, or was pregnant. Her off-spring were a persisting pleasure in the few hours she spent at home after her work. She wrote to brother Jozef in March 1905: 'The children are growing well. Little Eve sleeps very little, and protests energetically if I leave her lying awake in her cradle. As I am not a stoic I carry her in my arms until she grows quiet. She does not resemble Irène.'[5] They were to mature in very different fashions and she was to watch them grow uncritically and adore them both. But they were not the centre-point of her life.

Other interests that had once assumed prime importance now always took second place to her work. Politics and social science meant little to her. She did, however, watch with anxiety the progress of the Russian Revolution of 1905 since it held out the promise of a better future for Poland. She even sent a cash contribution in its aid via Kazimierz Dluski. But the wider implications of Marxism and any possible commitment had long since passed her by. She felt she could not be directly involved.

By June of 1905 she felt strong enough to travel again. Pierre Curie felt he should fulfil his obligations to the Swedish Academy of Sciences by giving the lecture in Stockholm which was a condition of the Nobel prize. He was still suffering from sporadic illnesses and easily tired. The Swedes, however, had responded to the Curies' wish for a minimum of publicity and the affair was carried out in relative peace.

Though Marie Curie was a joint recipient of the prize, it was her husband alone who gave the official lecture; she sat as one of the audience and listened to the sick man review their work together in his apologetic fashion. The mathematician, Henri Poincaré, said of Pierre Curie, 'he rose to glory with the spirit of a whipped dog'.

He began his speech with an apology for their being so late in visiting Stockholm 'for reasons quite outside our control'. By this, he meant their illnesses. He was never to know the true cause of their sickness. Again he carried samples of radium with him so that he could demonstrate its properties during his speech. He was by now more ready to admit the far-reaching conclusions for physics which such workers as Rutherford and Soddy had drawn from their, the Curies', fundamental discovery of powerful radiosources. He conceded at last that 'the existence of the atom is even at stake' – meaning that perhaps it might after all consist of smaller constituents.

The last years had been difficult and had not been his most productive. They had, however, caused him to think more deeply about the implications of his and his wife's work. He ended his lecture with a worried paragraph:

It might even be thought that radium could become very dangerous in criminal hands, and here the question can be raised whether mankind benefits from knowing the secrets of Nature, whether it is ready to profit from it or whether this knowledge will not be harmful for it. The example of the discoveries of Nobel is characteristic, as powerful explosives have enabled man to do wonderful work. They are also a terrible means of destruction in the hands of great criminals who lead the people towards war. I am one of those who believe with Nobel that mankind will derive more good than harm from the new discoveries.[6]

It was an arguable eulogy of Nobel, the armaments manufacturer, but it had a strange prescience. It showed that he and Marie Curie were beginning to see applications for radium beyond that of adding to physics' store of knowledge of the atom. The purity of discovery was their responsibility, but who would answer for the applications? Radium-therapy, or Curie-therapy as it became known in France, was already being employed by French doctors using radium loaned by the Curies. This was the optimistic face of the applications. But his pessimism had seen something foreboding ahead. Could radium and the knowledge derived from it have terrible applications, even for warfare?

Paris in the 1890s had seen the publication of a remarkably far-sighted piece of popular journalism written by a soldier, Émile Driant, under the pen-name of Captain Danrit. It was called 'The War of Tomorrow'.[7] In it Driant combined his knowledge as a military man and his interest in science to forecast in a racy Boys' Own style how physics and chemistry might be used in future battles. He predicted, among other applications, aerial warfare, a multiplicity of electrical death-dealing detonating devices and unimaginably vast explosives. Curie himself, as early as January, 1900, had had a letter from a Captain Ferrié at the Ministry of War, who had kept himself abreast of the Curies' publications on radio-activity, asking for advice on the possibility of using radium to make luminous gunsights and mine safety-catches for night fighting.[8]

The purity and 'disinterestedness' of the Curies' work was a difficult balance to maintain and one which both Pierre and Marie approached with a certain naïvety. They were shackled to the life they had to lead; only by this punishing routine could they afford to carry on their research. Marie had to be part-time teacher to support her salary as laboratory chief in Pierre's understaffed, still under-financed laboratory.

In February of 1906 Pierre thought he had found a rich bene-factress who promised them help, in cash. Clearly in a depressed and much dissatisfied frame of mind, he wrote to the woman, pouring out his problems: they were being tired out by the journey from their laboratory to their home; it was hard for Marie; ideally they wanted the children brought up in the country. 'Life at the centre of Paris is destructive for the children, and my wife cannot manage to bring them up under these conditions.'[9] He wanted a calm scientific existence away from the hurly-burly. He was plead-ing for a Radium Institute to be set up for them.

The irony is pitiful. The cost of radium salts in 1903 in English money was £400 a gram; by 1912 it was £15,000 and during the Great War, when demand for its use in gunsights and compass cards yet again inflated its price, it rose to £20,000. Just as Röntgen had not patented X-rays, the Curies had refused to patent commercial radium production. In 1906 they had derived not a penny in personal gain from any of the radium separated by the method Marie Curie had devised. It was her pride throughout her life to point to the fact.

They had had many requests for information on the radium separation process, particularly from America. They always gave information freely and willingly, for this was the traditional scientific approach to acquired knowledge. Whole industries were now being set up on the basis of the detailed techniques they provided.

The Central Chemical Products Company which first extracted pitchblende on an industrial scale under Marie Curie and André Debierne's direction, did so at a low fee, but gained inestimable information and experience in the process. Marie Curie naïvely felt the exchange was more than just. She rejected the economics of industrial research and development as not being her concern. The fact that the eventual marketing of the product might bring enormous profits to the industrialist at the cost of relatively little risk capital to himself was not a factor which she felt should enter into her reckoning. The application of science was too far removed from the purity of the acquisition of knowledge for her to feel that she need be involved.

Marie Curie had always admired the French industrialist, Armet de Lisle, who first took up the manufacturing process of radium. She considered him 'disinterested'. In 1904 de Lisle set up an industrial plant, liberally using the Curies' advice. In return he provided the work space and facilities which the government financed university had failed to make available. By 1906 de Lisle's factory had on its letter heading, 'Radium Salts—and other radioactive substances'. Alongside was a drawing of a hand holding a mysterious cylinder from which shone, on presumably radioactive rays, the words, 'Armet de Lisle, Radioactive Substances (Registered Trade Mark)'. By 1913 he was able to plan to float his General Radium Production Company with a nominal capital of £1,250,000.

The attitude of the Austro-Hungarian government had changed since the early days when a complicated procedure of diplomatic pressure had had to be exerted in order to extract a few sacks of pitchblende from Joachimsthal. In March 1905 the Austro-Hungarian ambassador in Paris wrote to Pierre Curie to thank him on behalf of his government for the gift of 200 milligrams of radium destined for a Viennese sanatorium. He assured Curie that 'the Imperial Royal Minister of Agriculture in Austria' was now prepared to send at the earliest opportunity, as many tons of pitchblende as the Curies had need of.[10] The Austrians too had seen the commercial possibilities.

And yet, while commercialisation went on all around them, the Curies were literally begging for money from a rich woman to set up a laboratory to meet their relatively simple needs. Marie Curie later told her physicist son-in-law, Frédéric Joliot, 'If we had had a fine laboratory we should have made more discoveries and our health would have suffered less.'[11]

There is no question that the Curies suffered more than they need have. A scientific worker who is involved in pure research sooner or later has to acknowledge that his work is going to be applied, if not by himself, then by others. Whether he likes it or not, he has a part in the responsibility of that application. He is the first in the line of knowledge, the custodian of the earliest information which can be used to warn those who are likely to suffer or to benefit from its applications.

The Curies saw the application of scientific discovery as being outside the bounds of their purity. They also felt it outside their sphere to take any safeguards, using simple commercial and legal principles, so that the application of their radioactive work could be used to finance their future work. Such a precaution would not necessarily have involved them in the reaping of what they saw as ill-gotten personal gain. They took no precaution, and they suffered in consequence. They were attempting to live out the life they had defined in those early days in Marie Curie's sixth-floor garret: 'our legitimate scientific dream'. But it was a dream which had nightmare edges to it.

In 1906 Pierre Curie's sickness was at its worst. The decline is reflected in the number of his publications which, throughout his creative life, he had always maintained in a steady stream. From 1883, with the exception of the two years when he and Marie were most fully occupied with the separation of polonium and radium, he published papers in every year until 1904. From July, 1898, when he published his first paper on radioactivity with his wife, until June, 1904, he, alone, and with co-workers, put into print in the accounts of the Académie des Sciences no less than 25 papers, almost all on some aspect of radioactivity. His last paper of 1904, done in co-operation with two medical colleagues, dealt with the experimental effects of radioactive emanations on mice and guinea pigs.[12] In their post-mortems they noted the intense pulmonary congestions in the animals and the modifications to the leucocytes of the blood – the white corpuscles responsible for protecting the body against infectious diseases. There was no doubt in their conclusions of the devastating effects of the gas given off by radium. The Curies saw no warnings whatever in this work as to what the effects might be of radium emanation on laboratory workers such as themselves. In the two years from 1904 Pierre Curie published not a single paper; one he had prepared on the radioactivity of gases from thermal spring waters was published posthumously.

Surprisingly, during this period he had taken an interest in spiritualism. Marie Curie was at first as intrigued as he and many other scientists in what was then a fashionable diversion; it was a timely accompaniment to the recent revelations to laymen of the mystery of X-rays and radioactivity. The Curies had been sufficiently interested to sit down at a séance table one evening with their friend Jean Perrin and the spiritualist medium who then had an international reputation, Eusapia Paladino. Paladino sat in the darkened room between the two men, her right foot placed on one of the physicists' left foot, her left on the other's right. It was the old 'boot trick'. A disembodied spirit, namely Eusapia herself, manifested 'fluidic emanation' and 'ectoplasmic materialisation' which drifted past and over the faces of everyone seated at the table.[13] With the lights suddenly switched on by one of the scientists, Paladino was revealed, naked of her weighted shoes, waving butter muslin in the air, and with her reputation in that small scientific community in little pieces. She continued her career unabashed, however, in countless other salons under the less wary scrutiny of some other of Europe's most distinguished scientists. There were still plenty of people with the need to believe.

Pierre Curie was one who desperately wanted to believe in some spiritual phenomenon that could be brought into the realm of the measurable. In one of his earliest letters to Marie he had written, 'I must confess that these spiritualism phenomena intrigue me a great deal. I think that there are things in these questions which touch closely on physics.'[14]

During the early months of 1906, depressed and permanently tired, Curie gave more disenchanted thoughts to the field of radioactivity: on paper it looked to be the successful accomplishment of their scientific dream, but it had brought him no real happiness. In this mood, he decided to take a short holiday with his family. Marie Curie later described how, 'quite ill and tired, he went with me and the children to spend Easter in the Chevreuse Valley. Those were two sweet days under a mild sun, and Pierre Curie felt the weight of weariness lighten in a healing repose near to those who were dear to him. He amused himself in the meadows with his little girls, and talked with me of their present and their future.'[15] He continued during the next few days to speak of the ideal that had evaded them: 'ideas on the culture that he dreamed of'.

That month the English magazine, *The Gentlewoman*, was to describe the Curies' way of life in the sugared terms which the outside world thought it deserved: 'the marriage of M. and Madame Curie was, like many French marriages nowadays, a union of very perfect sympathies. They were loving comrades in their life work in the laboratory, as well as in home life, which was not less charming because of their scientific achievements and distinction.'

The Spirit of a Whipped Dog

The undercurrents which strain a marriage in the conditions such as those under which the Curies lived can never have been seen, even by close friends, in any sort of perspective approaching truth; only the couple concerned knew the reality. This pair unquestionably experienced strain; others might not have survived what they experienced. But the strain on Curie's health was clear to all their intimate friends. At lunchtime on April 19th a group of them gathered in a left-bank hotel to discuss scientific administration at the Sorbonne. Marie was at home to give the children their mid-day meal. It was a wet day and the physicists sat inside the hotel. Shortly after the discussions ended Curie got up to leave. He shook hands with his colleagues, Jean Perrin among them and left to walk in the direction of the Seine and the offices of his publishers, Gauthier-Villars, on one of the quays near the Pont-Neuf. When he got there he found the doors closed; the printers were on strike. It was a wasted journey. Putting up his umbrella as he walked, he looked up the busy Rue Dauphine away from the Bridge, where a thick flow of afternoon trams and horse traffic, mixed with cars, was moving to and from the street intersection; he began to cross.

Chapter 13

Death in the Family

It was over in seconds. Only one or two people actually saw it happen. One man described the cranium as having been smashed into fifteen or sixteen pieces.

The driver of the large cart, the wheel of which had done the damage, described the incident in detail. He was in tears as he told his tale, surrounded by a group of reporters at the local gendarmerie. The tears were caused as much by the fear that the prefect of police might hold him responsible and keep him in charge for the night, as much as by the shock of the affair. He told newspapermen: 'He was walking quickly, his umbrella was up in his hand and he literally threw himself on my left-side horse.'[1]

The cart-horse driver's name was Louis Manin; he was about 30 years old. He had crossed the Pont-Neuf early that afternoon holding his pair of inexperienced percherons in tight rein, when he had to stop to let a tram pass in front of him. He then moved off at a steady pace down the right-hand lane of the Rue Dauphine with a load of military uniforms. A horse cab was passing him on the other side of the street when suddenly the man in the black suit with the umbrella appeared from behind it and immediately in the path of his left-hand horse. The man seemed to slip on the wet asphalt and grabbed at the horse as it reared. Manin instinctively heaved at his brake with one hand and dragged on the reins with the other. The man in black, in a tangle of harness, umbrella and human limbs fell between the two straining animals and between the moving cart's front wheels. The left rear wheel hit and smashed Curie's head.

A crowd soon gathered to watch the blood mixing with the rain in the gutter. A colonial brigadier, a grocer, a road-mender and a businessman had seen it happen and were prepared to witness that the carter's part in the affair had been an innocent one.

But the crowd, excited by the uproar, by the champing of the horses and the sight of the gore, began to jostle Manin; police had to move in to protect him. One or two of the watchers tried to get several passing cab-drivers to take the body to the police prefecture, but none would have the bloody corpse in his vehicle to stain the upholstery. It had to be carried away on a stretcher.

In spite of the frightful injuries to the head, the face was still recognisable. In his jacket pocket they found visiting cards with addresses at the Faculty of Science and at Boulevard Kellermann.

It was an elderly laboratory assistant of Curie's, Pierre Clerc, who was fetched to identify the body. When he saw the state the head was in he burst into tears. He said that often enough he'd told his employer that he never took enough trouble to watch the traffic when he crossed the street: always he had something else on his mind.

By this time Marie Curie was no longer at Boulevard Kellermann. She had gone to Fontenay-aux-Roses where another little colony of scientists lived, Paul Langevin among them; Langevin had said he wanted to keep his children away from the Paris traffic. It was decided that the news should be broken to Marie Curie by Paul Appell, as Curie's senior colleague and dean of the Faculty of Science, and by Jean Perrin, the next-door neighbour and friend. Marie Curie always hid her emotions, and she did so on this, the most pitiful of occasions. Intolerable as the tale was, she kept her feelings under her control, heard as much detail as the men thought fit to tell at that stage, asked Perrin if his wife would see to the children for the night, and was left to handle her grief alone.

The body, still in its wretched condition, was brought by ambulance to the house two hours later. There could be no hiding from what had to be done. It was laid out in a room on the ground floor. There she had to suffer the sight of the wreck of the man who had given her all the years of her life that had mattered. Whatever stress they had had to suffer together can now only have seemed of unutterably minimal importance. Pierre Curie had given her both the love of their early years and the access to a life she could otherwise never have known. What was left of that dream they had planned was now at its end, but the part they had succeeded in living out together had been truly shared. Curie had never taken so much as a tiny fraction more of this share of credit than had been his due. She, who could so easily have had to take second place when the honours were doled out, never did so as the result of any of his actions or wishes. His generosity had ensured her equal acknowledgement for equal achievement. The suffering too, both physical and mental, had been equally borne. Now 'the fragile brain', as he once called it, was broken and lying in front of her.

The pain of re-living the successes and the suffering would now begin. The tears to accompany that suffering would come privately. The inner woman had enough strength to close in on herself again for the time being at least. But this blow and the torment of having to look at what it physically had done was too terrible not to have pierced the protective shell.

That night saw a procession of carriages and cars at the house, stopping to let a visitor alight, and then moving on. The death of the physicist was an event calling for a major show of mourning and respect in the highest circles of the Establishment with which the Curies had so often felt themselves at odds. Callers during the next few hours included the President of the Republic and the President of the Council as well as senior representatives of the University of Paris.

During the days that followed Marie Curie presented a grieving but apparently inscrutable front to the mass of sympathisers around her. She avoided speaking of her tragedy. But her resistance was, over these hours, being badly eroded. Never at any time in her life since her early years had she allowed herself to sit down and write subjectively at length. Her writings and notes had been closely objective letters, scientific accounts and measured records. There was no measurement she could take for death. Now for the first time she felt the need to communicate what was inside her. Alone in the upstairs room of the house, she began to scribble a diary. What she was to write was a collection of guilty love-letters to a dead man which she could never have written in their past life together. She wrote not in her native language,

Polish, but in French, the language in which she and he always spoke together.

... What a terrible shock your poor head has felt, your poor head that I have so often caressed in my two hands. I kissed your eyelids which you used to close so that I could kiss them, offering me your head with a familiar movement ...

... We put you into the coffin Saturday morning, and I held your head up for this move. We kissed your cold face for the last time. Then a few periwinkles from the garden on the coffin and the little picture of me that you called 'the good little student' and that you loved. It is the picture that must go with you into the grave, the picture of her who had the happiness of so pleasing you that you did not hesitate to offer to share your life with her, even when you had seen her only a few times. You often told me that this was the only occasion in your life when you acted without hesitation, with the absolute conviction that you were doing well. [2]

The guilt, which is more than remorse, of the surviving partner of a marriage is a well-known psychological experience. It expresses itself in these sentences in which Marie Curie allowed herself privately to bathe in emotion. They were sentences the like of which she had never written before, and could now only address to herself. The guilt of the surviving partner is often more than merely that of having survived; it may be that of real or imagined infidelities or inadequacies. Marie Curie possessed feelings of this kind so strongly that, although she destroyed most of the papers that showed the intimacy of her life, she kept these infinitely personal writings so that somebody, somewhere could read them one day. Her family has preserved them in the Bibliothèque Nationale with a restriction on their being read, other than a small sample already published by her daughter, Eve, until the last decade of this century.

The guilty grief showed itself in other ways. Bronia, as in the other critical moments in Marie Curie's life, had been brought from Poland to help ease the stress. Years later Bronia told Eve Curie of the evening on which Marie made her symbolic gesture: the tribute brought from the depths of the guarded inner-self. Some weeks after Pierre's death, on a warm evening, Marie took Bronia into her bedroom where, in spite of the heat, a large fire was burning. Silently, Marie brought out a stiff, large packet wrapped in waterproof paper and tore it open. The contents were the blood-stained clothes taken from Pierre's body. Stuck to them were pieces of dried flesh. Marie took the pieces of cloth, began to cut them up, and then began to kiss and stroke them until Bronia took them from her and threw them into the fire. Marie then broke down and wept in her older sister's arms.

Marie had left one of her most personal, but inescapable tasks until after the funeral. The children had to be told, though only Irène, intelligent and advanced for her eight years, would be old enough to make any sense of the difficult conversation. Irène was playing in the house next door with the young Aline Perrin when Marie decided the time had come. Aline later always carried the memory of the black-clad woman who came in as they played and of how little it meant to Irène when Marie bent to tell the child that her father was dead. Irène listened, then without any reaction whatever turned to continue playing with Aline. 'She's too small; she doesn't understand,' Marie said, and was forced to turn, leave the children at their play, and quickly go out.[3] But suddenly Irène did understand and burst into tears. Henriette Perrin, Jean's wife, led her the few yards back to the arms of her mother. But for many years after this incident, Marie Curie could not bring herself to mention her husband's name to his daughters, nor discuss anything connected with their life together.

In the days after Pierre's death she hovered on the verge of breakdown. On the one side there was Bronia, with the large motherly arms, to turn to. On the other there was her diary, self-centred and self-pitying. The comparison between the full matronly figure of Bronia, with the thin, delicate body which Marie now presented to the public, its delicacy emphasised by the black and absolutely simple dress, was striking. It did not belie the physical privations to which she had both knowingly and unknowingly submitted herself during the past years. But it did disguise the resilience of Marie Curie. Within two weeks of the death she was dealing with correspondence concerning the future of her laboratory, and within a month her laboratory notebook starts again with her customary columns of figures of observations. Her jottings show that she was working at her bench in the Rue Cuvier, precipitating, purifying, observing emanations, and always measuring – hour after hour. Often during the next months she was in the small room working by artificial light, sometimes late at night, sometimes early in the morning. She would return to her diary and her introspection now and again, but gradually the guilt and the need to take recourse to the diary faded, and radium and its distractions returned to the centre of her life.

By May 8th, only two weeks after the funeral, Pierre's friend Georges Gouy, was writing thanking her for the couple of letters in which she had 'momentarily emerged from your sad thoughts to occupy yourself with scientific affairs so dear to Pierre',[4] and giving her details of an experimental electrical circuit she had asked about.

She had decided to take on the whole role she and her husband had once shared; she had now acquired sufficient political skills in the male-dominated scientific academic field to attempt it. But she never had any doubts, during these days when she was trying to sort out some sort of future for herself and her family, that if she was to survive, then it would be survival as an equal. She asked no favours and made it frankly clear that she abhorred charity. Pierre's friends had quickly rallied round and the suggestion was made by one or two of them that a subscription fund should be started on her behalf. She left Georges Gouy quite clear as to her feelings of 'repugnance' at the very mention of the idea.

When *Le Journal* (a newspaper with fickle loyalties, as Marie Curie was later to find to her cost), publicised the attempt of a group of Parisian women to make some sort of public gesture on her behalf – a medallion, a bust and a book of signatures were mentioned – she quickly made her blunt views known: 'I would like to make it clear in advance that I do not wish to have any sort of public testimony of this kind.'[5]

But what she did accept was the university post her husband had sought for most of his mature life, and had succeeded in occupying for only eighteen months. This was her total triumph over Establishmental tradition. Within a month of Pierre's death the Faculty of Science had offered her an assistant professorship, maintaining her in the chair specially created for Pierre Curie. She was the first woman in France to reach professorial rank, and within two years would be named titular professor. From May 1st, 1906, with a gap of only two weeks in the succession, she would have an annual salary of 10,000 francs and her own facilities for research.

Money, without which she could not hope to begin to run a family and a laboratory – particularly now that she had rejected anything with the taint of charity – was to be one of her first concerns. Georges Gouy, the man to whom Pierre Curie had poured out his troubles in his last years, took up the subject with Marie in their correspondence in the few days after Pierre's death. It was plain to Gouy as it was to many others, that in her laboratory in the Rue Cuvier, Marie Curie had now in her possession quantities of radium which were infinitely more precious than gold. Its exact value was not known. Rapid inflation in its price had already set in. As Gouy asked, what would it be selling at in twenty years' time? It was obvious even then that the sums involved might be vast and that there might be many contenders for ownership. Gouy's advice was that, 'It's absolutely necessary to make a sort of official inventory, signed by the Dean, in which it's specified that the Faculty has so much radium, and no more. Be quite sure that *in the inventory you do not mention your own radium* otherwise you might have to pay death duties. . . . Legally speaking, this radium belongs in part to Pierre, at least I think so, and one must divide the balance of the inheritance.'[6] He went on to suggest that Marie should get hold of a competent businessman to give her proper advice about any differences of opinion which the inheritance of the radium might stir up. Even if she had no thought of personal gain, she had the futures of Irène and Eve to consider. Ever after, she was to guard the rights of succession to her radium with a hawk-like eye.

The immediate problem of the children was solved by turning with her father-in-law, the now ageing doctor, to Sceaux: the little town where Pierre had first so proudly introduced her to his parents. There Marie began to look for a small house with a garden where she could install a distant relative from Poland as governess for the two girls and leave the old doctor to preside benevolently and tutorially over the establishment. It would mean half-an-hour's train journey to the laboratory for Marie every day, but it would be a satisfactory working arrangement. She could establish a routine, and with such a routine she always felt there existed a secure base for her life. In this case, besides providing stability for the family, it would also be a position from which she could prepare for the undoubted challenge of the professorial position she had now established for herself.

The symbolic acceptance of the new challenge was the inaugural lecture she was to give at the Sorbonne as Professor: the day of 'the first woman among the Masters', as one of her proud young lady pupils from Sèvres, Catherine Schulhof, described it.[7] It took place on November 5th in time for the beginning of the new term.

As a social occasion it was a highlight of the season, and the mistress of many a salon had gone to considerable trouble to secure for herself a seat at the public event. Although the lecture was not due to begin until 1.30, a crowd began to collect in the Place de la Sorbonne about mid-day, such a personage had Marie Curie now become. The doors to the lecture hall were opened at about one o'clock and within five minutes had to be closed, with the little amphitheatre full to capacity. Catherine Schulhof had succeeded in finding herself a place on one of the front benches, along with half a dozen other of her fellow students. She looked around at the incongruous audience that had gathered for this, the first lecture in a physical science course. Alongside the students were casual sightseers, journalists and distinguished professors from other faculties. The front rows, as one newspaper reporter was to point out, resembled the stalls of a theatre with its *toilettes*, its huge hats and its distinguished ladies beneath them, rather than the benches of a physics lecture hall. Catherine Schulhof noticed, that besides Jean Perrin, Paul Appell and others unaccustomed to sitting on the students' side of the fence, there were several other noteworthy faces, including that of Countess Greffulhe, a great patroness of the arts whose salon was amongst the most formidable in Paris.

Just before 1.30 Paul Appell rose to quieten the expectant hubbub. Madame Curie, he said, had expressed the wish that there be no official installation and that she should simply take up her husband's course where he left it.

On every occasion that Marie Curie appeared in public, even teaching a small class of girls, she suffered intensely from nerves. On this, the most testing of occasions, the tightly packed crowd which saw the thin figure enter, put down a few sheets of notes on the desk in front of her and begin a physics lecture, also saw a woman nervously stretched to her limit. Too frequently she rubbed together her fingers' ends, irritated by radium burns, and too often she shuffled her papers. Those at the back of the hall had difficulty in hearing her unprojected voice. Pointedly, she made no concessions whatever for the heterogeneous composition of her audience.

Nevertheless, in spite of the fact that by far the greater number of those present had no understanding whatever of the language of physics in which, during the next hour, Marie Curie reviewed the progress of the understanding of the structure of matter since the beginning of the nineteenth century, they felt that they had shared nothing less than an epic experience. With Marie's last thinly enunciated sentence the crowd broke into tumultuous applause and, icy faced as she had entered, she glided out.

The rapture of *Le Journal*'s reporter, who had managed to squeeze himself into a corner of the hall, knew no bounds. To him Marie Curie's high forehead was reminiscent of one of Memling's Virgins. Another enthusiast described the day as 'the celebration of a victory for feminism. If a woman is allowed to teach advanced studies to both sexes, where afterwards will be the pretended superiority of man? I tell you, the time is near when women will become human beings.'[8]

Chapter 14

The Widow

If the feminists took her as a figurehead, that was their affair. Marie Curie had no intention of fitting her life into what others thought should be the pattern for women as human beings. For her the centre of her human relationships was in Sceaux with her children. Besides these two and her father-in-law, there were now only two other people, Henriette Perrin and Jacques Curie, to whom Marie used the French familiar 'tu'. It was a severely restricted set of intimate relationships.

Now she had to make decisions on the children's behalf. Her object above all was to give them maximum liberty to mould their own futures. She had deliberately avoided having them baptised; her own experiences as a child during her mother's last years had sown the seeds of doubt which had grown to disapproval though not intolerance of religion. Once she went so far as to admit to a friend that, 'I would like to have believed, but I cannot, I cannot!'[1] Later in life she made it quite clear to the children that if they wanted to take religious views she would not dissuade them.

Equally, she wanted to prepare the most fertile soil in which their minds could develop. On this subject of education she had the strongest of views. Irène was already nine years old and her education had now to be taken most seriously. Marie Curie believed that the measure of a nation's civilisation could be based on the percentage of its budget it spent on national education.[2] France, at this time, ranked low in her league table. Her answer to the shortcomings of the nation was to devise an educational system calculated to give products of the right calibre. It would be an educational élite, but then Marie was herself attracted to élite groups. In one case, that of her own child, the experience of such a group would have remarkable results.

Marie Curie sat down with her friends from the Sorbonne, all much the same age as she and mostly married with young children, and planned a school curriculum which they themselves could operate. It was an eclectic group: Jean Perrin, the physical chemist; Paul Langevin, the physicist: Edouard Chavannes, the Chinese scholar; and Henri Mouton, the naturalist. However, they were all prepared to give a certain amount of time each day to modelling one another's children in educational images which they considered to be an improvement on anything achieved by the existing systems.

The result was that eight or nine infants joined the 'Co-operative' and spent a relatively small amount of time every day being intensively educated by the highest quality minds, and a relatively large amount in games and physical exercises of one kind or another, of which Marie Curie passionately approved. A still larger part of the children's time was spent in travelling from one professor to the other. Langevin and Chavannes lived in the suburbs at Fontenay-aux-Roses, and it was there that mathematics and culture were taught: for physics they sometimes travelled to Sceaux and sometimes to the laboratories of the Sorbonne. Literary gaps were filled in by Mme Perrin and Mme Chavannes.

As a system designed by an élite for an élite it was a success. It was scientifically overbalanced, but the children's memories of it during its brief two or three years seem to have been nothing but happy. Its effects in the case of Irène Curie were salutary. The genetic inheritance from her parents was considerable, but there was some risk that this refined environment might saturate her love of science. The opposite proved true and she thrived on the staple diet of mathematics, physics and chemistry. These years laid the foundations for future success.

Irène was a strange young creature: green-eyed, with short-cropped hair, rather awkward in her movements. She had the shyness of both parents as well as their abilities; the introversion of her father was obvious in her character, but it had an insensitive edge: unaware or uncaring of the attitude of others. She always had great difficulties in greeting and dealing with strangers.

One day, shortly after the 'Co-operative' had been abandoned and Marie Curie was teaching mathematics to Irène and the young Isabelle Chavannes, in an upstairs room of the house, Marie turned to her daughter, whose concentration had slipped, and asked a relatively simple question. Irène had no reply. Marie, with a sudden uncharacteristic loss of self-control, grabbed the girl's exercise book from the desk and threw it out of the open window. Irène stood up, walked down the two flights of stairs into the garden, picked it up, climbed back to the room, sat down, and answered the question.[3]

There was seven years' difference between Irène and Eve. The younger girl had an obviously different style from the elder, even when she was not much more than a baby. Prettier, easier in manners, she was approachable, where Irène tended to repel intimacy. The friends and the visitors who came took to her instantly, yet the outward signs of the contented child hid something Eve was not prepared to reveal until she was a mature woman. Already she was separated by age from the intellectual relationship between her mother and her elder sister. It was this sort of mental communion which Marie Curie preferred to more obvious physical bonds. She taught her children to be affectionate, but always restrained, and always undemonstrative: never to raise their voices either in anger or in joy. Eve Curie later wrote of this period of her life, 'In spite of the help my mother tried to give me, my young years were not happy ones.'[4]

The strong daily human bond of affection being forged during these years was that between Eugène Curie and the children, particularly Irène. By the time she was twelve, the old doctor had already imprinted his democratic and social ideals on to the older girl. They were the political ideals with which he had joined in the Revolution of 1848, and taken a rifle ball on his jaw for his pains; and they were the social ideals with which he had organised a hospital behind the barricades of the 1870 Commune. Some of them were similar to those which had inspired Marie as a girl. They had been the basis of the mutual respect Marie and the old man felt for each other. But in Irène's case they were eventually to have a fuller importance in her adult life.

The responsibility for the routine of family life was left to

Dr Curie and to the Polish governesses who came in succession to look after the girls. The re-establishment of the routine of her laboratory life not only enabled Marie Curie to survive, it enabled her to thrive. Her fame, which so far her romantic and tragic life-story had given her through the popular press, still brought intrusions to her personal privacy, but at least she was now learning to use some of them to her advantage.

During this period she first discovered America—or at least, what America could do for her. In its way it was to be as important a discovery as any other she was still to make. Andrew Carnegie, the owner of apparently countless dollars, author of *The Gospel of Wealth*, patron of the arts and the sciences and advocate of the simple life, had met Marie Curie in Paris not long after Pierre's death, when she was still the centre of public attention. Attracted by her outwardly plain manner, by the immobile and unselfpitying face which she presented in this grief, and also approving of the simplicity of her life and the aims of her work, he decided to endow her research. In November 1906 he dispatched to Paul Appell 50,000 dollars in 5% gold bonds to found Curie scholarships. For her it was a magnificent solution to the problem of financing the staff she needed for research, and it gave her a nucleus round which she could base a school of radioactivity work in Paris. Moreover, there was no taint of personal charity to herself involved since it was money to be given entirely to her students.

Carnegie had been impressed by the woman and particularly by her attitude as a scientist on equal footing with men. She had somehow conveyed to him her precise role in her laboratory's past, and what she intended it should be in the future. 'Might I venture to suggest,' he wrote to the Rector of the Academy of Paris, 'that so long as Madame Curie is alive and capable of conference her wishes be respected.' For the name of his new institution he suggested that it 'should simply be The Curies Foundation, created by Andrew Carnegie. Making it plural will include Madame, which I am anxious should be done.' He also added, with peculiar modesty 'I could not endure my name being coupled with the two immortals, the Curies.'[5]

Many others during this period joined in to see that Marie Curie was well-provided for. The faithful Lord Kelvin, at the age of 82, had set sail for Paris within hours of hearing of Pierre's death. Now he meant to make quite sure that the widow was not short of the right sort of company. His visiting card would again be carried into the laboratory, but scrawled on the reverse side would be such notes as, 'Introducing my friend, The Countess of Winchilsea'.

However, although he saw to it that his aristocratic friends were looking after Marie Curie's social well-being, he himself was coming dangerously close to upsetting her scientific peace of mind. As it happened he was merely exercising the old man's traditional privilege of having his errors tolerated in public, but being an extremely distinguished old man, they were unfortunately errors that had to be exposed. What was more they were the kinds of errors that would drive Marie Curie's work during the next few years into yet more exacting and even punishing channels.

The medium in which Kelvin elected to launch a broadside on August 9th, 1906, was nothing less than the correspondence columns of *The Times*. Although he could have chosen any of the specialist scientific journals for his attack, such at that time was the public interest in radium and everything connected with it, that he chose the leading daily paper. Kelvin's *Times* theory was based on the discovery of Sir William Ramsay and Frederick Soddy that radium spontaneously and continuously gives off the inert gas helium. This discovery had been an important step in the understanding of the nature of the disintegration process of radioactive substances. Kelvin's hypothesis was also based on the fact that the humble metal, lead, is found among the disintegration products of radium. What he suggested to *The Times*'s readers, therefore, was that radium, far from being a new element, was probably nothing more than a molecular compound of perhaps lead, together with 5 helium atoms. If he was right his theory would leave in ruins the whole of Marie Curie's work of several years: the work in which she had purified radium chloride, then determined radium's atomic weight, so raising it, she believed, to the indisputable status of an element.

But there was more than Marie Curie's work at stake. If Kelvin was right, then Rutherford and Soddy's theory of radioactive disintegration was also in tatters. Through that summer the thunder of the public battle ranged through the leader columns of *The Times*, and then into the pages of the magazine more accustomed to this type of warfare, *Nature*. It involved such British scientific heavyweights as Sir Oliver Lodge, Sir William Ramsay and Rutherford and Soddy themselves. Rutherford, no matter what his mother's views on the nearness of Lord Kelvin to God, was as crushing as ever in his rational attack on the peer's heretical views.

Rutherford, among other arguments, pointed out that, if Kelvin was right, then the compound Kelvin believed radium to be was of a type completely unknown to chemistry. 'Radium,' Rutherford said, 'has fulfilled every test required of an element.'[6] But in spite of the fact that good reason, and all who mattered in modern radiochemistry, were on her side, Marie Curie was drawn into the correspondence. She wrote, 'I see no use in combating the theory (that radium can no longer be regarded as a simple element) enunciated by Lord Kelvin.' Nevertheless, she was intellectually deeply affected by the fact that doubt could still be cast on the brilliant assumption on which her career had been based: that radioactivity is an *atomic* property of the *element* radium. She still was driven to prove herself. Five years later she admitted that, for her, 'It was of real importance to corroborate this point as misgivings had been voiced by those to whom the atomic hypothesis of radioactivity was still not evident.'[7] And the only way to do this beyond what she had done already, was to produce radium: not the pure radium chloride which she believed she had, but radium metal. To make it would mean a repetition of many of the laborious tasks she had already carried out, and more exacting work in addition. It was the nose-to-the-grindstone activity at which she had no contemporary equal. She set about it with the same resolution and obsession with which she had attacked her first sacks of pitchblende.

The work that had always been the centre of her life was now to be her saviour in the vacuum left by her dead husband. With the facilities she had at her disposal through Carnegie's riches she could begin to build the little school of people around her who would become her scientific family. She could use her laboratory personnel as a substitute family for the one at Sceaux from which she was so often absent. And all the substitute children during the years that followed developed the same fierce loyalties to 'La Patronne', as they called her. For the young people, particularly the young women, who worked for her in the Rue Cuvier laboratory she was the mother-figure who guided and freely gave. Several of these in later years looked back on this period as the happiest and most productive of their lives. She had a great deal to offer those who could easily accept her in this matronly role. Though those who could not, and there were to be many, often found themselves in conflict with a masculine toughness which, under certain circumstances, could be unattractive and even repulsive.

Her own work, once she had re-established it in a routine, began with yet another purification of radium chloride. By the same dogged process of the preceding years, she produced in 1907 four decigrams of what she felt she could now describe as 'perfectly pure radium chloride',[8] from which she could determine an even more reliable atomic weight for radium – assuming it to be an element.

Then with the faithful André Debierne, she set about trying to prove beyond doubt the credentials of polonium as an element. A few years previously, just as Kelvin had doubts about her radium, she had made the mistake of doubting her first major discovery's reality as a true metal. Worse, she had embarrassingly put her doubts in print. But she had long since returned to her original conviction. However, the problem as far as polonium was concerned, was that there was 5,000 times less of it in pitchblende than there was radium. None the less, knowing that even a ton of the best mineral she could lay her hands on contained only a few thousandths of a gram of polonium, she began the long process of extraction, first in the factory, then in the laboratory.

Eventually she and Debierne succeeded in getting a sample of polonium salt which was 50 times more radioactive than an equivalent amount of radium salt. It was in sufficient quantity to identify polonium as an element from its spectrum, though she knew full well that the Kelvins of the scientific world were not prepared to accept these new-fangled mathematical methods as final.

Already in the past she had had to go into the attack to defend polonium for what she knew it to be. In Germany in 1902 the chemist Willy Marckwald had produced what he believed was a new radioactive substance which he had called radiotellurium. Marie Curie was convinced that what Marckwald had gone to such formidable trouble to produce was nothing more than her own polonium. During the next few years, she had put her uncompromising bull-dog teeth into Marckwald's work and had begun to wear it down. She had even gone so far as to publish a paper in German to show ruthlessly to Marckwald's countrymen, if not Marckwald himself, how great was his error.[9] After a study lasting ten months and ending in 1906, Marie Curie had published a definitive refutation of the German. Marckwald had to capitulate like a gentleman – though a slightly grudging gentleman 'The great services of Mme Curie in the discovery of the radioactive substances justify us in considering her wishes in a question of no wide-ranging importance. For this reason I propose in the future to replace the name of "radiotellurium" by "polonium".'[10] He had even sought out the comfort of an English bard to rub in his one remaining point:

> What's in a name? that which we call a rose,
> By any other name would smell as sweet.

Marie Curie was unaware of how much she had hurt Marckwald's pride.

There still remained the question of radium which, in spite of the fact that reason suggested it was an element, was under suspicion as a bastard substance. Four years after Kelvin's attack she reached the position that even the doubting Thomases had to acknowledge as being unassailable. By the tedious process of separating more large quantities of radium chloride and making a radium-amalgam with mercury by an electrolytic process, then by distilling the minute amount of the substance she had obtained, she managed to condense infinitesimal, but recognisable amounts of a shiny white solid: radium itself. She showed that it was indisputably a metal and measured its melting point: about 700°C. Finally she had satisfied any of the old guard who still doubted – Kelvin had died in 1907 – that radium was what twelve years ago she had said it was: an element.[11] The words she used to indicate the mountainous problems hindering this ultimate step – 'considerable difficulties were involved' – were typical of her in their understatement.

During these years Marie Curie had grown into more than a public celebrity with a tragic history: she had become a figure of no mean account in the wider scientific world. This was a period of relative world peace and stability and one when international co-operation among scientists was at its height. There existed a real international scientific community and a full exchange of information. Unlike Pierre Curie, who had a reluctance, even a repugnance, to shift himself from his own little world of the Latin Quarter, Marie had moved out to take a leading role in this international group of physicists and chemists. She had a special part to play.

For any research worker involved in making measurements with radium, it was vital to know the purity of the radium which he was using. Hospitals too, using radium in the treatment of cancers, could only operate their treatments if they had an exact knowledge of the amounts of radium, and therefore of the doses, they were applying to tumours. It was essential, therefore, that an international standard of a precisely known amount of radium should be prepared, and then secondary standards could be prepared for individual countries.

International standards of any kind are never arrived at without the intrusion of maximum national rivalries and minimum compromise. The establishment of a Radium Standard was no exception. It was, however, eventually agreed that because of Madame Curie's eminence and undoubted expertise, she should prepare the primary International Standard. This she did in 1911, and the thin glass tube a few centimetres long with her pure salt inside it was eventually deposited by her at the International Bureau of Weights and Measures near Paris.

But the road to the decision as to what the Standard should be, who should prepare it, and where it should be deposited had been full of pitfalls. The human relationships Marie Curie kept up in her own laboratory, where she had easy and friendly, though near-reverential treatment from those who worked under her, were quite different from the relationships she had to build up in the international community among her intellectual equals. Some of those who saw her on the international stage, at meetings and conferences throughout Europe, saw not the soft and sympathetic woman of the 'family' laboratory, but the tough, uncompromising figure in black, often wearing an icy expression, difficult to engage in conversation, and not only needing, but sometimes demanding respect. Several young workers attending their first international conferences were hurt by the way she rebuffed any attempts at casual conversation. One young English physicist, E. N. da C. Andrade, was so put out by her frigid and unhelpful response to him that even until a few months before his death at a ripe old age he remembered her as 'not a very nice person'.[12]

Some of the older school knew how to handle her sensitivities better. Rutherford had a gentle touch with her that worked smoothly. But many of her contemporary intellectual equals took exception to her autocratic front and, like George Jaffé so many years before, were conscious of a crown, or even a halo hanging over her now greying hair. Bertram Borden Boltwood was one of these. He was an American who himself was capable of the occasional lofty attitude. He was a bachelor, often given to fits of depression, or 'lonesomeness' as he called it, but had opposing manic moods of cheerfulness which attracted Rutherford. The New Zealander had put him into his category of 'thundering good fellows' and admired him for his skills as a radiochemist; they had become firm friends.

Boltwood and Marie Curie's personal chemistry did not mix at all well. Boltwood took no delight in any brushes he had with her cold front; he took a plainly disapproving objection to her queenly, rather than motherly attitude to her place in the ranks of the radiochemists. During this time Rutherford and Boltwood were exchanging letters with a frankness of phrase which never entered any of their published works.

Boltwood had discovered that the Curie laboratory was not the generous source of material and information it had been when Pierre was alive. In 1908 Boltwood had tried to get Marie Curie to let him compare one of his radium solutions with her own radium standard but, as he told Rutherford, 'The Madame was not at all desirous of having any such a comparison carried out, the reason, I suspect, being her constitutional unwillingness to do anything that might directly or indirectly assist any worker in radioactivity outside her own laboratory. ... It is a great pity that some people are so darn sensitive about criticism and the Madame apparently has the idea that anyone associated with her laboratory is a sort of holy person.'[13]

Rutherford of the soft touch, however, had no difficulty in persuading Marie Curie to lend him her standard when he needed it several months later. But although Rutherford's personal liking for the woman never varied, his opinion of her work was changing. He admired her obvious diligence and thoroughness as a laboratory worker, but he was in some doubts as to the originality and even the necessity of the slow hard labour to which she was submitting herself. He was not the only one with a sceptical eye. He would have been unusual if he had not experienced some sense of self-satisfaction when, as long ago as 1904, he had received a letter from another American, Henry Bumstead, saying, 'I haven't seen Curie's last paper yet; I am never very eager to see them for I usually find that I have read the same things about a year before in one of your papers.'[14]

In 1910 Marie Curie published her *Treatise on Radioactivity*. Again it was a work of great labour, ran to almost 1,000 pages, and was a comprehensive summary of progress in radioactivity since she, to all intents and purposes, started the subject by her observations of 1897. Rutherford reviewed it for *Nature*. He gave the two volumes a favourable reception. But what he had to say about them in the privacy of the pages of a letter to Boltwood was in a different tone from the respectful one he reserved for the scientific journal.

They are very heavy and very long, but she has got a great deal of useful information collected together. I think she makes a mistake of trying to include all the work, old and new, with very little critical discussion of its relative importance. I have not had time to read more than parts of it, but, as a whole, it would appear that she has been reasonably generous in the recognition of those outside of France. At any rate, I should judge that I have not been neglected. In reading her book I could almost think I was reading my own with the extra work of the last few years thrown in to fill up. . . . It is very amusing in parts to read where she is very anxious to claim priority for French science, or rather for herself and her husband. Long quotations are given to show their mental attitude at the times under consideration. . . . Altogether I feel that the poor woman has laboured tremendously, and her volumes will be very useful for a year or two to save the researcher from hunting up his own literature; a saving which I think is not altogether advantageous.[15]

Rutherford was privately patronising. But no matter how critical he was of the progress of Marie Curie's work, he watched her progress through life with a sympathetic eye. That September he had been with her at a scientific Congress in Brussels where the International Radium Standard was under discussion. Rutherford watched her arrive with Jean Perrin. The contrast between the gay and generous 'jack-in-the-box' Perrin, as Rutherford called him, and the withdrawn and grey figure alongside could not have been more discomforting. Rutherford wrote to his mother to tell her how 'wan and tired and much older than her age', Madame Curie looked. 'She works much too hard for her health. Altogether she was a very pathetic figure.'[16]

1910 had not been a good year. Her health fluctuated from bad to indifferent, improving when she spent periods away from the laboratory much as both hers and Pierre's had a few years earlier. Considering the concentrated quantities of radium and polonium she was handling at close quarters during this period it is scarcely surprising that her body was behaving as though it were receiving bouts of punishment. Her state of mind had not been improved by the death of old Dr Curie in February. He had been an integral part of her household and her life for fifteen years. Several doctors at the Brussels meeting told Rutherford that they thought Madame Curie looked in a bad nervous state.

However, not every physicist believed that the Madame's frequent absences from crucial discussions were altogether involuntary. Stefan Meyer, the Austrian physicist suspected her of bringing on her frequent attacks of nervous exhaustion when it best suited her. It all seemed part and parcel of the unfortunate scientific gathering they were both now involved in. The Congress as a whole had been disorganised from the start. When resolutions and counter-resolutions were being attempted in three languages on its final day under a weak Belgian chairman, the audience got out of hand and began whistling and booing. As a Committee member, and the only woman, Marie Curie had to bear her share of the displeasure of the crowd of dissatisfied scientists with the same equanimity as her male Committee member colleagues.

She herself had been at the centre of one of the disputes, concerning the adoption of the International Radium Standard. She had been flattered by the fact that the name 'Curie' had been suggested as the unit of measurement for the Radium Standard, but there was no agreement as to what this unit of measurement should be. On the day that a definition was adopted she left the meeting feeling ill. But she was nevertheless not beyond making her dissatisfaction with the proceedings quite plain. She sat down in her room and, on a piece of the 'Hôtel du Grand Miroir' notepaper coldly wrote down her, as usual, uncompromising position. If the name of *Curie* was to be adopted as the unit, then it must be she who defined it: 'the quantity of emanation in equilibrium with one gram of radium'.[17] She had her way; her bald dictatorial statement was accepted. But she created her critics, some of whom were becoming less tolerant of her mistressly attitudes. They were not surprised when she failed to attend the Congress's gala dinner with a 'bad cold' as her excuse.

But Rutherford was not so quick to condemn. He had sat next to her at the Opera on the previous evening and he could see that she was not well. Halfway through the performance she left on his arm. He deposited her, worn out, at her hotel.

Marie returned next day with Jean Perrin to Paris, and to the days of quiet that Sceaux and her children could give her until the driving urge to work returned, as it would. The girls were growing, and she was seeing too little of them. 'Ma douce Mé,' the young Irène wrote during her holidays that summer, 'WHEN ARE YOU COMING TO JOIN US? . . . I shall be so happy when you come because I badly need to caress somebody.'[18]

The sight of the children sometimes depressed her when she let herself slip into the self-pitying belief that the time she and they had left to spend together, might be limited. Earlier, she had written to her Polish childhood friend Kazia, the woman who twenty years before had been used as the repository for Maria Sklodowska's depressed and hypochondriac musings: 'When I think of the younger one's age! I see it will take twenty years to make grown persons of them I doubt if I shall last so long, as my life is very fatiguing, and grief does not have a salutary effect upon strength and health.'[19] But there were hidden reserves of strength which even she did not know she owned.

Chapter 15

Academic Miscalculation

At Pierre Curie's death Marie was 38 years old; a widow of an awkward age with two children. Rutherford noted she looked older than her age. But photographs taken in the early years of the century show a striking contrast between the adopted severity of her dress, and the developing serenity of her face. She was passing through a period of beauty. The romantic would call it the beauty of suffering; the unromantic would suggest that her illnesses took her skin closer to her bones and showed their facial structure to better advantage. No matter whether internal or external changes were the cause, with her slim figure and greying hair, she had become a striking woman. Her appearance complemented the romantic image of purity of purpose which popular legend had built for her.

Those who worked close to her during these years saw that the mask of mourning hid a driving urge for work. Now that she had taken on the full masculine role her uncompromising nature emerged more forcefully. In international scientific circles there were many who made no concessions whatever because she was a woman, since her attitudes demanded that this was how they should react. And in her Parisian circle, there were those whose reactions were suspicious and even unfriendly towards her reputation and behaviour.

Marie sensed these reactions. She was no different from most widows in that, during this period more than any other, she needed close friendship and some substitute for the companionship that Pierre had given her. Curie had been a good man and a good scientist, but he was a totally scientific animal and in some senses a restricted man. He had channelled Marie's interests into a scientifically very productive life: but he had also left gaps. During the years just before and just after her husband's death Marie came into close contact with a man who, at the same time as having some of Pierre's scientific brilliance, was more of a philosophic and political animal who could reawaken old interests for her. He was Paul Langevin, Curie's ex-pupil.

She had first met him as the enthusiastic student whom Pierre introduced to research and then appointed as his young co-worker. Later at Sèvres, teaching long hours of physics to the young girls, she had worked alongside Langevin, both of them sacrificing time they would have preferred to have spent in their laboratories in order to earn living wages. Then too she had seen him in different circumstances again as one of the group which, before Curie's death, used to sit admiringly at the Master's feet in the garden at Boulevard Kellermann on Sunday afternoons.

This was a rarified group of scientists which had in it the attractions, the failings, the weaknesses and the strengths of any other group of individuals. Their familiarity with logical argument gave them no special protection from the pitfalls of life. They had their enthusiasms, their eccentricities, their jealousies and their marital problems, as did any other collection of men. Marguerite Borel, daughter of Paul Appell, the Dean of the Faculty of Science, was first introduced to the members of this group as an attractive nineteen-year-old when she married the mathematician Émile Borel. She had no scientific small-talk, but was in the privileged position of the pretty insouciante. She did, however, have literary pretensions. As a source for her literary observations, she used the characters of the young men who, after a day's work in the laboratories and lecture halls of the Sorbonne, relaxed in the cafés of the Boulevard St Germain with her husband, or who put in an appearance for distracting conversation in her salon.

Marguerite, far from feeling an outsider to the group, was enchanted by it. She used her ignorance to advantage. She would flirt with 'the archangel', as she called Jean Perrin, and take from him as much reassurance as she needed whenever she felt it necessary to question the presence of an uncomprehending woman in a gathering of scientists. 'And what when they don't understand the conversation?' she would ask. 'Flowers don't understand either,' he would dutifully reply. 'They don't need to.'

Perrin she adored; she adored the bunches of flowers he brought her, and she adored his sometimes riotous behaviour with his great friend Langevin. They would turn up in her maple-lined drawing-room late in the evening after a day's work and, Perrin sitting at her piano with Langevin alongside him, would release the day's tensions with a burst of Schubert or Wagner.

Marguerite had an observant eye for the wives of these scientists, just as she had for the scientists themselves. She had watched the Curies appear together at the various gatherings, drifting in 'like two shadows' and she was attracted by the withdrawn woman under the short greying hair. She watched Henriette Perrin's gentle tolerating smile, and she noted the fact that Langevin never came with his wife.

Marguerite was half Marie Curie's age and belonged to the generation which, unlike Marie's, would eventually expect emancipation to include sexual emancipation. She not only knew of her husband's premarital sexual adventures, when she came face to face with one of his ex-paramours, she took some pleasure in letting the woman know that she felt not the slightest pang of jealousy.

Marie Curie, educated in Polish society with its Victorian inhibitions, belonged to the generation in which women, in the normal course of affairs, did not discuss sexual behaviour. If it had to be mentioned at all, then it was referred to by euphemism. It was the generation which Freud was to use as his mine to prospect the sexual unconscious of middle-Europeans.

That age in which Marguerite Borel built her salon was one when sexual conversation between the sexes was confined within certain bounds: when Anatole France would compliment her on her sensual shoulders and legs, and make cynical comments about the pleasures of love. It was the age in which the existence of the discreetly rented bachelor flat for illicit affairs was common knowledge, but not discussed in mixed company. There was, of course, gossip which many of the 'advanced' young women enjoyed among themselves. Much of it concerned the rich, the famous and the aristocratic. It was said that General Boulanger had had a small place tucked away where he could take Sophie,

Comtesse de Trêmes; Clemenceau was reputed to share the Duc d'Aumale's mistress, and the carryings-on of the francophile Prince of Wales, even as 'Kingy', with the wife of an officer of the Norfolk Yeomanry, was familiar subject matter in Parisian conversational pieces. But this behaviour was, apparently, that of a rarified stratum, and the possibility of its existence in other less exalted, more purposeful and more hard-working society was hypocritically not accepted: nor was it generally acceptable. Men might, with discretion, occasionally walk where they wished and escape social odium; women who overstepped the mark of propriety did so at their peril.

Marie Curie never approved of Marguerite's gossip, though they were to remain good friends. Marguerite observed Marie closely during the few years following Pierre's death, and what she saw could, by those with a mind for it, be turned into gossip. She began to suspect that there was some sort of relationship developing between the new widow and Paul Langevin.

Langevin pleased Marguerite a lot. He had a wide smile under his waxed moustaches and his intelligence was impressive. He was from a humble background, very different from Marguerite's. He had struggled to give himself a good scientific education and, dressed formally in his morning coat and stiff white collar, would take a perverse pleasure in being mistaken for a cavalry officer and a member of the privileged class although his political inclinations were far to the left.

After his work with Pierre Curie, Jean Perrin and others in Paris, Langevin had set off in 1897 for the Cavendish laboratory in Cambridge to become the first of the non-British in the new category of 'Research Students' that had been instituted at the University. It was during the year that the creative influence of J. J. Thomson was at its height and when some of the most brilliant of young physicists were being attracted to the laboratory. There Langevin worked on X-rays alongside the young Rutherford. As the first foreigner Langevin had been a popular success. He took in his stride the comradeship of the place, which was so vital to this, one of the most fertile periods in its fertile history. At one of the annual Cavendish dinners in a Cambridge hotel he rounded off the evening with a spirited chorus of *La Marseillaise* with such enthusiasm that the French head-waiter was moved to tears as well as to embracing his fellow-countryman.[1]

Langevin's life as a physicist was a story of outstanding achievement. In 1905 Pierre Curie saw his young protegé succeed him as professor at the School of Physics and Chemistry. Langevin's work on the theory of magnetism was in the direct and brilliant line of Pierre Curie's own early work. In another field Langevin independently came to the same conclusions as to the equivalence of mass and energy as those just published by an unknown patent clerk in Berne, and in France Langevin later took up and publicised the revolutionary implications of this young Albert Einstein.

Inevitably Rutherford and Langevin struck up a friendship at Cambridge and Langevin saw the good sense in Rutherford's early conclusions concerning the nature and origins of radioactive energy. Through the years they exchanged friendly letters in an easy style, very much in contrast to the stiff and formal ones Marie Curie and Rutherford passed between one another.

Outside physics, Rutherford and Langevin had a common characteristic: both had a keen interest in money. Rutherford, however, was noticeably more successful at both making it and keeping it. He counted the pennies carefully, and budgeted accordingly. Langevin was miserably less successful, and it was his worry over money matters which first attracted Marguerite Borel's special curiosity.

Marguerite's husband had become scientific director of the École Normale and the couple had now set up house in the apartment once occupied by Louis Pasteur. It was there in her study hung with yellow striped wallpaper that Langevin would call after a day in the laboratory to chatter to the pretty girl. As with the rest of the scientists and young men of letters who appeared on her doorstep Marguerite presented an ever open ear for his triumphs and a ready word of consolation for his failures and problems. Langevin's love of literature gave him an easy conversational link with Marguerite and she would watch 'his brown eyes – so beautiful' light up his face as he talked over a wide range of subjects that interested him, in and out of science. Some of the problems he carried into Marguerite's study were mundane: he had a bad stomach and he craved cups of tea which she dispensed with sympathy. But this ailment, it was not difficult to divine, was a symptom of much deeper problems.

In 1898 Langevin had married a girl called Jeanne Desfosses. Like him, she had working class origins but had not had his access to advanced education. Before her marriage she helped her mother in a grocer's shop they owned at Choisy-le-Roi where her father worked in a pottery. Between 1899 and 1909 Paul and Jeanne Langevin had four children, two boys and two girls. The scholarships and salaries he had struggled on in Paris and in Cambridge had never adequately kept pace with his family's growing needs.

Langevin poured out his confidences to Marguerite. He had a classic line to deliver to his confidante: he was not understood at home. There his wife and his mother-in-law could not begin to comprehend why it was that he avoided the apparently simple solution to their financial problems. He had already had magnificent offers from industry which recognised his high skills as a practical scientist and was prepared to offer salaries to match. But to Langevin this was the temptation of the devil, and he was between it and the deep blue sea of his love of 'pure' scientific research. Regrettably, the purity of his passion for science would, for the foreseeable future, always be accompanied by inadequate academic salaries. Unlike Marguerite and her husband, Langevin and his wife had no supplementary incomes to depend on.

Langevin's wife could never forgive him for not having succumbed to industry's tempting offers. It was, to her, culpable behaviour considering they had four children and 'you would get four times more than they give you at the University'.

Langevin emerged from the bruising of the family quarrels to Marguerite's yellow salon where she could comfort 'this man whose intelligence embraced a world of intellectual problems, but who was defenceless in daily life'. When, as often happened, Langevin told Marguerite he could not go on and had had enough of life, Marguerite and her husband or Jean Perrin hauled him off to a theatre, to a public meeting, or to late-night onion soup at Les Halles: anything to distract him from his nervy introspection.

Marie Curie

Marie, Bronia and Helena with their father in 1890

Jacques and Pierre Curie with their parents

Pierre and Marie Curie in 1895

Inside and outside the shed in which radium was separated

Pierre and Marie Curie shortly after their marriage

Pierre Curie

Marie Curie with her daughter Irene in 1908

Delegates to the Solvay Conference in 1911. On Marie Curie's right is Perrin, on her left Poincaré. Behind her is Rutherford; to his left are Kamerlingh Onnes, Einstein and Langevin

Marie and Irene in the laboratory

Marie Curie with pupils from the American Expeditionary Force
in 1919

Irene and Frédèric Joliot-Curie

Eve Curie in 1939

Marie Curie with Albert Einstein, Geneva 1925

Marguerite was a confidante, but she was no secret-keeper. She discussed Langevin's worries with his closest friends. They could all see that Langevin was genuinely worried to illness about the dilemma of his personal situation and his scientific preferences. He was becoming more nervous and unpredictable.

But among the group of scientists whom Langevin regularly met there was one who, to the surprise of the rest, was beginning to show a more deeply involved interest in Langevin's state of mind. Marie Curie had in her own life never been touched even by the fringes of the dilemma which tormented Paul Langevin. For her the purity of scientific research was absolute. Extending the boundaries of pure scientific knowledge was the noble ambition she had struggled for and achieved. She had been aware of some of Langevin's troubles as long as most of his friends. She had seen him regularly for several years before Pierre's death but was now prepared to reveal that she was more than a casual and respected colleague. Marguerite had the first hints of this one evening in the dining-room of the Perrins' house in Boulevard Kellermann. She had seen Marie wear dark or black clothes during the five years since her husband's death. Now Marguerite saw that a metamorphosis had taken place. 'It was a rejuvenated Marie Curie, in a white dress and with a rose at her waist. She sat down, silent as usual, but something signified her resurrection, like the spring following a frozen winter, declaring itself suddenly by these small details.'[2]

That an interest in Langevin and his affairs had stimulated this resurrection became more clear to Marguerite when shortly after this incident she shared the same hotel as Madame Curie in Genoa. Émile Borel and Marie had accepted invitations as part of a French delegation to a scientific conference. They had turned the visit into a family affair. Borel had taken along Marguerite, and Marie had taken her two children and their Polish governess.

One evening while Borel was preparing his work for the next day's conference Marie Curie asked Marguerite to come to talk to her in her bedroom. Marguerite sat by the bedside and soon sensed that the older woman had some sort of confidence she needed to share. The normally over-talkative Marguerite controlled herself in silence on this and several other evenings they spent together.

I forced myself to say nothing so as not to startle her confidences, and she began to discuss Langevin.

'I know he trusts you. He's sad.'

I discovered, evening after evening, that underneath the austere scientist there was a tender and animated woman, capable of crossing fire for those she loved. She was afraid that Langevin might give in to the pressures on him and give up pure science:

'He is a genius!'

Or, giving in to despondency and lassitude, he would come to grief.

'He is so worthwhile!'

Her thin hands shook as she took hold of mine:

'We must save him from himself. He's weak. You and me, we're strong. He needs understanding, gentle affection . . .'[3]

Marguerite saw the newly revealed relationship in the rosy hues of blossoming love, though she was by no means the only observer to reach this conclusion. And these other observers were not limited to the intimate group of scientists. Langevin had taken an apartment in the city; it could be described as the bachelor flat. It was small and unpretentious: two rooms in a grey-shuttered five-storey tenement block in the Rue du Banquier opposite the School of Physics and Chemistry. It was therefore convenient for his work and saved him late-night journeys to and from his family home in the suburbs. It was also convenient for Marie Curie to visit him: only a ten-minute walk from her laboratory. She did so, and was seen to do so on many occasions by residents of the apartment block, who watched her easily recognisable, and now well-known figure enter the wide entrance to the courtyard, and climb the stairs to his rooms.

The relationship, such as it was at this stage, between the woman Nobel laureate and the distinguished physicist five years her junior, would probably have continued without comment had it not been for a scientific event which brought Marie Curie once again into public view. She had been proposed for election to the

Académie des Sciences. Under normal circumstances the Académie's elections of its members carried no great interest for the French public. But this occasion was significant because Marie Curie, were she to be elected, would be the first woman to cross the threshold of the hitherto male preserve.

The press picked up the news that she was seeking election before any formal announcement had been made and when only the earliest rumours had leaked out. They were the first warning shots in a two-year spell of publicity which was to be even more embittering than the exposure which had so seared her at the time of the Nobel award of 1903.

During this period the French press had been experiencing a revolution in style and content, just as had the newspapers of Britain and America. The cause had been the application of late nineteenth-century technology to the methods of newspaper production. Linotype, invented in 1885, reached the Paris presses in 1900. Combined with the electric telegraph and the telephone, the new machinery was capable of turning out a new form of paper: one with more pages at a cheaper price, with headlines and sub-headlines, with pictures and, above all, with content in which news now took precedence over doctrine. It was a technology eminently suitable to take newspapers to the lower social orders in a form that would make mass circulation easy and high profits a certainty for those who were able to corner the market. *Le Journal* was founded by Fernand Xau in 1892 and aimed quite deliberately at the clerks and the tradesmen, and above all at the women of the country who, he believed, had the leisure to read undemanding prose. His belief made Xau a prodigious fortune.

The Parisian scandal sheet had already arrived before the turn of the century. The early years of the century saw the rise of a right-wing, nationalist and anti-semitic press in *L'Action Française* and *L'Intransigeant*. The first issue of *L'Action Française* had appeared in March of 1908. Its editor, Léon Daudet, possessed a savage and reactionary pen, pro-Catholic, and anti-Jewish.[4] He had a wealth of personal invective at his literary command and, within the limits imposed by the laws of libel, was capable of attributing sordid sexual behaviour to any of his opponents.

In 1910 these were concerns which seemed remote from Marie Curie's scientific ivory tower. Science journalism however was just beginning and *Figaro* in that year published a leading article in praise of ultra-violet ray research and its applications to the control of epidemics; it saw science as the legitimate crown of nineteenth-century intelligence.

Beyond the points where journalism touched scientific work Marie Curie had neither need nor wish to be involved in the columns of newspapers. Occasionally she had taken up her pen to address a paper's editor when it was imperative to her that she did so. In 1905 she had written to the editor of *La Patrie* about a published interview which one of his reporters claimed to have had with her at the time of Pierre Curie's election to the Academy. In answer to a question concerning the rewards she expected from her own work the reporter described how she replied, 'Oh! I am only a woman and nothing more than a woman. I shall never have a seat under the Cupola.' He went on to add that Madame Curie had said that her only ambition was to help her husband in his work. The supposed interviewee was quick to nail the story before it too became legend. In her letter to the editor she described the whole interview – its reflections on her submissiveness in her scientific role, and the suggestion that the shade of the Institut de France's Cupola over the Académie des Sciences as being beyond her expectations – as 'purely imaginary'. The editor apologised.[5] Other editors with whom she later crossed swords were not to be so accommodating.

Figaro, on November 16th, 1910, first broke the news that Marie Curie was preparing to submit her candidature for the newly vacant seat in the general physics section of the Académie des Sciences. Since its re-foundation in 1795, the Institut de France, which housed under its domed palace its five academies, of which the Académie des Sciences was one, had never admitted a woman. *Figaro* pointed out that Marie Curie's absence from this academy meant the exclusion of the person who was probably France's most illustrious physicist. However, feminist pressure was causing walls to crumble around other male bastions. The independent literary academy, the Académie Goncourt, had just elected Madame Judith Gautier.

But why did Marie Curie want to be elected? The humiliating experiences of Pierre Curie when he had been first rejected, then at the second attempt only narrowly elected, had left Marie even more bitter about the process of election than her husband. But in spite of the lingering scars, there were good practical reasons for her to have the seat. She expressed these reasons as 'the advantage an election could have for my laboratory'.[6] Membership would give her access to the Académie's sessions, and through her, her laboratory staff would have a direct route to rapid publication of their work in the Académie's journal.

But there can be no doubt that the ambition to succeed, to tread a scientific path on which no other woman had stepped, must have been a strongly motivating factor. And she would not have entered the lists had she been unsure of her position in science. Internationally her scientific reputation was unassailable. But she was either unaware of, or seriously underestimated the reaction her personality engendered in many people – even amounting to hostility. She decided to offer herself as a candidate.

Immediately the decision became front page news. *Figaro* led with an article over three columns, signed by 'Fœmina', which extolled the virtues of Marie Curie and used her as a symbol of the inevitable rise of feminism: 'Her glory has such nobility and beauty! Including the poignant poetry of her suffering, she has nothing short of a perfect and pure image to display to us.'[7] Effusive as the article was in praise of the Madame, it was correct in pointing out that the Academy had among its members some very mediocre scientists; if ability was all that counted, Marie Curie could not fail to be elected.

But ability was far from being the only quality at issue. By the end of November most of the popular dailies had jumped on *Figaro*'s bandwagon, but were not all intent on driving it in the same direction. *L'Intransigeant* held a mock poll for readers to choose women most worthy of election to the Institute. Most of the names submitted were writers, with Colette's name prominent. Marie Curie's name featured rarely. Editors encouraged the subject matter into the correspondence columns of their papers where heavy-breathing gentlemen treated the business as being more akin to a Miss World contest rather than a serious election depending on scientific merit. One reactionary soul summed up his and many others' attitudes to women's club membership in the shortest of the letters: 'Sir, None and never. Affectionately yours.' *Figaro* responded with a half page cartoon of a glamorous girl holding the Institute's cupola over her flowing hair and captioned, 'What a pretty hat the Cupola would make'.

The whole affair was in danger of being turned into a circus. The sober and respectable *Le Temps* entered the fray in December but, whilst being well disposed towards Marie Curie, pointed out that 47 years earlier George Sand had refused to let herself be used as 'a battering ram against the doors of the Institute'.[8] It was to the editor of this newspaper that Marie Curie wrote confirming that she intended to put herself forward as a candidate, but pleading for no more press comment or interest. But it was too late, and in any case a vain hope. Already the affair had the look of battle and those with influence were beginning to take sides. Newspapers had begun to align themselves. *Le Temps* took the wholly unprecedented step of giving one and a half of its long columns to the permanent secretary of the Académie des Sciences, Gaston Darboux, to write in support of Marie Curie's election.[9] Darboux carefully reviewed Madame Curie's career, listed her honours, and explained in simple terms to the lay public the advantages of the speed of publication of the Academy's proceedings (five days after each Monday's session), and therefore the advantages to the Curie laboratory. There is no equivalent in modern times of a scientist having gone to such pains to explain to a general public the workings of esoteric scientific politics in order to benefit one of his colleagues.

But less moderately expressed opposition to Marie Curie was mounting in the right-wing press. There existed a vocal group very ready to revive the view that Marie Curie had ridden to success on her husband's coat-tails; it maintained that the discovery of radium and the subsequent work leading to the award of the Nobel Prize had been carried out by Pierre Curie, with his wife sharing all the honours but being responsible for none of the creativity. It was an accusation Marie Curie had long feared might be levelled and against which she had guarded by the careful wording of her scientific papers. But this had not laid the ghost. The accusation was coming from those who had never read her papers. On January 11th *L'Intransigeant* made its position clear. One of its reporters had failed to get past the doorkeeper now permanently posted outside Marie Curie's laboratory, but had managed to get a seat at her weekly lecture course. Public feeling and interest was high, as was obvious the moment Marie Curie entered the lecture room on what would in the normal course of events have been an ordinary workday. She was greeted by loud applause from students, reporters and other inquisitive visitors. Nevertheless *L'Intransigeant*'s reporter turned in his copy as a succession of pinpricking innuendoes describing how he sat through a tedious hour and a half of the lady discoursing on 'her dear radium'.

A battleground had been prepared and on it was a challenger. All that was now needed was an enemy. His name was announced on January 15th – Edouard Branly. *Figaro* prepared its readers for the fun to follow. It would be 'the war of the sexes'.

Edouard Branly was 66 years old. He was a mild-mannered, pince-nezed, white-haired and devout Catholic French gentleman who had behind him a long and distinguished, though unspectacular scientific career. He had taught at the Catholic Institute for 30 years and had turned out scientific publications on a wide range of subjects. The discovery that won him fame was the phenomenon he called 'radioconduction'. He found that he could make his 'radioconductors' from tubes of iron filings which were capable of receiving electromagnetic signals. The discovery earned for him, in France at least, the title, 'the father of wireless telegraphy'. Marconi had incorporated Branly's device into systems capable of receiving radio waves over large distances.

Branly entered the lists of the Académie des Sciences' election with as much caution and as little sense of *Figaro*'s fun as did Marie Curie. The daughters of both candidates would later leave accounts of the scars left on their families by the welter of publicity which hinged on the characters of their parents.[10] Branly was as undemonstrative and as retiring as Marie Curie, but equally he could summon as many, as influential, and as militant supporters as could his internationally famous woman opponent. His press support was substantial and came from the right. It was in the main that same rabidly nationalist press that had condemned, and still did condemn, Dreyfus as Jew and traitor. Its leading editors such as Léon Bailby of *L'Intransigeant* and Léon Daudet of *L'Action Française* were capable of a greater range of invective than the more sober papers' editors who gave their favours to Madame Curie.

Besides his scientific achievements, which made him a very strong contender for the vacant Academy seat, Branly's circumstances, like Marie Curie's, commanded an emotional response. He was an old man whose great contribution to modern technology, carried out in 1890, seemed to have been given scant international recognition. There were many who felt that he should have had a share in Marconi's 1909 Nobel Prize in physics. Twice before he had tried for election to the Academy, and twice had been rejected. He announced that this was an old man's last attempt. He even had an emotive personal claim on the vacant chair; Gernez, whose death had vacated it, was one of Branly's close friends.

Branly's scientific supporters from within the Academy were themselves seasoned campaigners. Significantly, one of his leading champions was Émile Amagat, the man Pierre Curie had defeated in the 1905 election. Another was Paul de Cassagnac. Just as Gaston Darboux had pleaded Marie Curie's case to the world at large in *Le Temps*, so too now de Cassagnac looked to the popular press. *L'Autorité* was only too accommodating with its columns in which he was allowed to list the desirable qualities of his candidate. Just as the benefits of the wonders of radium had been displayed as the product of the mind of Marie Curie, so too now the visions of humanitarian and even imperial benefits of *Télégraphie Sans Fil* were conjured up as being the products of the cerebral activity of Edouard Branly:

On top of the Eiffel Tower are antennae which transmit

electric waves across thousands of kilometres, to posts established over the whole seaboard, to all the ships in our war squadrons, and to all our liners. And they are captured by Branly's observation.

Thanks to these waves, in only a few seconds, our Ministers can be in communication with our African colonies. . . . Wireless telegraphy has already saved hundreds of lives by making it possible for ships to call for help . . .[11]

For the Parisian press there were heady days to follow. Each newspaper aligned itself in one of the two available ranks. Between the two there was a clear delineation. On one side were the liberals, the feminists and the anti-clericals, and on the other were the nationalists (Marie Curie's undesirable Polish origins were recalled) the pro-Catholic (Branly had been created commander of St Gregory the Great by Pope Leo XIII), and the anti-semitic (there had been murmurings about Marie Curie having Jewish origins notwithstanding her Catholic parentage).

The candidates had common ground on two points. First, in 1904, when their relative merits were not in dispute, they had shared the Osiris Prize of 50,000 francs. Secondly, the pen portraits which their championing newspapers were separately painting, bore remarkable sentimentalised similarities. Both Branly and Marie Curie were being represented as impoverished, modest, and disinterested workers in the cause of science, who wanted nothing better than to be left in peace to continue their researches. If these descriptions were in substance true, it is nevertheless worth remarking on the fact that neither Marie Curie nor Edouard Branly had been able to resist the temptations, or the pressures, to put forward their own names in an antiquated and debasing system of election.

During the next few days Marie Curie walked from apartment to apartment and from laboratory to laboratory, ringing door bells and leaving visiting cards. She had to perform the humiliating and impossible task of combining self-aggrandisement with modesty as she touted for each scientist's vote. Grey-haired Branly had to follow the same route and the same routine, often in front of men half his age. And when the ritual was over and done with, such was the interest aroused, nobody with a vote intended to miss the opportunity of using it.

The scene in the hall of the Academy on the afternoon of January 23rd, 1911 – the election day – was one never before witnessed in that sober scientific society's home. The session attracted not only France's most distinguished scientists, but, as so often now with events concerning Marie Curie, many others besides. Curious crowds gathered at the doorway to watch the full complement of fifty or so members arrive. Available space not filled by natural philosophers was occupied by journalists and photographers. At one point the crowd became so dense that a man was overcome by the heat, slipped to the floor, and had to be ushered out by a convoy of functionaries, followed by a doctor.

The Academy's session was intended as a normal scientific meeting. Several papers were scheduled to be read, and an hour of attempted serious discourse by well-intentioned physicists had to be passed through to a background hubbub from bored and uncomprehending spectators. By the time the clock struck four to signal the election, the hubbub had risen to an uproar and Armand Gautier was unable to bring the session to silence. Only the advance of a group of ushers carrying ballot-boxes eventually converted the unseemly noise into an atmosphere of expectancy.

During the voting the hubbub rose again. Somebody had noticed that Marie Curie's supporter, Gaston Darboux, the Academy's permanent secretary, had slipped a paper into the hands of the aged and almost blind member, Monsieur Radau. Rumour quickly spread that Darboux had substituted Marie Curie's name for Branly's on Radau's voting slip. What actually happened, as Radau later explained in a letter to *Le Temps*, was that one of his neighbours in the hall had tried to persuade him to vote for Branly; but he, Radau, was already firmly decided on Curie. Because of his 'extreme myopia' he had approached Darboux of his own free will to ask him to vote on his behalf.

By the time Armand Gautier came to count the votes the noise was deafening and only subsided when it was clear that he was ready to announce the result. 28 votes had been cast for Madame Curie: 29 for Branly – with one vote for a third candidate, the distinguished physicist Marcel Brillouin. A second vote would be necessary to give a clear majority.

The tension mounted as in a staged melodrama, its script liberally sprinkled with theatrical effects. As the second vote began, a disrespectful photographer lit a magnesium flare which blinded all eyes, then sent a cloud of acrid smoke to hang over the hall. Beneath it the leading Curistes and Branlystes moved to lobby their weaker brethren in a final attempt to sway the unknown floating voter. One scientist was seen to cross the hall and speak to a colleague who then altered his ballot paper.

The recount was definitive. Marie Curie remained at 28 votes; Branly moved to 30. As his daughter put it, 'The Academy had at last opened its doors to the father of T.S.F.'

The battle was at an end. The 58 Academicians rose to their feet and a crowd gathered round Amagat to congratulate him on his successful campaign on behalf of Branly. Henri Poincaré, an active Curie supporter, as a good loser should, went round shaking his adversaries' hands and consoled his colleagues with the thought that, 'She will be elected next time.'

But there was to be no next time for Marie Curie. When the news of the result reached her she was deeply hurt. In the Rue Cuvier the bunch of flowers bought by her laboratory assistant to celebrate her victory remained where it was under the bench.

Her friends consoled her. Edouard Guillaume told her that he thought Branly had been elected by methods that would have made a monkey blush.[12] Georges Gouy assured her, somewhat unconvincingly, that she had had a moral victory and that her scientific stature had actually increased with the defeat. She herself was convinced that politics and the press, and not a proper assessment of academic abilities had been responsible for her humiliation.[13] She had to face the fact, however, that she had rashly miscalculated the esteem of her Parisian physicist colleagues.

Ernest Rutherford, hearing the news in Manchester as he was composing one of his long letters to Bertram Boltwood, wrote, 'You will have seen that Marie Curie was not elected to the Academy. I do not suppose it will worry her much.'[14] He was wrong. The hurt never completely disappeared. She never again submitted her own name for consideration for any honours, and accepted none that were not spontaneously given. She was not willing to have her candidature put forward for a second vacant seat in the Académie des Sciences which became vacant within a few days of her abortive attempt to gain entry, nor for any other seat which subsequently became vacant.

But the wound she carried from this affair, though it pained her ego, ought not to have been crippling. The reason why it was to be in the end so devastating was that it made her extremely vulnerable. The Academy uproar and its publicity had put her and her every action on view for public scrutiny. And it had done so at a time when she could least afford to have her so-far carefully secured private life exposed.

Chapter 16

The Breath of Scandal

Her work had always been her life-jacket. This was another occasion when she could take comfort in the distractions of the laboratory. She was making the initial attempts to prepare a Radium Standard, was carrying out a series of experiments on the variation with temperature of the activity of various radio-elements, and was planning to co-operate in research with colleagues she had found sympathetic on her visits to international meetings, besides directing the work of her research students. However, Marie Curie was to allow none of this work to be presented at any of the Academy's sessions, or to appear in the *Comptes Rendus de l'Académie des Sciences*. It was ten years before a paper carrying her name again appeared in that publication.

But if she felt that her own leading national scientific institution had snubbed her, she could justifiably claim that the fountain of international discovery that had sprung from her early experiments had changed the nature of growth of physical science. This change would continue, and the consequences for the twentieth century would be profound.

These years had been crucial in the history of atomic physics. 1911 had been particularly important. It was the year in which Ernest Rutherford conceived his picture of the atom as a small positively charged atomic nucleus surrounded by a sphere of electrification. Like Becquerel's original observation of radioactivity, Rutherford's nuclear theory of the atom attracted scarcely any attention. But its tremendous significance would soon become apparent.

Between 1896 and 1911 radiochemical and radiophysical research had moved at a phenomenal pace, simply because of the quantity and quality of research workers attracted to the field. The alpha and beta rays given off by radioactive elements were now well understood. In Rutherford's laboratory it had been confirmed in 1909 that the alpha rays given off in radioactive decay were the once mysterious source of helium gas, and that alpha particles were positively charged helium atoms. Becquerel and Marie Curie had shown beta particles to be negatively charged; they were fast-moving electrons. Paul Villard's uncharged gamma rays would before long (in 1914), be shown to be rays of even shorter wavelength than X-rays.

The understanding of the chemistry of the radio-elements had advanced at the same pace as that of the fundamental nature of matter. The idea that radioactivity was the result of atoms disintegrating and turning themselves into lighter atoms by emitting particles as radioactive rays, encouraged chemists to look for more of the radioactive disintegration products. Many radioactive species had been found with half-lives ranging from weeks, to days or minutes, and which varied greatly in the amounts of alpha, beta and gamma rays they gave out. Details of what happened during radioactive change were now beginning to be worked out. Marie Curie's earliest inspired guess that radioactivity was a property of atoms was no longer in doubt and it was realised that in each atom was stored vast amounts of energy. Rutherford recognised the brilliance of her assumption and had glimpsed some possible consequences in 1903 when he had written, 'There is no reason to assume that this enormous store of energy is possessed by the radio-elements alone.'[1] They were words with more than an edge of prophecy. In this same article, written with Soddy, Rutherford had used the words 'atomic energy'.

Rutherford produced a theory for the series of changes which were responsible for one radioactive element producing another, for this producing a third, and so on in a branching family tree. In the case of radium, its first product was radon (radium emanation); this in turn produced radium A when it gave off an alpha particle; and as alpha, beta or gamma rays were emitted from subsequent products, radium B, C, D, E, and F would be produced, with lead the final decay product in the chain. Radium F was none other than Marie Curie's polonium.

Some of the most spectacular work carried out under Rutherford's aegis had been that of Hans Geiger and Ernest Marsden, who had shown that certain alpha particles in a thin beam aimed at a fine metal foil could be significantly deflected in their path. 'It was,' said Rutherford, 'quite the most incredible event that has ever happened to me in my life. It was almost as incredible as if you fired a 15-inch shell at a piece of tissue paper and it came back and hit you.'[2] Rutherford had realised that what their alpha particles had hit was the dense central core of the atom, and it was on this and other experiments that he based his theory of the structure of the atom.

So by 1911 there existed a picture of the atom which bore some resemblance to the picture we have today. It was simple and it was inadequate. It was based on the work of men (and very few women) who had great practical physical and chemical skills. But the age of classical physics was having its apparently solid foundations undermined. That period of productivity in which physicists could use mental pictures of mechanical models to deduce what they believed to be the inner workings of the atom had reached its zenith. New concepts in physics had begun with the beginning of the twentieth century and were now throwing new light on intractable classical problems. In 1900 Max Planck had made the crucial assumption that, like matter, energy was not infinitely divisible. He assumed that energy must exist in 'packets' which he called *quanta*. Albert Einstein first applied the quantum theory in 1905 to explain the phenomenon of photo-electricity. Then in 1913 Niels Bohr used the quantum theory, with Rutherford's classically based model of the atom, to formulate the ideas on which current understanding of atomic structure now rests. The nucleus of Bohr's atom is surrounded by electrons moving in orbits; when these electrons change orbits, energy is emitted or absorbed in fixed quanta. His work led to an understanding of the spectrum of each atom and through it, detailed knowledge of atomic structure.

The quantum theory dates the beginnings of modern physics. Marie Curie's education, technique and style had been acquired during the classical age, and her great work had derived from its traditions. Her discovery of radioactive elements, the purification of polonium and radium, her atomic weight determinations and her preparation of metallic radium were all carried out in the classic mode of nineteenth-century chemistry and physics.

She had always been intellectually at her happiest when she was with those whose methods and manner of thinking were rooted in this tradition. Always her deepest and most satisfying relationships, until recently, had been with men considerably older than herself. With her father and grandfather, teachers by both instinct and profession, she had enjoyed the intellectual companionship. Pierre Curie had been eight years older than she. The international scientists with whom she began to mix when she herself was less than 40, were in the main mature men; many were distinguished old men and they had reached that distinction only after years of dedication in a classical craft. One of the most trusted and respected colleagues she had found on her European travels to scientific congresses was Kamerlingh Onnes, the Dutch physicist who had carried out brilliant work in low temperature physics. During the spring of 1911 Marie Curie was able to distract herself with plans for a series of experiments to be carried out at Leyden with the 57-year-old Onnes, investigating radiations from radium at low temperatures.

Marie Curie was no reactionary. The new concepts were attracting a fresh breed of physicists, but she had the necessary grounding in mathematics to keep pace with what was going on. She also had a strengthening link with a representative of the new generation. Her relationship with Paul Langevin was the only significant one she was to have with a man who was not many years older than herself. Langevin was five years her junior, and was one of the physicists responsible for ushering French science into the new age. Already by 1911 he had seen the important implications of the special theory of relativity, and was later to become one of Einstein's main champions when anti-German feeling in France was running at its highest.

And so, besides adding much that was enriching to Marie Curie's middle years, including a keen interest in politics, a love of literature and music, as well as (in spite of his stomach upsets) a love of good food, Langevin was able to provide an intellectual bridge to the emerging new physics. As a pair with suitable common interests to fill the gaps each had in their lives, they were an ideal mix.

Langevin's relationship with his wife had become so bad that he had now left her. Marie Curie was far from indifferent to other people's views of her. She craved privacy because she was sensitive to opinions, no matter from what source. When what she did was wrongly interpreted or incorrectly reported she would quickly jump to her own defence.

Marie Curie often naïvely misinterpreted what she believed to be other people's reactions to her. Her judgement of her chances of election to the Academy is an example. That she believed that she could have a private relationship with Langevin in which only a few colleagues would show interest, was perhaps her most disastrous miscalculation of all.

Marguerite Borel recalls a date in spring, 1911,[3] when she was woken by her maid. Jean Perrin and André Debierne were at her door wanting to see her on an urgent matter. It is possible that her memory is at fault and that the visit was later in the year. Whenever it happened, it was one of several visits which Marie Curie's close friends were paying on one another in a sudden flurry of activity. Marguerite, propped decorously on the pillows of her bed, immediately realised that both Perrin and Debierne were most agitated, and no doubt each showed his agitation in his own style: Perrin voluble and active, his arms and his papers swept into a windmill of confused motion: Debierne lip-biting and tongue-tied and avoiding the eye.

The substance of what they had to say was that some letters sent by Marie Curie to Paul Langevin had been stolen, were incriminating, and that there was a possibility that they would be published by a newspaper. There was no question that, if the news was true and the letters were published, a press sensation of unimaginable proportions would be stirred up.

Whether or not the letters had been stolen was a matter of semantics. The lock to Paul Langevin's study had been broken and a drawer forced, and Madame Langevin and her brother-in-law, Henri Bourgeois, had got possession of the letters. The letters stayed in Madame Langevin's possession for several months and she used them in an attempt to get a separation order from her husband.

For Marie Curie it was intensely worrying. Letters, signed and anonymous, genuine and faked, had been at the root of many of the most recent of sensational French scandals. The possibility that she, Marie Curie, could be involved in publicity of this kind, which dragged both innocent and guilty under the most intimate public scrutiny, was now real. The prospect was frightening.

It seems likely that during the autumn months she believed the dangers in the situation were easing. She had spent much of the summer outside France at Zakopane where sister Bronia now ran a sanatorium. In late October she set off for Brussels to attend a Radiation Congress financed by the Belgian industrial chemist Ernest Solvay. It was to be the first of the celebrated Solvay Congresses. Rutherford came across her there. He thought she was looking well: much better than she had at the conference of a year ago[4] and he took particular trouble to be thoughtful to her needs during the meetings. Marie was touched. He had heard, along with other delegates to the conference, of the rumours spreading in Paris about some business between her and Langevin, and breezily dismissed them as 'moonshine'. But Marie was a troubled woman before that conference ended. She did not attend the final day's sessions. She let it be known she was ill again. Nevertheless before she left Brussels she found time to write a note to Rutherford thanking him for all his little kindnesses.[5]

Rutherford's tenderness, however, besides having a genuine humanitarian motive, had a sharp practical reason. He was concerned about the International Radium Standard which Marie Curie was preparing, and one evening that week spent until midnight with her, gently moving her from the stubborn position she was adopting. She had prepared the original Radium Standard but, 'for sentimental reasons which I quite understand,' said Rutherford[6] wanted to keep this Standard in her own laboratory. With tact and patience Rutherford tried to persuade her that a truly international Standard could not properly be held in the possession of one individual. He recognised that the fee of 1,000 francs which she was proposing to charge individuals who wanted duplicates of the Standard was high, but he felt this was fair reward for good work done. He never under-estimated the monetary worth of applied physics.

Even so Rutherford had still not achieved his main aim with regard to the location of the International Standard and he explained his worries about the Madame's position in a confidential letter to Bertram Boltwood. 'I am sure it is going to be a ticklish business to get the matter arranged satisfactorily, as Mme Curie is rather a difficult person to deal with. She has the advantages and at the same time the disadvantages of being a woman.'[7]

The news which pushed all scientific problems out of the woman's mind broke on November 4th, while she was at the Congress. It was Fernand Xau's *Le Journal* which prepared Paris for the scandal to come.

Chapter 17

The Terrible Year

The headline, 'A Story of Love. Mme Curie and Professor Langevin' appeared in *Le Journal* on November 4th, 1911. For all its inaccuracies the story had the essentials of the relationships between the two families. The article was accompanied by a fetching photograph of Marie. 'The fire of radium,' the story went, 'had lit a flame in the heart of a scientist, and the scientist's wife and children were now in tears.' The reporter, Fernand Hauser, claimed to have visited Fontenay-aux-Roses to interview Langevin's elderly mother-in-law, Madame Desfosses, and he had asked whether Madame Langevin was contemplating divorce. 'You know,' was the reply, 'when you have several children – six children' (Hauser had invented a couple) – 'you hesitate before doing something irreparable.' Hauser also claimed to have asked Madame Desfosses whether she had in her possession letters which had passed between Marie Curie and Langevin. Madame Desfosses confirmed that this was the case.

By the next day every Parisian paper had the story and the news of the elopement of Madame Curie and a physicist father of four was winging its way by wireless telegraphy to the tabloids of London, Berlin, New York and San Francisco. *Le Temps*, with its customary discretion, hid away the scandal on an inside page, but once again allowed itself to be used as the Curie mouthpiece. At the Solvay conference she had given one of *Le Temps*' reporters a statement which she had composed referring to her supposed disappearance with Langevin. It read, 'In the rumours spread by a Paris newspaper it was said that my address was not known. Since I had sent from my laboratory in Paris for some graphs and photographs which I needed, it was well known in Paris where I could be found.'[1] She added that she attached no importance to the reports and that they were 'pure folly'. *Le Temps*' reporters confirmed from the worried Debierne at the Rue Cuvier laboratory that she was in Brussels. Langevin, it was discovered had spent August in England with his two sons, had stayed most of September with Émile and Marguerite Borel and, according to Émile, Madame Langevin was well aware of her husband's whereabouts. Langevin was now also in Brussels.

So the elopement was, as *Le Temps* put it on behalf of Marie Curie, a 'pure invention', and left it at that. But other papers were not willing to do so. They had had too strong a scent of blood. *L'Intransigeant* reported on the well-known quarrels within the Langevin family[2] and said that both Marie Curie and Paul Langevin were preparing to take legal action against the rumour mongers. But this was not the only relevant article which this Janus-faced journal placed on its front page. The column immediately adjacent was headed 'For Monsieur X' and was composed by the sharp pen of Léon Bailby, the editor. It addressed an unnamed physicist, telling him that the publicity he was now getting was his just deserts; it assured him that the press could only conclude that 'the friend who was your confidante, is quite simply your mistress'.

Marie Curie had already seen enough. Again *Le Temps* accommodated her and printed her unambiguously phrased warning. 'I consider all intrusions of the press and of the public into my private life as abominable. . . . Henceforward I shall rigorously take action against all publication of writings attributed to me. At the same time I have the right to demand as damages considerable sums which will be used in the interests of science.'

She also gave to *Le Temps* Fernand Hauser's letter of apology which her threat of legal action had rapidly extracted. 'Madame,' it said, 'I am most distressed and want to present my most humble apologies to you. Trusting in certain information, I wrote the article as you know; I was in error. In any case I should not have written this article, and I cannot understand at this moment, how the fever of my profession was able to lead me to such a detestable act . . . There remains a sole consolation for me; it is that, humble journalist that I am, I do not know how, by any of my writings, to tarnish the glory that crowns you, nor the esteem that surrounds you . . . Your very chastened, Fernand Hauser.'[3]

She had made him grovel. But that was all she could salvage from the situation. The popular press sensed it was standing on too secure ground to need to flinch. *Le Journal*[4] now published an unsigned interview with Langevin's wife who said that for a year and a half she had had material proof of her husband's infidelity. *L'Intransigeant* weighed in with a critical attack on Marie Curie's threat of a claim for damages; the damaged party, it was soon hinting, was another woman: the suffering wife of Langevin, mother of his four children.

Marie Curie had slipped back to Paris unnoticed by the press. On November 8th she was handed a telegram. She must have thought it was yet another demand for an interview or a statement. It was datemarked Stockholm, however, and its simple message also was almost identical to one she had received eight years earlier:

'Nobel Prize for chemistry awarded to you. Letter follows. Aurivillius.'

It was the announcement of the most important recognition given any scientist so far during the twentieth century. She was the first person – not merely the first woman – to be awarded two Nobel Prizes in science. It was a marvel of success against all odds. The news ought to have reassured her that her abilities were now acknowledged internationally. It ought to have been uplifting to her spirit just as it should have been an immediate source of pride for her fellow-countrymen. Instead any warming pride was lost in the worry over what next day's papers would produce and where the thing would all end.

The press had reason to neglect the Nobel Prize announcement. Several newspaper editors now had a source of much more exciting copy. Moreover, it was sufficiently circumstantial to make them entirely confident of their ground. They had succeeded in laying their hands on the Curie-Langevin letters. Léon Daudet's *L'Action Française* led the attack, intent on turning the scandal into a new Dreyfus affair. Daudet's 'organ of integral nationalism' displaced from pride of place its stories of German Jewish espionage against France, and the sexual peccadillos of the liberal intelligentsia. It substituted long articles pleading the case of an honest

Frenchwoman whose home had been systematically destroyed by a foreigner: a Polish woman. Fouquier-Tinville's famous words which had sent Lavoisier to the guillotine, 'The Republic has no need of scientists', were regurgitated by Daudet who protested 'Today, republican dreyfusism has need of a dogma of virtue from scientists.'[5] Dreyfus, science and immorality were now one.

Marie Curie had influential friends and they were willing to use their influence on her behalf. On November 16th Jean Dupuy, President of the Paris Press Syndicate, telephoned the leading newspapers asking them to impose a voluntary censorship on any comment concerning the Curie-Langevin affair. *L'Action Française* relished the fact that it had been omitted from this appeal to responsibility and took enormous pleasure in pointing out to its readers that the distinguished lawyer and ex-Minister Raymond Poincaré (within a year to become Prime Minister), who was Marie Curie's and Paul Langevin's legal adviser, was also employed by the Press Syndicate.

There was no doubt that in addition to having copies of the letters *L'Action Française* had also a ready source of ammunition from Poincaré's opponent, Madame Langevin's legal adviser. The paper pointed out that Madame Langevin, on October 26th, had instigated proceedings against her husband and 'another woman' and that a Sûreté enquiry was under way. It revealed also that Émile Borel had called a meeting, in front of the prefect of police, with Madame Langevin's legal representatives; that Borel claimed to have a mandate from both Paul Langevin and from the Sorbonne; and that he had demanded the sequestration of all the incriminating documents which Madame Langevin had in her possession. Needless to say, Madame Langevin had been advised not to relinquish her main armament.

So the affair rolled on day after day throughout November. At the centre of it all, visibly blenching under each day's revelation, was Marie Curie. The strain was mounting. This uproar had followed with scarcely a break on the fracas of the Academy election. She stayed at home at Sceaux watching anxiously over the effects on her children as she shepherded them to their classes past the eyes of curious sight-seers. There were now too many inquisitive spectators round the laboratory for her to venture into Paris. Her friends and advisers were rallying round – the Perrins, the Borels, the Chavannes, Debierne, and others – but there was little any of them could do for her state of mind.

Everybody was in suspense to see what would be done with the letters. So were the papers, most of whose editors now had full knowledge of the letters' contents. But were these genuine? Would Marie Curie's bluff of legal action be called? And if so, by whom?

The suspense was broken for Marie Curie on November 23rd, when a little red-backed magazine, *L'Oeuvre*, under the title of 'The Sorbonne Scandals', published long extracts from the letters. For Marie Curie the revelations were calamitous. The journalist who had decided to push in the knife as far as it could go was Gustave Téry. He was an unpredictable, aggressive little man: wire-rimmed spectacles, goatee beard, roll-pointed moustaches over thick lips. It was said that his doctor had prescribed green beans for his digestion, and that he so hated the things that there was a mark on his office door where he had thrown a plateful at his servant.

He had more than digestive problems in common with Paul Langevin. They had been students at the École Normale, knew each other well and, according to Téry himself, had been comrades. Téry's academic career at various institutions had been less distinguished than Langevin's and his political activities had led to his dismissal early in 1910 as a teacher of philosophy at Laon. His weekly magazine *L'Oeuvre* and its distinctive red binding had quickly become well-known. It was a salacious, quasi-intellectual scandal sheet, virulently anti-Jewish, xenophobic and seeing traitors to France in every foreign or Jewish bed.

In this case Téry was entirely sure of his information; sufficiently so to give up almost the whole of one issue of *L'Oeuvre*[6] to the Sorbonne scandal, to the letters and to his outraged views of the behaviour of Marie Curie and Paul Langevin. If camaraderie had ever existed between the two men, then from its first line this publication was calculated to end it, and much more besides. Téry took up the theme of the new Dreyfus affair, with Science the modern idol and with its grand priest practitioners adopting attitudes of infallibility and creating their own taboos. *His* pen, he let it be known, was 'in a hand which does not tremble' in the face of these scientific gods. The truth, as he told it, was that Madame Curie, 'the vestal virgin of radium', using perfidious and vile suggestions, had detached Paul Langevin from his wife and had separated this lady from her children. For Langevin, '*le chopin** de la Polonaise*', his pen showed little compassion. Addressing Marie Curie Téry wrote; 'Having received your letters and followed your advice, today he drags, or allows all his friends to drag in the mud, the woman who carries his name: the woman who is still the mother of his four children; this man, even though he is a Professor of the Collège de France is no more than a cad and a scoundrel.'

Téry followed his accusations with what he claimed was the text of the writ of separation to be read in court on December 8th. It baldly stated that Monsieur Langevin had had adulterous relations with Madame Curie 'in conditions which constituted the maintenance of a concubine in conjugal domicile'. The dates of Langevin's tenancy of the Rue du Banquier apartment were given and it was stated that the adulterous pair had met there daily, having their meals together. Information as to Marie and Langevin's movements in and out of the flat had been given by neighbours who had observed that they 'behaved like lovers'.

The letters themselves, a dozen pages, were clearly those between two people on intimate terms, used the familiar 'tu', and were mainly concerned with Langevin's domestic problems. He described how,

Yesterday in my room I had yet again explanations from eleven until four in the morning. Still without any result, I was able to make some progress, since my wife confirmed that she would withdraw her threats and leave me free to choose between you and her. Without agreeing to give back the stolen letter, she said she was ready to swear in front of witnesses that she would not use it publicly and that she would stop threaten-

---

*The argot meaning a piece of good fortune, particularly an opportune conquest by a woman.

ing you. So there's some progress. . . . I am trembling with impatience at the thought of seeing you again at last and of your saying how much you have missed me. Tenderly I embrace you and wait for tomorrow.

And from Marie,

Goodbye dear Paul. I take your dear head in my hands to caress it gently with tender and maternal affection.

For the most part the long letter dated 'Sunday' from Marie to 'My dear Paul' is advice on how he ought to handle his wife under the extreme difficulties of their family life together, what in the end would be best for the children, and insisting that for the peace of his mind and for his scientific future, he should demand his liberty. The rest of the text is fond, but apart from the tough advice concerning the firm line he should take with his wife (with a particularly strong warning about the dangers of getting her pregnant in moments of reconciliation), scarcely unambiguously incriminating.

We are joined by a deep affection which we ought not allow to be destroyed. Isn't the destruction of a sincere and deep sentiment comparable to the death of a child which one has cherished and seen grow, and couldn't its destruction in certain cases be a greater misfortune than such a death?

What couldn't we extract from this instinctive and so spontaneous sentiment, which is so consistent with our rights and compatible with our intellectual needs, to which it's so beautifully adapted? I believe we've extracted a great deal: some good shared work, a good solid friendship, courage in our life, and even more beautiful children of our love, in the best accepted sense of that word.

Téry arranged his material in such a way as to leave no doubt in his readers' minds that Madame Curie and Langevin had frequently shared a bed, and that only Madame Langevin's sense of propriety had prevented the lovers being caught *in flagrante delicto*.

The letters have an unreal air about them and several points about them are questionable. The source of letters from Marie Curie to Langevin is known, but what was the source of the letters of Langevin to Marie? If Madame Langevin and her brother-in-law removed documents from Langevin's drawer was it possible that these would include either copies of letters he had written, or even the letters themselves? And why is not one of them fully dated?

Téry would have had no scruples about altering the stolen letters if it suited his purposes to do so, and if he could have got away with it. But in this case he was by no means the only editor to have seen the documents. By this stage it seems that they had been made available to half Paris. However, the fact that none of the letters are wholly incriminating, that the contents more or less corroborate undisputed evidence, and that sentences in them show that whoever composed them was initially familiar with the Faculty of Science as well as with the Perrins, the Chavannes, and the Borel families, suggests that the published paragraphs, if not true quotations, were at least based on original letters. Marguerite Borel, who was to be deeply involved with Marie Curie within a few hours of *L'Oeuvre*'s appearance on the bookstalls, later wrote that the letters 'had been truncated, cleverly separated by ellipsis in a way which perverted their sense',[7] and interpreted the malevolent interpretations of their contents as being due to Marie Curie's frank Polish use of written French. But the existence of the letters was never denied.

By the standards of half a century later Marie Curie has not a great deal to answer for. Langevin's marriage had been a running fight for several years. Her greatest mistake was to give somebody else advice about their failing marriage. Paul Langevin was a brilliant and emotional man, of whom she was, of her own admission, admiring, and with whom she had developed a tender relationship. That there was a sexual attraction is certain, but it also seems equally certain that, in Marie Curie's state of health, companionship and not sex was the dominant reason for the relationship. She had been a widow for five years and his marriage had been breaking up for a good portion of this period. Coquetry was no part of her make-up; she detested the quality in others. There is no worthwhile evidence that she set about enticing Langevin from an otherwise happy household.

Only they know whether they were lovers, though under the circumstances in which they regularly met it would seem extraordinary if they were not. Today's moral code might just find the affair worthy of a few private tut-tuttings, but scarcely fit for public scandal.

But the standards by which they were judged, and by which Marie Curie judged herself, were not today's. Repressive attitudes towards sexual behaviour persisted as strongly as ever. Marie Curie had been revealed as having a clandestine relationship with the husband of a woman with four children, one of them a babe-in-arms. Langevin was displayed as the owner of a 'bachelor apartment'. For him it meant he was the butt of some ridicule. But for her, the exposure of her guilt as a *woman*, meant that she had to face the vicious contemporary judgement of society on the erring female.

The effect on Marie Curie of *L'Oeuvre*'s decision to publish was shattering. The results in the end were to be more traumatic than the sight of her dead husband's mutilated body. She felt, and several newspapers had not shrunk from suggesting it to her, that she had besmirched the name of Curie. Even if she were guiltless of everything else of which she was accused, she could not answer the accusation that she had not prevented that good name from being dragged in the gutter of penny journalism.

The scandal had still a long course to run. Rumours of all kinds began to spread. The history of the Marie Curie–Paul Langevin relationship was examined in more detail. It was noted that they had taught together at Sèvres in the year preceding Pierre Curie's death: a death which had occurred under peculiar circumstances. Had the clandestine affair been going on for some years? If so, the widely published words of the frightened carter, Louis Manin, that Curie 'literally threw himself on my left-side horse', could now be seen in a new light. Had the great physicist been driven to suicide by the carryings-on of his wife with his former pupil? There is no documentary evidence whatever to support this rumour, but it was strong enough for its ripples to persist to this day. Whether it had any foundation in truth, or had a simply malicious origin, it was only one of many surrounding the activities of the pair of now worried and confused scientists.

The immediate results of Gustave Téry's work were physically rather than psychologically frightening. The gathering of sightseers which in the past few days had occasionally collected near the gates of her Sceaux home suddenly thickened and the stares of the curious now became more openly hostile. From inside the house she could hear cat-calls and shouting. Some of the sentences were distinguishable: 'Get the foreign woman out. Husband stealer.' Somebody threw a stone at the wall.

Before the situation could get too far out of hand Marguerite Borel, in her most favoured role of ministering angel, arrived in a taxi with the staunch André Debierne. Émile Borel, on reading *L'Oeuvre*, had immediately packed off his wife and André to bring Marie back to the safety of his apartment, where there were two rooms she could occupy with her family.

Marguerite and Debierne, when they arrived at the house, pushed their way past the crowd at the gates. Once inside they found Marie, frightened but as usual outwardly controlled. She was worried about Irène, who had set off for a gymnastics class with the young Chavannes children. After some time she allowed herself to be persuaded to move outside holding the hand of the uncomprehending little Eve. Debierne quickly ushered them both, with Marguerite and a suitcase of clothes, into the taxi saying he would collect the older child. As the cab moved off past the crowd Marie's face was petrified: 'white, as if it were a statue', according to Marguerite, who wanted to take the distraught woman's hand, but dared not.

During the journey Marie said nothing and, when the cab arrived at the École Normale, she slipped across the college courtyard to the Borel apartment.

Her children were her immediate cause for concern. Eve was too young to begin to understand. Irène at fourteen was more vulnerable. Debierne had found her in the gymnasium. But a copy of *L'Oeuvre* had arrived before him and was already in Irène's hands. The child was numbed. When she reached the Borel's flat she clung to the neck of her mother. Both were dry-eyed; both were prostrate. Eventually Irène was detached and taken off to

Boulevard Kellermann by Henriette Perrin. Marie was persuaded by Marguerite to lie down quietly with her younger child, now being looked after by a maid.

If all inside the safety of the École Normale's walls was muted, then outside interest in the Curie–Langevin affair had by no means died its death and the atmosphere was noisy with symbolic male trumpetings. Several parties felt that their honour had been impugned and, irrespective of the sufferings of Madame Curie, Madame Langevin or any of their children, were determined to have retribution for themselves. Retribution, however, in this male dominated scene of the popular Parisian press, was normally won by animal posturing followed by a situation from which one male could emerge as dominant. Libel actions were not in favour; they were too expensive. The popular alternative, duelling, was not only much cheaper, it was considerably quicker: and usually far less dangerous.

A duel in this, the most inglorious period in the history of the art, usually meant the ritual appearance of contestants and seconds, all suitably dressed and prepared with épées or pistols. Only in the most extraordinary circumstances were either of the participants seriously hurt; the slightest drop of blood drawn from the least painful part of the anatomy was enough to settle the most bitter of quarrels.

Unknown to Marie Curie a duel was being fought, ostensibly on her behalf, on the very day of publication of the letters. Henri Chervet of *Gil Blas* and Léon Daudet of *L'Action Française*, like so many polemicists of their day, when news in the cause they were championing ran thin, had taken to demolishing one another in print. Chervet had taken exception to Daudet's bitter attacks on the two scientists, and the journalists, now tired of crossing pens, were crossing swords.

Le Temps reported the duel, as it did so many others, in the tolerant, if somewhat impatient style of *The Times* reporting a qualifying round at Wimbledon. The Chervet–Daudet duel, however, was uncommonly vicious. Daudet, though much experienced at this sort of encounter, suffered a 'six-centimetre deep' wound at his elbow. It affected a reconciliation between him and Chervet, but it also delayed his taking up another 'affair of honour' with a second member of *Gil Blas'* staff, Saul Merzbach, who had demanded satisfaction.

Gil Blas was staffed by a fractious group of writers responsible for its satirical columns. On the following day its editor, Pierre Mortier was challenged to a duel by none other than Gustave Téry, offended by Mortier's criticisms of his part in publishing the Curie–Langevin letters. The duel, again with épées, took place at the Parc-des-Princes bicycle stadium, with Madame Langevin's brother-in-law as one of Téry's seconds. The ritual ended in a well-controlled fashion when Mortier was slightly wounded in the forearm. Several other duels were also now being mooted.

The whole situation had an abandoned air of farcical Grand Guignol about it. The play-acting richly deserved the superior stifled yawn of 'yet another duel' from *Le Figaro* (whose journalistic standards were infinitely superior to any of its competitors). But behind the posturing of a few second-rate journalists with time on their hands, was a great deal of mental anguish for the parties at the real centre of the affair. The sight of true catastrophe suddenly loomed on the horizon when Langevin, seeing the struttings of the fighting cocks, felt the urge to conform to this behaviour. He had had the whole of his private life turned inside out for the benefit of the Parisian newspaper readership, and he had watched another man challenge Gustave Téry, the journalist who that day had publicly described him, Langevin, as 'a cad and a scoundrel'. The pressures were too great. He decided to take action *à la mode*.

On the morning of November 24th Langevin appeared on the Borel's door-step wearing his morning coat and saying, 'I've decided to challenge Téry to a duel. I know it's idiotic, but I've got to do it.'[8]

It was idiotic. Langevin only realised the true idiocy of his decision when he spent the morning touring Paris in a horse-drawn cab trying to find himself a pair of seconds to deliver his challenge. His academic friends were polite and understanding, but not at all inclined to be involved in the silly extremes to which the affair seemed to be dragging. Langevin's first approach to

Haller, the Director of the School of Physics and Chemistry, was unsuccessful. Haller was sympathetic, but had no wish to be hauled into the mêlée. It was only when the suave Paul Painlevé, mathematician and shortly to be Socialist deputy for Paris (and the second future Prime Minister to be involved in the affair), agreed to act for Langevin that Haller was drawn in, against his better judgement.

The morning of November 25th dawned with Langevin and Téry's seconds having fixed the terms of the encounter: pistols—one round at twenty-five metres. The Parisian duel has probably provided as many occasions for wit as it has caused injuries. George Moore, the novelist, used to tell his friends that he had once fought a duel in Paris with pistols. When Sir William Geary asked him whether it had been at ten or fifteen paces Geary replied, 'That would have been dangerous. We were at thirty-five paces; each of us went unscathed.'9 Nevertheless, pistols had the reputation of occasionally causing much more than slight injury. Accidents were not unknown; lives had been lost.

At ten to eleven on that cold morning Langevin stood on the open track of the Parc-des-Princes bicycle stadium with an unfamiliar weapon in his hand. He would have been an insensitive man had not some sense of foreboding caused his crew-cut scalp to tingle in uncertain anticipation. It was covered, as it happened, with a bowler hat. His waxed moustaches were at 25 paces from the waxed moustaches of his old school-friend, Téry, also bowler hatted. The figures nearby, like himself, were all uniformly in black, though sartorially contrasting: Haller and Painlevé in morning coats and top-hats, the opposing seconds in jackets and felt trilbys. Less conspicuous and at a safer distance though nevertheless somewhat menacing, were the black figures of a pair of doctors. Further distant still on top of the cyclists' changing rooms sat a line of newspaper reporters. They had reached their perch from outside the locked stadium by means of a ladder specially brought along on occasions such as this.

At eleven o'clock precisely Painlevé called the bowler-hatted pair to attention. He then began to count the order to fire. But he was unfamiliar with the routine of the ritual. He took all present, seconds, doctors, journalists and, more important, contestants by complete surprise when he suddenly began to count in unusually quick time.

'*Un ... deux ... trois*'

The spectators waited for the crack of the guns. But not the slightest noise disturbed the cycle track's tranquility. The pigeons which the journalists observed pecking peacefully at the grass in the middle of the stadium went about their business with their concentration unbroken. Langevin was pointing his weapon at – and staring at – Téry, who still held his pistol pointing to the ground. Langevin lowered his gun, half lifted it again, then lowered it.

Nobody was sure of protocol. The seconds conferred with one another, then with their men, then with one another again, and then with their opposing seconds. *Brouhaha* reigned as black-coated figures pirouetted back and forth across the cycle-track. What had transpired, as Téry later revealed to his readers, was that he had felt that he could least serve the cause of Madame Langevin by killing her husband, and his scruples prevented him from 'depriving French science of a precious mind, no matter whether the owner preferred to use it on his own behalf, or whether he preferred to run back to the gracious go-between, Madame Curie'.[10] He refused to fire.

The seconds took off their hats and wiped their brows, one of them cautiously took the pistols from the unfulfilled contestants and fired them into the air to make sure they did no harm; the pigeons rose, the doctors closed their bags and the reporters put away their notebooks. The farce for that day was at an end.

In the Borel apartment there was no hint of farce. Marie Curie was taking the news of the succession of events badly. Henriette Perrin now stayed permanently alongside her. Marie Curie later told her daughter that it was during this period that she began to think of suicide.[11]

Friends were gathering in the hour of need. Already the message had gone out to Poland. Bronia was by now travelling across Europe, but on this occasion, so obviously desperate was the situation, she was accompanied by brother Jozef and sister Hela.

The pressures on Marie Curie to take some definite action were at this point enormous. Within the Sorbonne itself there was a faction which had decided views on where the guilt lay and how it should be expiated. Émile Borel was at once under fire from the Minister of Public Instruction who told him that his post of scientific director of the École Normale did not give him the right to use it as a haven for Madame Curie.[12] Even Borel's father-in-law, Paul Appel, the Dean of the Faculty of Science, the man who had broken the news of Pierre Curie's death to Marie, and who had sponsored her Academy candidature, was furious that his daughter and her husband should have involved themselves in a scandal as sordid as this had been made to seem. Appel was of the view that it would be better if Madame Curie took herself off to Poland where she would have no difficulty in getting both a professorship and a laboratory. Several others in responsible university positions shared his opinion.

There was now brought to bear on her the influence of her two sisters and her brother: all that was left of her close family. They too wanted her to go away with them. The emotional magnet drawing her to Poland – to home – was strong, quite apart from the pressures pushing her out of France. But something made her cling on. Her children were French, her husband had been French, and all that she had achieved that had been worthwhile had been in France. Moreover, to take to her heels now would have been tantamount to a confession of guilt. The others around her, the Perrins, the Chavannes and the Borels, were in favour of sitting things out. But there was a serious question at issue if this course was taken; would Marie Curie's condition let her ride the storm? Not only was she mentally broken, she was physically in very poor shape and began to lose weight.

In the end, however, in spite of her condition, she braved it out. Not only that, she decided that in two weeks' time she would go to Stockholm and take the Nobel medal in her own hands. Mentally and physically the effort involved would be enormous. It was another example of the amazingly substantial bodily resources she was able to call on in times of need.

In the meantime Téry continued his campaign for three successive weeks, though he was now having to spread his fire by attacking the moral degeneracy of the whole of the Sorbonne Faculty of Science. Then too there were the music-hall song composers and the satirists who were making hay with 'le chopin de la Polonaise'. But the worst of this, like the worst of morning and evening newspapers, could be hidden from Marie Curie. As the days passed and as public interest waned, a more hopeful light began to shine through, and the results of sitting things out quietly, began to show. Early in December it became clear that an amicable settlement in Madame Langevin's proceedings against her husband was likely. On December 9th came the news, not only that an out-of-court settlement was likely, but that if the affair came before the courts, then Marie Curie's name might not even be mentioned in the legal proceedings. The storm was blowing over.

On December 11th Marie Curie was in Stockholm to receive her Nobel Prize. She had taken with her sister Bronia, the unfailing prop; but also she had taken the young Irène. The fourteen-year-old had responded to the events of the past few weeks with sudden maturity and understanding. She was a link with stability and with the happy past. Irène only partly understood the nature of the uproar that surrounded the family during this period, but she was sufficiently aware to know that the crisis through which her mother was passing was the most awful of her life.

The public acclaim of the Nobel Prize too was a rock for Marie Curie to grasp at in the whirl of ocean which had swept round her in a fashion which even she did not fully understand. However, that rock was placed there by scientific well-wishers. It would not have appeared had not Marie Curie been involved in such personal and political stress during these months of 1911. The science she had carried out since 1903 and her first award of this great prize, cannot rationally justify its being handed out on this second occasion.

The system of award of the Nobel Prizes is one which is usually cloaked in secrecy. Nominations for the awards are solicited from leading scientists throughout the world (Marie

Curie had in the past been asked to make nominations) and the awards are recommended to the Swedish Royal Academy of Sciences by an Awards Committee. The deliberation of the committee and the qualities on which they judge a candidate are not published. Through the years many distinguished scientists have been honoured, but several awards cannot escape the accusation of being a scientific-political compromise. Pavlov was awarded the prize in physiology and medicine in 1904, not for the controversial but brilliant work on conditioned reflexes he had begun, but for his work on the physiology of digestion. Rutherford, to his enormous amusement, had in 1908 been given not the prize in physics, but in chemistry. And in 1921, 16 years after publishing his first paper on special relativity theory, Einstein was given the physics award, not for that momentous work, but for his studies on the photo-electric effect.

The sympathy for Marie Curie among many foreign scientists during 1911 was very great when the humiliation of her rejection by the Academy became known and when, following so quickly on this, some sordid rumours of an imminent newspaper scandal had begun to circulate. The Swedish chemist, Arrhenius suggested to the Nobel Committee that the discovery of radium had been 'the most important during the last century of chemical research'. The Nobel Committee justified its decision to give the prize because, it said, 'the discovery of radium had not yet been made the subject of an award'[13] and that the previous prize in which Marie Curie had shared had been for 'the discovery of radioactivity for which the prize was given; no mention was made of the new elements discovered in pitchblende'.

It was a hair-splitting argument, even if it was popular and concocted for the best of sympathetic and humanitarian motives. The discovery of radium cannot be underrated. Just as the discovery of X-rays heralded the atomic age, that of radium heralded the nuclear age. Nevertheless, the 1903 Nobel Prize citation, without actually daring to mention the element by name, had already acknowledged the value of the discovery. It is difficult to avoid the embarrassing reality that Marie Curie was awarded the Nobel Prize twice for the same work, once for physics and once for chemistry. The work she had done since 1902 had been first class chemistry which had established radium and polonium in the periodic table of elements: but it had not broken new scientific ground.

The gesture by the Nobel Awards Committee was generally approved of in international scientific circles. Planck, Rutherford and most of Marie Curie's distinguished colleagues immediately wrote off their congratulations on hearing the news. Rutherford also had a friendly word of comfort to add: 'My heartiest congratulations on this recognition of your scientific work. Only a few days ago, I mentioned to Langevin that I thought you should be awarded the prize.'[14] But again what he had to say to Boltwood had a slightly different emphasis: 'I was very glad to see that she got a Nobel Prize, but I had thought Richards would be the nominee. He certainly deserves it.'

Theodore Richards's unsurpassed work on atomic weight determinations at Harvard had to wait until 1914 for Nobel recognition. There were others too who might have expected an earlier place in the queue. Some, such as the Frenchmen Grignard and Sabatier, eventually reached the queue's head and collected their medals; others, the American Robert Wood and the Englishman Sir James Dewar, waited in vain and in disappointment.

There were many other potential candidates for the prize, and there were some who had no sympathy whatever with the 1911 business. 'Mme Curie is just what I have always thought she was, a plain darn fool, and you will find it out for certain before long,' Boltwood told Rutherford.[15]

Marie Curie bore the Nobel ceremony with dignity in spite of her weakened state. Six years earlier she had sat in the same hall, with Royalty, with ambassadors and with the world's leading scientific figures to listen to her husband give the speech of acceptance for the award in which she had had a full share. Now she gave her own speech. It was carefully worded and strongly influenced by her experiences of 1911. She left no doubts in the mind of those who listened to this speech as to what work she could lay claims for herself, and for herself alone. Because of the frequent accusations of having ridden to glory on Pierre Curie's brilliance, she introduced the subjective and possessive pronouns on every occasion where she wanted to make clear to both her audience and to the world at large, what it was that belonged to her. She named the subject as being the one which '*I* have termed' radioactivity[18] and she talked of '*my* hypothesis that radioactivity is an atomic property of matter'. She did this without the intention or result of diminishing Pierre Curie's work and recalled for her audience that 'the discoveries of radium and of polonium were made by Pierre Curie in collaboration with me'. She also added, 'The chemical work aimed at isolating radium in the state of the pure salt, and of characterising it as a new element, was carried out specially by me, but it is intimately connected with our common work. I thus feel that I interpret correctly the intention of the Academy of Sciences in assuming that the award of this high distinction to me is motivated by this common work and thus pays homage to the memory of Pierre Curie.' But it was her own interpretation and nobody else's. It was an emotional public display of the strong union between herself and the dead man at a time when her own fidelity to the memory of Pierre Curie was in question.

This effort at Stockholm, however, drained her. Once back in Paris she did not feel strong enough to return to the house at Sceaux. In spite of the diminished public interest in her affairs, her friends watched her sinking during the next two weeks into a depressive state. She had planned to take an apartment in the city before the year ended, but was now in too bad a condition to think of it. On December 29th she was carried off on a stretcher to a nursing home: a woman at her mental and physical limits.

1911 had been a terrible year.

Chapter 18

Recovery

She was gravely ill. A serious chronic infection of the ureter had been diagnosed and she was having acute attacks of fever. Whether any or all of this suffering was due to the radiation to which she had exposed herself, will never be known. A decision whether or not to operate would have to be made. She was kept undisturbed. As the fever worsened her children were not permitted to visit. Only the faithful few were allowed in to talk with her over her most pressing problems. André Debierne was frequently at the bedside or having notes of reassurance sent in addressed 'Dear Madame and friend' and signed 'your devoted, A. Debierne'. She had entrusted to him not only her laboratory affairs, but her personal affairs too. When he came she was reassured about how things were at home, particularly with the children, who adored this gauche and bashful 'uncle'.

Debierne and Jean Perrin passed round the news of her state both to her friends in Paris and to those abroad. At last, after several days of anxiety, the worst crisis was over and Perrin immediately wrote off with the good news to Rutherford. But Perrin had other things to tell:

The news is good. The fever has fallen and it isn't necessary to operate on Madame Curie immediately, which worried us a great deal in view of her weak condition.

The judgement of separation between Langevin and his wife makes *not a single mention* of Madame Curie, but the *'injuries'* are attributed to Langevin (who didn't take the precaution of getting evidence which he could have used against his wife, without involving the name of Madame Curie in the process).

The two boys have their lunch every day (between their school classes) with Langevin. The four children sleep at their mother's, except every second Thursday and every second Sunday . . .

After the age of 19 the boys can live with him. In the end he will look after 'the intellectual direction' of the four children. Such are the obligations of the judgement (plus an allowance to his wife, naturally).

And now I hope that we can all get down to some work!? . . . Jean Perrin.

(Langevin was very much aware of your friendship. Madame Curie also has been very touched by your attitude.)[1]

Thus it was that Perrin signalled the end of the affair. Any relationship between Marie Curie and Langevin had been torn up by its roots. Langevin may not have had any wish to further the liaison beyond the point it had reached. If he had, then he now had no choice other than to abandon it. The effects of the public exposure on Marie Curie were so severe that she would never again contemplate a relationship with a man other than on a scientific basis. The spectre she feared most, that of having her name dragged into some divorce action, had been laid. Langevin would have to look elsewhere for any emotional relationship.

Psychologically the relief to her tense state of mind was enormous. Initially her health improved. Still feeble, she was back in her home and reunited with her children by the end of January. The operation was to be delayed until she gained strength.

She did gain strength; but too soon, by the first week of March, she was back at her laboratory bench. The kidney operation, when it came later that month, left her again in a feeble condition and in a profoundly depressed state of mind.

She was obsessed by the deep guilt of having besmirched the name Curie. She had her sister take a house in Bronia's married name of Dluska at Brunoy, near Paris, and there she closeted herself for several weeks in the grip of melancholia. She kept her address a close secret from all except the few friends who were looking after the children and adopted the name 'Madame Sklodowska'. Debierne was sworn to secrecy and told not to disclose her whereabouts even to the members of her laboratory.

In May she allowed a Polish delegation to visit her, led by Henryk Sienkiewicz (Poland's best-known author as a result of

Quo Vadis, and a fellow Nobel Laureate) which tried to persuade her to return permanently to Poland. But on that subject she had already made her decision.

Throughout this desperate period the single-minded habit of recording the measurable events of her life never left her, even though there was no work to record. Meticulously she still wrote down every minute detail of her household accounts. The habit she could not abandon, even under these circumstances, perhaps helped her to survive. She itemised the cost of laundry, pharmacy, music and English lessons for the children, shoes for Eve, gloves for Irène. Everything that was accountable was there. She even copied into her account-book her expenses for December, 1911; and there, covering the most tumultuous event of her life, was the short sentence, 'Expenses L. affair, 378 francs'.[2] It was the only written reference to these momentous days that she was to leave behind.

Towards the end of June she had a relapse and was taken to a sanatorium at Thonon in the mountains of Savoy. On every day of the month in which she lay in this hospital, she kept an account of her illness in her immaculate hand. Morning and afternoon she recorded her intake of water, her temperature, the regularity and the degree of pain in her ureter, the amount of pus she was discharging, the state of her urine indicating the progress of her illness and the frequency of the attacks of fever.

During the worst of this crisis Irène wrote to her mother at the sanatorium, the address of which, like that at Brunoy, was being kept secret. 'My darling Mé, Yesterday I read in *Le Matin* of the death of Henri Poincaré. I believe it's correct that he died after an operation. The idea that there could possibly have been a similar article about you sent a shudder through my scalp.'[3]

It was a time of trial for Irène. As a girl on the very edge of turning into a young woman she was still only partly able to understand the true nature of the events that had enveloped her family. But she was very vulnerable to the sufferings which she now had to share with the mother she adored.

She only realised the great depth of her mother's wound when she was told by Marie Curie that in future Irène must address letters not to Madame Curie but to Madame Sklodowska. Un-wittingly the mother was passing the wound to the daughter. The girl was painfully hurt by the knowledge that the name she had been taught to adore should now be hidden away as if in shame. She had no conception of her mother's reasons for not wanting to use her father's and her own name any more, and pleaded with her to let her address her letters to Madame Curie which once she had been so proud to do. But Marie Curie refused.

Irène played little mother to Eve, watched over the seven-year-old when she had a slight fever, and reported her temperature of 37.2°C. with the accuracy with which she knew her mother would approve. She wrote frequently and in an adult fashion: she discussed mathematical problems, reported on her progress in English and assured her mother that she had remembered to pay for her German lessons. But during that summer the sense of shame implanted itself as securely as it had in her mother. The consequence was that it drew mother and daughter even closer together in spirit. 'Thank the postman who brought you my letter,' she wrote to her at Thonon, 'in spite of the way I have to address it.'[4] In her schoolgirl diary for 1911 she noted what had happened to the family by two words only: 'Langevin affair'.

By August Marie Curie felt physically improved and able to venture out of her morbid solitude. What she needed was a complete change of environment: a place free from the feeling of siege and one where she would be unrecognised and unknown.

Earlier that year when she was at the depths of her most depressed period, Marie Curie had agreed to a request, which, had it come from some other source, she would have refused without a second thought. Hertha Ayrton, the Englishwoman she had met during her visit to the Royal Institution in 1903, had written asking Marie Curie to put her name to an international petition asking the British Government for the release of three women suffrage leaders, then on hunger strike during a nine-months' gaol sentence. 'They are,' Mrs Ayrton said, 'persons of the utmost nobility of mind and greatness of purpose.'[5]

It was the period when in Britain women's suffrage activities were at their most militant and violent. Hertha herself had become a vigorous champion of Mrs Pankhurst, had taken part in the first suffrage procession through London and, in a march on 10 Downing Street, had only been prevented from reaching the door by a policeman who held her unceremoniously by the neck, which she described as 'an attempt at strangulation'.[6]

In the first place Marie Curie doubted the value of militancy in suffragist affairs, and in the second she never let her name be used to further 'causes'. Yet there was something about Mrs Ayrton, whom she had met on several occasions during the past few years, which made Marie Curie reply that she had enough confidence in everything she had seen Hertha do, inside and outside of science, to let her name be used as Hertha thought fit. Beside that, it was a consolation to know that the currency of her name abroad had not dropped in value.

Hertha was an extraordinarily talented, if eccentric, woman. As a slim girl with bright green eyes and a thick frizzy brush of raven hair she had deeply impressed George Eliot, who based the character of the young Jewess, Mirah, on her in *Daniel Deronda*. The fact that Hertha was a physicist and the recent widow of a physicist had given her a natural bond with Marie Curie. Whenever she was in Paris, a slight but distinctive figure in a flowing pre-Raphaelite robe, she would visit Marie and discuss her work with a self-assurance unusual in women scientists.

Hertha too had faced accusations that her own work in physics was the collection of crumbs from her husband's laboratory bench. Sir William Ramsay had even used the Curies and the Ayrtons as good examples of his point when he told a *Daily Mail* reporter that, 'all the eminent women scientists have achieved their best work when collaborating with a male colleague'.[7] Whenever she had been able, Hertha had taken every opportunity to defend Marie Curie's originality. When British newspapers persistently referred to Pierre Curie as the discoverer of radium she wrote, to the *Westminster Gazette*, 'Errors are notoriously hard to kill, but an error that ascribes to a man what was actually the work of a woman has more lives than a cat.'[8]

Another bond which drew Marie Curie much closer after her Academy experiences of 1911, had been Hertha's failure a few years earlier to achieve recognition by the senior scientific body of Britain, the Royal Society. It had refused to recognise Hertha's work in the obvious fashion by making her a Fellow. With a hypocrisy that can only have made Marie Curie indignant, and her French male colleagues roar with laughter, the Society had rejected Hertha's candidature, not because she was a woman, but because she was a *married* woman. Legal Counsel's opinion had even been sought on the matter and had verified that Mrs Ayrton's unfortunate condition was not one provided for by the Charters of the Society.

Until Marie Curie's breakdown the pair had been in frequent correspondence and Hertha, hearing in early January, 1912, of the scandal and of its effects, had immediately written off to Bronia offering a safe haven.[9] It was agreed that, as soon as she was well enough, Marie Curie would slip quietly into England and let Mrs Ayrton be responsible for her protection. Hertha was well-equipped to do this. Her suffragist activities had taught her how to handle both the press and the detectives who, on several occasions in the past few years, had besieged her Hyde Park home. Now that she had sacrificed her drawing-room by moving her laboratory there from the first floor, she had made plans to take a house on the Hampshire coast as soon as Marie was well enough to come. There she would minister to the patient and her needs.

Marie arrived at the house near Christchurch worn out by the journey and having suffered severe pain en route. But Hertha's campaign to rehabilitate Marie Curie was an outstanding success. The true identity of Madame Sklodowska was never discovered by the press and Marie Curie's visit to England went completely unnoticed. She gained strength; the children came to visit; Hertha played the piano for Eve to sing her nursery songs, and talked mathematics in an appropriately adult fashion to the grave-faced Irène. It was not long before the dark-cloaked figure of Madame Sklodowska was seen walking on the cliffs near the house, and by September Hertha had organised an outing to London: incognito and successful.

Hertha was the last in the short line of friends who had rallied in the long hour of need. These friends, together with Marie's inexplicable resources, saw her through the great crisis. By the beginning of October it was over. She was well enough to face the Dover–Calais ferry again and within a few days of reaching Paris felt sufficiently strong to begin quietly picking up the disarrayed threads of her life.

She had taken a small apartment on the third floor of an eighteenth-century house in the city on the Quai de Béthune. It had a clear view of the Seine and the passing river traffic. It also had a view of the commanding dome of Le Panthéon, the sight of which is as important to those who love the life of Left Bank Paris as is the sound of Bow Bells to Cockneys. Here, for the good of her health, she would have to keep a peaceful routine. But she had no intention whatever of letting the same restrictions apply to her cerebral activities. She was already ready for the mental fight.

By October 17th she was again sitting at her desk in the Rue Cuvier writing to thank Rutherford for his letters. Not merely that, in that first letter she straight away launched herself into a blistering attack on Sir William Ramsay – no favourite of hers, Hertha's, or Rutherford's for that matter. Marie did not like some of the things now revealed to her, that had been going on in her absence from the scientific scene. She told Rutherford:

Perhaps you have seen that Monsieur Ramsay has published some work on the atomic weight of radium. He arrives at exactly the same result as I did and his measurements are less consistent than mine. In spite of that he concludes that his work is the first good work on this subject!!! I must say that I was astounded. Moreover [he] made some malicious and incorrect comments [about] my experiments on atomic weights.[10]

Rutherford had kept her informed about the progress being made in the agreements on the International Radium Standard. At the last meeting on the subject in Paris in March, when she had been too ill to attend, in spite of her strongly worded wish that the conference be delayed, it had gone ahead with Debierne acting as her representative. Although Rutherford saw Marie Curie on that visit and noted how feeble she looked, he nevertheless breathed a private sigh of relief that her hushed, but entirely dominant personality, and her stubborn will, would for once not prevail on the vexed question of the Standard. As he told Bolt-wood, whom he knew, along with several other physicists of his acquaintance, had a firm dislike of the woman: 'I think we perhaps got through matters very much quicker without Mme Curie, for you know, she is inclined to raise difficulties.'[11]

The problem on this occasion was that both the Viennese, Stefan Meyer, and Marie Curie had prepared primary Radium Standards. If these were true Standards, and if both the Austrian and the Frenchwoman had done their work accurately, then their Standards would be identical. If not, and if one was wrong (but which?) Rutherford foresaw hurt pride on an international scale. That 'sensible person' Debierne, as Rutherford called him, set up the apparatus in his scientific mistress's absence to test the Standards against each other. There was a deep sigh of relief when it was found that, to all intents and purposes, the two Standards did agree. Marie Curie let it be known that she ap-proved of the Committee's work in the matter, and Rutherford considered that this incident was a major contribution to the preservation of Franco-Austrian relations. At long last the Standard could be laid to rest at the International Bureau of Weights and Measures.

Two more months' recuperation and Marie felt strong enough to begin her experimental work again. The last entry she had made in her day-to-day notebook on Radium Standards had been on October 7th, 1911. Her next entry was December 3rd, 1912. The date marked the beginning of a new life: a life with one important contact removed from it. Hypocrisy and sexual con-vention had prised Langevin out of the position of intimacy which seemed to have held so much promise for them both. In the year ahead they would meet often, as it was inevitable that they should, in the physics laboratories of the Sorbonne and at the conference tables of international scientific symposia. But no man, and certainly not Langevin, would ever again fill that unique gap in her intimate relationships.

Over-indulgence in morbid reflection might have been one of her faults, but she never succumbed to the sin of inactivity. Early in the spring the familiar figure, now once more having adopted its black-dressed simplicity, could be seen flitting towards the lecture rooms of the Sorbonne, like some apologetic moth, though seeking out the shadows, avoiding inquisitive eyes.

As her confidence returned she began to risk some public exposure. In the autumn of 1913 she kept an old promise to visit Rutherford, and at the same time put in an appearance at the British Association meeting in Birmingham and collected an honorary doctorate from the University. She wrote to Irène to tell her about the ceremony: 'They dressed me in a beautiful red robe with green facings, as they did with my companions in misery, that's to say the other scientists who were receiving doctorates.'[12] She also made sure to tell Irène, who was taking a most serious interest in these matters, that eminent scientists such as Lorentz, Rutherford and Soddy were also present. Even more important, Irène was mother in her absence. Marie wrote off with detailed instructions of how Irène should bathe with ethyl salicylate an infectious rash which Eve had developed on her scalp.

But the happiest news for Irène was that her mother had at last dropped the pretence of trying to protect the name of Curie by dissociating herself from it. Madame Sklodowska was gone, and Madame Curie had returned. She told Irène, 'Don't write to me at Birmingham any more but to London at Mrs Ayrton's, 41 Norfolk Square, Hyde Park W., London, for Mme Curie. My name is now well known here by the servants, who are the sort you can employ without any problems.'[13] Irène was overjoyed.

Marie Curie was at last learning to live with the paradox that her withdrawn personality attracted attention, and that the attention had sometimes to be accommodated. A. S. Eve, a friend of Rutherford's, noticed the results in Birmingham; she was, he said,

> ... shy, retiring, self-possessed and noble; everyone wished to see her, but few were successful. The press were eager for interviews, and Madame skilfully parried their questions by singing the praises of Rutherford. It was not quite what they

wanted, but it was all that they could get. 'Dr Rutherford,' she said, 'is the one man living who promises to confer some inestimable boon on mankind as a result of the discovery of radium. I would advise England to watch Dr Rutherford; his work in radioactivity has surprised me greatly. Great developments are likely to transpire shortly, to which the discovery of radium is only a preliminary.'[14]

Marie Curie's predictions were accurate. Rutherford's work was to have far-reaching applications, and Niels Bohr's remarkable and important theory of the atom, the earliest developments of which she was clearly fully aware of, was about to emerge.

But the press was much more interested in interpreting her remarks in terms of the immediate applications of radioactivity. And at this time this meant applications to cures for cancer. For almost ten years now malignant tumours had been treated by rays from radium sources; recently some spectacular successes had been reported. It was Marie Curie's part in the discovery of radium, the 'wonder cure', which was now adding enormously to her international fame.

Most countries in Europe were in the process of setting up Radium Institutes. She herself had agreed to be honorary director of the Warsaw Institute and made the journey to the opening ceremony in November. But the emotive interest in radium as a cure for cancer was beginning to act against the interests of the very research workers who had discovered its peculiar properties. Many of the new institutes were financed by donations specifically intended to provide radium for medical applications. Such now was the demand for radium that its price was rocketing. Rutherford complained to Marie Curie that a large quantity of radium ordered by the British Radium Institute from the Austrian Government had been backed by a personal request from the King of England.[15] The result was that physicists working on the Radium Standard had to wait in a queue whilst this kind of demand was satisfied, and watch the metal's price inflate with every new and urgent demand.

The cost of science was beginning to increase. The price of materials which the Curies had discovered and separated was now enormous. Many physicists were dependent on these materials and on increasingly sophisticated equipment with which to carry out research. Forming a nucleus of research workers, moulding them into a productive laboratory team and keeping them financed and equipped was to take up a major portion of the rest of her life's work.

Her laboratory report to the University of Paris for the 1912–13 academic year, now that she had rehabilitated, began as she intended to continue, irrespective of the Sorbonne's attitude to her over the past months. She had complained bitterly of the lack of adequate funds for research and research workers, which were only maintained at their present levels by the funds she herself had brought in from rich men such as Carnegie and Solvay.

The Sorbonne's memory for her supposed adultery was conveniently short-lived. The idea that Marie Curie should have a laboratory built for her own use by the world-famous Pasteur Institute had been mooted some years earlier. In 1912 an agreement was reached between this institute and the University that a new establishment, devoted entirely to the science of radioactivity, should be founded. It would be divided into two parts: one directed by Marie Curie and devoted to physical and chemical research, supported by the University from a government grant; the other directed by Dr Claude Regaud, and given over to medical and biological research, supported by the Pasteur Institute.

At last she was to have total independence: her own institute built, appropriately enough, in the newly named Rue Pierre Curie. During the next two years it would provide the outlet she needed to distract her from the trauma of the past. She was determined, however, that if this independence was to be real, she would be responsible for everything connected with that independence. Even when the scaffolding of the new laboratory was only just beginning to rise from the ground, Marie Curie was needling the University authorities with the reminder that her existing laboratory staff arrangements were quite inadequate. Both the funds and the space on the site alloted to her were parsimonious. From its very conception the situation was an ideal battle-field on which she could take up a position of command.

She had sat looking over the shoulder of the architect from the moment of the first completed drawings, and now she was not only willing but determined to clamber over scaffolding and piles of bricks with anybody involved, whether he was an executive or a manual worker. The winter of 1913–14 was particularly wet, delaying work considerably on the skeleton of the 'Pavillon Curie'. Each week throughout the winter a meeting on site was held between architects, contractors and construction workers. Always leading it between the track which wended its way through pools of mud and between the rising outlines of laboratory walls, would be the figure in black dress and cloak. Nobody doubted who was in command. Each man listened and deferred to sentences which, though they were not issued as commands, could be interpreted as nothing else. Antoine Lacassagne, a young doctor of 29 brought by the 43-year-old Claude Regaud as his assistant, recalling one of these occasions in the mud and rain, noted how Regaud listened to her as though he were her pupil; Lacassagne himself felt like a small child as he looked down on this frail invalid.[16]

The place was finished and ready for occupation by the last day of July of 1914. But on August 2nd the only man she had at her command in the pavilion's empty shell was an elderly laboratory assistant with heart trouble. He was the only member of her laboratory staff who had not been mobilised for war.

Chapter 19

War

Paris was in uproar. The little white notices of mobilisation had appeared on the streets at about 5 o'clock at the end of a wonderful day of summer sun. Before darkness fell, parades with massed tri-colors accompanied by bands pouring out *La Marseillaise* were sweeping up and down the cobbles. Before the night was out a few German-owned shop-fronts were smashed in and a few stores looted. The Government, it was rumoured, was to move to Bordeaux, and within hours, trains crammed with women and children were, like the Government, steaming out of the capital to the safety of more distant places. Marie Curie herself had been at Montparnasse station and had seen some sign of panic there which she found unbecoming in her fellow-countrymen and women.

For these *were* her fellow-countryfolk now, and this, after having spent half her life in it, was her country. She intended to serve it with the patriotic spirit which she felt was appropriate for the moment. But she had first to make decisions about what to do with what was nearest and dearest to her. Her family was in Brittany on holiday. Her other charge was sitting in the Rue Cuvier laboratory: one gram of radium – a very considerable fraction of the total world supply at that time. Decisions were necessary on both counts.

The children were well-cared for where they were and in theory it would be best for them to stay out of Paris, in l'Arcouest. She had first been to the place two years earlier. It was the holiday retreat of a few of her friends from the Sorbonne who centred themselves on the jolly scholar Charles Seignobos. Seignobos, beloved by both the intellectual clan of holidaymakers as well as by the Breton villagers, who remember him well today, was known to all and sundry as *le Capitaine*, not merely because he organised the holidays around his barque, *l'Eglantine*, but because also he was the natural captain of this little team of intellectuals.

The Perrins, the Borels and the others had taken cottages in the pines near the peaceful fishing settlement. Irène, Eve and their Polish governess were with the Perrins on the day that the white mobilisation orders were nailed up round the village. A message from Paris was already on its way to the children from their mother, who was so ready and eager to further the spirit of patriotism which this serious situation merited, and which she wished particularly to pass on to her daughters. She told them to be 'calm and courageous ... You and I, Irène, we'll look for some way to make ourselves useful.'[1] Irène was flattered to be treated no longer as a child, but now completely as an equal. She kept her mother fully informed of the situation in Brittany.

Sunday morning, (August 2nd), My darling ...

The local people are panicking. They are confusing war and mobilisation. We've tried to calm them a bit explaining that they aren't the same thing. Eve came up to me yesterday evening in tears because some little imbecile of twelve who plays with her had told her that war had been declared; I had to explain it to her too. I think she was worrying about Maurice and André.[2]

Their cousin Maurice Curie, Jacques Curie's son, and André Debierne were the children's favourite 'uncles' who, it seemed, would be the pair in the age bracket most likely to be engulfed by war. But Irène too now saw a role for herself, and was overcome by the feeling of involvement in which her mother's sentences had embraced her.

When the Germans crossed the French border, again Marie sent off a stiff-upper-lip note to her daughters imploring them to be courageous and calm. But the feeling of impending doom hanging over Paris had not reached the intellectuals of l'Arcouest and Irène's main concern was not one of maintaining calm, but of seeing the promise of involvement fulfilled. 'I know it's not sensible,' she told her mother, 'but my one desire is to return. I daren't tell anybody that here, since everybody will say that it's silly and that I'd only serve to hinder, and yet I don't know what

would become of me if I was here for the whole of the war. I'd
so like to see you, darling.'[3]

During the next few days Irène continued to bombard her
mother with suggestions of how she could be involved: nursing
with the Red Cross, as a secretary with one of the commissions,
or even teaching. Her letters became even more anguished as she
got into arguments with other adolescents who accused her of
being Polish and not a true French girl.

Marie Curie shared her child's anguish. For her there was the
double irony that Poland had again been marched over. But she
persuaded Irène not to take the taunts to heart and to wait
patiently. 'If you can't work for France at present, work for her
future. A lot of people will, alas, be missing after this war and
they will have to be replaced. Work on physics and mathematics
as best you can.' But Marie Curie was genuinely missing her
daughters who were fast becoming the main props to her emotional life. 'I'm well aware,' she told Irène, 'how much you have
already become a companion and a friend.'[4]

Marie Curie's immediate preoccupation, however, was with
her other off-spring, radium. As soon as she was able she joined
one of the overcrowded trains leaving for Bordeaux carrying its
bewildered selection of territorials, government officials – and
others: others who, it seemed to her, were 'those who could not,
or would not, face the possible danger of German occupation'.[5]
She herself had no intention of being out of Paris a minute
longer than necessary. She boarded the train in Paris with her
precious gram of metal prudently protected by twenty kilograms
of lead. As she sat in her compartment she was plainly embarrassed by the ridiculously heavy bag alongside her, which she
could not even lift unaided. Guiltily she felt and looked like one
of 'the others', fleeing with her most expensive possession. The
journey was painfully slow. The train made unscheduled stops
lasting many hours, in the middle of abandoned countryside.
From her seat she could see that the arterial roads were full of
expensive private motor cars carrying their owners away from
Paris.

At Bordeaux the crowd swept off the train and along the platform. It left behind the solitary woman with the bag she could not lift. Eventually a man from the Ministry helped her find a hotel. She stayed in it overnight with her gram of radium alongside her bed. Next day she had it deposited in a Bordeaux bank vault. By the evening she was back on board a military train heading for Paris.

When Marie Curie finally sent a telegram saying that she had found something useful for Irène to do and giving her permission to risk the journey to the capital, Irène could scarcely contain herself. Nor could she move. A rock which one of the playing children had accidentally dislodged had damaged her foot badly enough to keep her from stepping out anywhere for two weeks.

Henriette Perrin, one of the few people with whom Marie Curie allowed herself to be on first-name terms, and who had helped nurse her through the worst of her crisis, wrote a letter of reassurance to Paris by the first post. It was clearly aimed at preventing another nervous upset to Marie's system. Five times in the letter describing how the accident had happened, Henriette assured her that there was nothing whatever to worry about and that the injury was a minor one.[6] But Henriette need not have worried. Marie Curie's recovery was now complete. She was back in full command of herself; moreover she was again in command of others.

Within a few days of the Belgian border being crossed by German troops she had come to the conclusion, not shared by all her colleagues, that the war was going to be long; she also realised that the number of wounded was likely to be immense, and that the nature of the injuries as a result of modern technical warfare was likely to be very different from that experienced in any other major war. She realised that her own radiochemical work could not possibly have any immediate widespread application, but the use of X-rays to locate bullets, shrapnel and broken limbs, a technique still only used on a small-scale in civilian life, would be necessary on a vast scale should the war last. Not just X-ray units, but some method of transporting them to the front-line, would have to be used if suffering men were not to be dragged back to a base hospital for examinations.

She had little difficulty, this now thin, collected and distinguished figure, in quietly convincing harassed and uncertain officials in government offices that there was a role she could play. Within ten days of the war beginning she had in her hands a formal request from the Minister of War to equip operators for radiographic work.[7] It was the signal for her to begin yet another sustained burst of work.

She spent the next few days touring Paris on public transport, in horse-drawn cabs, and in motor vehicles when she could get hold of them. Her first ports of call were the houses of the rich and the famous, or of the friends of the rich and the famous. There was no question here of going cap in hand, begging for the benefit of 'disinterested' science. She took whatever she could get for the *application* of science and 'for the good of our country'. Patriotic princesses and baronesses, pleased to be involved with both the war-effort and the distinguished Madame Curie, now rehabilitated with the official title of Director of the Red Cross Radiology Service, handed over their cash. When they could be persuaded, by the quiet authoritative voice, they handed over their larger town cars or open-tourers, reassured by the Madame herself that they were 'to be returned at the duration'.

Next were the scientific instrument makers: manufacturers of portable X-ray machines, of dynamos and of induction coils. Where possible she commandeered useful pieces of physics equipment from the empty Sorbonne laboratories. Paris hospitals, already beginning to receive large numbers of wounded, were persuaded to co-operate by supplying the few trained radiologists they could spare for the initial stages of her scheme. Car-body manufacturers were co-opted to convert the chassis she had begged into useful vans.

Irène arrived in Paris at the beginning of October when work on the first radiological car was well under way. Her mother quickly removed any doubts the girl might have had about the full nature of her involvement in the scheme. One of the first tasks they did together was to hire a horse-cab to begin transferring at least some of the equipment along from the Rue Cuvier to the new laboratory in Rue Pierre Curie. Later they were able to use one of the converted radiological cars as a removal van for the heavier equipment. Their driver was a sick man, so that most of the carrying had to be done by mother and daughter.

When Marie Curie began her work the whole of the French Army was equipped with a single radiological car.[8] She was eventually to be responsible for putting more than 200 on the road, the first of which rolled towards the front-line at Creil in late October. In it was a 110 volt, 15 amp dynamo, a Drault X-ray machine, photographic equipment, curtains and some primitive screens with a few pairs of gloves to act as protective barriers for the operators from the X-rays.

The vehicle was never able to go at much more than 50 kilometres an hour, even over decent roads, so that every journey it made was bound to be long, crowded and uncomfortable for its occupants: Marie Curie, a doctor, two assistants, one of them Irène, and a driver-mechanic. On November 1st, Radiological Car 'E' brought its cargo to a halt at the door of the Creil military hospital and the little team began its routine – the first of many such routines – finding a suitable room, making it light-proof, carrying in the X-ray machine and connecting it by cable to the dynamo operated by the driver from the car.

Until then, war for Marie Curie had been a process of energetic administration. That day she was to see the reality of blood and gore, and so too was her daughter at seventeen years old. Together they handled the first of the wounded, manoeuvring him in front of their elementary equipment. Marie Curie formalised the situation and so blunted the shock for the girl by bringing out a notebook and recording the details. A few terse words sum up what they saw, beginning in the morning with the simple cases to better their technique: 'Bullet in the forearm', 'Numerous shell splinters and fracture', 'Ball shrapnel in right hand', 'Rifle bullet in left buttock. Depth of round, 10.9 cm', 'Examination of cranium. Rifle bullet in central region viewed in profile.'[9]

It was only the beginning. The number in the notebook reached 30 that day; it progressed into many hundreds as the car

moved from place to place, as new cars and crews were brought
into service, and as they changed cars: Anglo-Belgian ambulance
at Furnes, 5 Dec. 1914; Joinville, 20 Feb. 1915; Anglo-Ethiopian
hospital at Frévent, 28 March, 1915. And so it goes on, the
numbers rising, and sick men becoming cold statistics in the
handwriting which, like that in the early laboratory notebooks, is
interspersed with annotations; not now with those of her husband,
but written in the adolescent script of her daughter.

Many of the bodies which they processed were those of boys
not much older than Irène herself. One British politician visiting
Paris, who had once earned his living as a journalist, was taken
to see a casualty clearing station behind the French and British
lines at Aubers Ridge at the height of a battle in the spring of
1915. Though accustomed to warfare, he wrote of this experience
with an undulled eye:

> More than 1,000 men suffering from every form of horrible
> injury, seared, torn, pierced, choking, dying, were being sorted
> according to their miseries into the different parts of the
> Convent at Merville. At the entrance, the arrival and departure
> of the motor ambulances, each with its four or five shattered
> and tortured beings, was incessant: from the back door corpses
> were being carried out at brief intervals to a burying party
> constantly at work. One room was filled to overflowing with
> cases not worth sending any farther, cases whose hopelessness
> excluded them from priority in operations. ... An unbroken
> file of urgent and critical cases were passed towards the operat-
> ing room, the door of which was wide open and revealed as I
> passed the terrible spectacle of a man being trepanned. Every-
> where was blood and bloody rags.[10]

The writer was Winston Churchill. Marie Curie spoke little
and wrote less of the emotional effects of what she saw. The deep
impression only revealed itself occasionally after the war talking
in unguarded moments in the laboratory to close colleagues – and
once when she read through the typed draft of the few sentences
of autobiography which describe her experiences in military
hospitals, written in her customarily detached fashion. As though
as a confession to herself she added to it in handwriting:

I never could forget the terrible impression of all that destruction of human life and health. To hate the very idea of war, it ought to be sufficient to see once what I have seen so many times, all over those years: men and boys brought to the advanced ambulance in a mixture of mud and blood, many of them dying of their injuries and many others recovering but slowly, in the space of months, with pain and suffering.[11]

Worries that Irène might not have the same mental and physical resilience were soon dispelled. In the end the girl was as capable of detachment as her mother. Now, for the first time in her life, Irène was able to watch at close quarters her mother working with men. She watched the technique carefully and noticed that it was not without cynicism. On one occasion when Marie Curie was giving a tour of her radiological posts to the Inspector General of the Military Health Service Irène saw the method operating at its most effective. 'I remember having to suppress with difficulty a strong desire to laugh,' Irène said, 'when I heard my mother speaking to this inspector, and referring to the posts she had installed "with your gracious authorisation".'[12] Irène had found that the name of this same inspector had often come up in her mother's private conversations when she was speaking of the obstructionist attitude of the military health authorities.

Irène soon learnt from her mother's example under what conditions she could face a man as an equal. There was a considerable resistance at that time, particularly among older doctors, to the use of X-rays as a means of diagnosis and both women during these early months of the war experienced resentment to their presence in military hospitals. Marie Curie later described how on one occasion the girl assistant radiologist,

... who had only been in the hospital a short time, located the position of a piece of shrapnel which had passed through, and crushed the femur of a man's thigh. The surgeon ... did not want to probe for the shrapnel from the side from which the radiologist indicated it was accessible; instead, he probed from the open wound side. Finding nothing, he decided to explore the region indicated by the radiological examination and immediately extracted the shrapnel.[13]

What Marie Curie did not reveal in this account was that the girl radiologist was her daughter. Irène was already beginning to apply what she had learned. Quite soon she had enough skill to correct, if not actually cross swords with military surgeons old enough to be her grandfather. In one hospital she sat down and delivered a brief lesson in elementary geometry to a Belgian doctor who had failed to understand the principles of locating projectiles in the body by use of radiographs.

Before long, when her daughter was not yet 18, Marie Curie considered that she could leave her as her own substitute at the front. And there she remained: like mother, like daughter – in command, and choosing to be over-worked. Also, unsuspected by either of them, she was being over-exposed to X-rays. The protective measures which they used, a few small metal screens, cloth gloves, and making sure to avoid the direct beam of the X-rays whenever possible, were quite inadequate.

Moments of relaxation during those first uncertain months of the war were few. Contact with old friends was contact with an age, its style, its values and its inhibitions, which, though they none of them yet realised it, had gone for good. One happy January day early in 1915 Marie Curie and Jean Perrin succeeded in meeting in his radiological car not far from the front-line. Together the former next-door neighbours retired to a Dunkirk hotel which had once called itself de-luxe. They sat at a rickety table, celebrating with a cup of black tea, and there they decided to let Paul Langevin, who had gone into the army as a sergeant in a pioneer battalion, know that they were thinking of him. Perrin began the sheet of paper to '*Mon cher Paul*', and ended it, '*A toi, Jean*'. It was a typically cheery letter, trying to persuade Langevin that his talents could be infinitely better used elsewhere. 'If you could only use your intelligence as a PHYSICIST you could be of more service than a thousand sergeants, in spite of all the esteem I have for that honourable rank.' Marie Curie added on the other side of the paper three friendly sentences, neatly written in spite of the rickety table, addressed '*Cher ami*'. She added her best wishes and ended, very unusually for her, with a scrawled signature which might be 'M.C.'; or it might be 'Marie'.[14]

It was not long before Marie Curie was back in Paris, having now successfully got several of her cars on the roads leading to and from the trenches. The problem at this stage was not with the cars and their equipment, but with the staff which had to go with them. Trained radiologists were rare and certainly not available on the scale she had in mind. So far she had staffed her units with the few available medical personnel along with any professionals, such as teachers or university research workers whom she could recruit to the service and who could be quickly taught the simple principles involved. There was, however, one ready source of suitable high quality manpower, of which Langevin was only one example. The difficulty was to tap it. Already the French army had recruited scientists, as had the British, without thought for the possible loss of technological skill. She herself was that year to lose her favourite young Polish co-worker, Jan Danysz, who had spent several years of research with her in the Rue Cuvier. He was killed serving as a captain in the artillery. And Rutherford too was grieving over the foolish waste of his brilliant Harry Moseley, 'shot clean through the head'[15] in the Dardanelles campaign. Poland had lost its best French-trained radio-chemist and England the rising star of physics to whom there were few contemporary equals.

Andre Debierne's case had been more happily solved. From the first few days of the war, the faithful shaggy friend, who had become perhaps one of the oldest corporals in the French infantry, had written soulful letters to his 'Dear Madame and friend', complaining of the senselessness of it all, of his constant colds, of the stupidity of the officers left in his unit, and of his hopes of release now that some territorials, younger than he, had been discharged. He was soon withdrawn into the radiological service. Not all scientists were so well accommodated.

Marie Curie was having a regular supply of letters from the front from her nephew, Maurice Curie, who had adopted her as a second mother since beginning research as a young chemist in the Rue Cuvier laboratory.

23 Feb. 1915. Dearest Aunt . . . I'd love to get out of this village where I am now or I shall end up by being ruined through living among the ruins . . . I'd willingly give away my blanket for an hour at the window of your apartment on the Quai de Béthune. Dear Aunt, I go off again this evening, for three days we think, to a firing position along with my old chum, my 90 mm. gun. How I love you. Maurice.[16]

Yet he had never dared join the little band of people who called Marie Curie '*tu*'. It had always been '*vous*' ever since he was a child. Not directly – that would perhaps have been too informal – but tactfully through Irène, Marie Curie now gave him permission to *tutoyer* her, as she saw the increasing misery of each letter and the beginnings of his disillusionment in the war and his role in it.

11 June, 1915. Dearest Aunt . . . It seems that the Germans are making many more technical advances than us . . . And to be able to survive here, I'm quite sure that the question of men is, within certain limits, less important than the question of shells and offensive armaments. At the moment there is some movement in this direction, as far as I can establish from the papers. They have already asked for chemists with experience of toxic materials from my regiment; it isn't my subject, but I'll put my name on the list if they ask for less specialised knowledge. Then also I've had more than two months of bad winter in the trenches and have a certain apprehension about the new campaign . . .[17]

But in spite of the newly invited intimacy he did not yet dare to go so far as to ask his aunt directly to use her influence on his behalf. As her nephew well knew, her name had immense pulling power. By early 1915 the mail was bringing appeals for permission to use her name in newspaper fund-raising campaigns for hospitals, and as Vice-President of organisations for the wounded and for other war charities. Loïe Fuller, past the age of the best of the *Folies Bergère*, was now doing her bit in England, making use of Marie Curie's name. In an article in *Queen* Loïe described a non-existent 'radium' hospital at the front and touched many hearts of many middle-class ladies of the Empire, who sent along their one-pound notes in response to the magic of the words 'Madame Curie'.

During 1916 pressure on her radiological organisation was at its worst when the demand for replacement of staff by trained personnel was at its highest. One doctor, after the Somme offensive, in sentences composed between visits to the wounded told her he was 'occupied from morning until night. I was able to carry out 588 radiological operations during July ... I don't think I can continue for much longer with this sort of responsibility.'[18]

During this same period Marie Curie had to deal with a letter from the British Ambassador who, in some embarrassment, had been made to ask for her and Pierre Curie's autographs which his King wanted to attach to photographs taken from *Vanity Fair*. Quite apart from the inopportune timing of the request, she was left in some doubt as to whether whoever originated this royal request realised that her husband was long-since dead. She eventually sent off a copy of his signature, along with her own, and returned to obsessions deeper than those of stamp and autograph collecting.

She had found a war-time use for her new Radium Institute, though for the time being it would be unconnected with radium. She decided to found there a radiological school to teach simple X-ray technique to young women. On this occasion Marie Curie's social catchment area was wider than it had been when she was seeking money and equipment. She persuaded young ladies of fashion, nurses, students, and even chambermaids if they had the potential, to enroll at her *ad hoc* academy to keep the radiological cars rolling. During the next two years she was to give a basic education in elementary mathematics, physics and anatomy to 150 girls whom she could then feed into the front-line organisation.

There was nothing *ad hoc* about her methods. She presided over this, the first class in her own Institute, with the same efficiency as she had once shown in her Sorbonne courses. She now stood in front of a group of twenty or so young people of considerably lower average educational standard than that in classes she had been used to. To some of these girls she had an impressive, even angelic appearance. To others, this figure, which wasted no energy on unnecessary physical movement except to rub at the irritating skin on the fingers' ends, seemed strangely inscrutable.

She occupied them all day and every day for two months moving them from theory to practice. When she saw the teaching load was going to be heavy she brought Irène back from the front to help her. Marie Curie quickly learnt to sort the wheat from the chaff – and rejected the chaff without ceremony. In the end some of the girls learnt to worship the quietly dominant woman and eventually wrote intimate letters to her from the front-line to which she sent them, and to which they willingly went. Others, as had many with greater intellects before them, remained intimidated, some of them with their sensitivities bruised. She suffered no fools gladly; it was an expression she herself used against the name of one of the girls in the inevitable notebook she kept of their progress. Of another she wrote in impatient disbelief, 'Tried to leave the course because of harmful effect of rays (???).'[19]

Between organising the teaching course and making tours of inspection to some of the hospital bases which she had established, she was now giving some thought to how radium could be used in the war-effort. Already some of the spectacular results of the treatment of malignant tumours by radium were well known, and early in 1915, at the Grand Palais, now a military hospital, radium was being used to treat scar tissue, bad cases of arthritis, neuritis and other assorted ailments.[20]

Radon had already been found to be one of the most useful sources of curative rays. If the gas was drawn off from the radium in which it was formed, and sealed in thin glass tubes about one centimetre long, these could be put inside platinum needles and inserted in the body at the point where it was judged they would be most effective.[21] However, the technique was still in its infancy and the whole operation was very much a hit or miss affair.

Marie Curie had now retrieved her radium from the Bordeaux bank vault: the same radium she and her husband had separated together so many years before. She installed it where symbolically it belonged: in the Curie laboratory of the Institute of Radium. There she began the first French radium therapy service, providing tubes of radon to both civil and military hospitals.

She trusted only the most skilled and experienced operators to draw off the radon from its then incalculably valuable source. Whoever did this work invariably found it fatiguing, since, as we now know, they were inadequately protected from either radiation or from radon leaking to the air they were breathing. Some found the work so exhausting that they had to take off to the countryside or the mountains to recuperate.

By this time it was becoming obvious that there was a likely causal connection between exposure to a radioactive atmosphere and the physically and mentally depressive states of so many of the laboratory workers. But since a few days in unpolluted surroundings gave them back their lost energy there seemed no special reason for alarm. When there was nobody left to do the work, as often happened, Marie Curie did it herself.

There was little scientifically skilled manpower for her to call on if she needed help. Jean Perrin was now in charge of National Defence Research in Paul Painlevé's Ministry of Inventions and was involved in work using sound echoes to locate aeroplanes by night. Painlevé himself had personally intervened on behalf of Paul Langevin, the man whose duelling second he had once been; Langevin had, as a result, been transferred from the army to research work, and was brilliantly applying himself to the detection of submarines by ultra-sound. André Debierne, having collected the Croix de Guerre as a sergeant, had at last been commissioned, and was in charge of the Chemical Warfare Service.

Marie Curie's scientific friends in Britain were just as deeply involved in applying their work to war. Hertha Ayrton had invented 'Mrs Ayrton's fan' which troops, who were lucky enough to survive long enough to employ it, used as a hand-operated device to clear their trenches of poison gas. Rutherford, like Langevin, was involved in submarine detection.

One day Rutherford turned up in Paris to talk at the Ministry of Inventions on his submarine work. He was in his hotel preparing his lecture when, to his delight, 'about 12.30 a taxi driven by a soldier turned up in which were Perrin, Langevin, Mme Curie and Debierne, who took me to lunch and treated me in Royal fashion'.[22]

When his lecture was done, Rutherford went off with Langevin and Marie Curie. Sitting opposite the pair whose brief but exceedingly stormy affair now must have seemed a world in time away, Rutherford drank tea at a bench in the Curie laboratory. Looking at her he saw that her physical condition had not changed for the better; yet again she was 'rather grey and worn and tired'.

She was indeed tired. But it was the condition she now accepted as part of her own system's chronic malfunction. She let the pressure of work stay on her as long as the war lasted. She still kept up her visits to the chain of hospital radiological stations she had set up. During the summer of 1918 she went to Italy to report on Italian radioactive sources. Meanwhile, Irène, from a laboratory now in range of enemy bombardment and protected with sandbags, kept her posted with news of the war's progress.

As late as June 1918 conditions in the city were nerve-racking. Irène had taken to moving out to Brunoy to sleep so as to get some rest from the whining sirens of the Paris night alerts. She told her mother:

The German advance is putting us all in quite a troubled state of nerves. Let's hope the situation improves.[23]

It did, quite suddenly. By early August, when Irène had heard of the failure of the German offensive, she was writing, 'Darling, I think that at last the moment has come we've all been waiting for; the moment when, having passed the bottom, we're climbing up again.'[24] And so they were. A few weeks later Radiological Car 'E' recorded the location of a small piece of shrapnel in the left shoulder of a wounded soldier. He was the 948th, and the last man to be examined in that one car. The total number of men who passed through radiological posts in 1917–18 alone was more than 1,100,000.

Chapter 20

Missy

It was all over, including the shouting. Armistice Day, like mobilisation day, had been surprisingly fine and warm for November. Like mobilisation day, too, the streets had been packed with people and with bands parading over the cobbles, thumping out *La Marseillaise*. A few lights had timidly shown themselves on long unused street lamps: Parisian citizens, who had spent some of the last year under bombardment, had embraced each lamp standard that had succeeded in accommodating a glowing bulb. Tipsy soldiers had addressed captured German cannon being dragged through the streets. Slowly in parade behind had followed streams of vehicles with happy crowds clinging to every available handhold. In the front of one van, a converted radiological car, with waving bodies and flags on roof and bonnet, had been a smiling Marie Curie peering, in rather short-sighted confusion these days, at the mass of swaying and singing humanity.

Now that it was done, she was left in silence in the laboratory she could at last truly call her own. The office was simply furnished. In it there was with a desk, a few straight-backed chairs and two or three bookshelves. On the desk were her pen, spectacle-case and slide-rule. Nothing around her was functionless, and nothing was decorative. It was almost the entire equipment she needed for the remainder of the significant part of her life's work.

But her plan for the rest of the laboratory – that it should house the beginnings of an important French school of radioactivity – meant that she would need to find for it equipment as sophisticated and expensive as any in use in any physics laboratory in the world at that time. Apart from her one gram of radium, the essential nucleus for the work, and then worth she reckoned a million francs, she had little else beside bare walls and the remains from the young ladies' radiological classes.

When the first few months of readjustment were over, she took her first real holiday since the days at l'Arcouest before the war. She took off for the warmth of the Midi with Martha Klein, a woman who had helped her with her radiological classes during the war. The brief interlude was a great success. For the first time for many years she found it possible to relax. She bathed, walked and spent several nights sleeping outside in the warmth of the southern nights. She was refreshed, and with the refreshment came optimism. She was even cautiously optimistic about her lifespan, which for many years now she had been underestimating. She told her adored daughters, 'You are really both a great source of riches for me and I hope that life will still keep for me several good years together with you.'[1] As for the laboratory she had only the highest hopes: 'I often think of the year of work opening up in front of us and my only wish is that something good will come out of it.'

But it was to be a year of frustrations. Again she needed financial aid, but now the war was over, social pressure and moral rectitude were no longer on her side. Even had she been disposed to go out again, cap in hand, she would have found that many of the early war-time sources of money no longer existed. The princesses and the baronesses who had provided the funds for her radiological cars were many of them now in quite different circumstances. Many private sources of funds had disappeared with the war. The public purse was particularly badly equipped to encourage scientific research in the face of the innumerable demands being made on it. Even before the war's end, Marie Curie had written to the Ministry of Inventions pointing out that France, the birthplace of radium, had only five factories producing the metal; at the war's end the nation which was potentially the richest in Europe, stood to be the loser in this highly profitable but competitive industry, as it did in many other scientifically based enterprises.

The public will was at least in evidence, even if the way was not yet clear. In a letter of considerable foresight addressed to Madame

Curie, the government's newly appointed director of Scientific, Industrial and Inventions Research said that henceforth science and industry must march forward together, not just in warfare, but in the inevitable postwar economic struggle. He told her that his Board would put at her disposal 'all the necessary credit, indispensable apparatus and other means which it possibly can'.[2]

They were brave words. Nothing of substance came from governmental coffers bled white by four years of warfare made expensive by sophisticated technology. She would again have to provide for herself if there was to be provision at all. By March, 1920, having got together little equipment and little money, she was writing to as many sources as she could think of for war-surplus materials for her laboratory – Coolidge tubes, ammeters, voltmeters, electric motors, typewriters, desks – at the smallest possible price, or preferably free. She also needed two vans for the laboratory's use. She even got in touch with the Minister of Finance to try to get him to intercede in her bargain over a pair of ex-government vehicles. She did not hesitate to remind him that it was she who had equipped the wartime fleet of radiological cars, 20 of them entirely through voluntary subscriptions. Now she was having to beg to get a couple back at cut-price.

But there was one area of research which was still capable of attracting funds. The 'war against cancer' (already a popular phrase), found considerable financial support even in the most austere year of 1920. During the Great War medical successes in cancer therapy using radium, now suggested that the cancer war might not be interminable after all. Marie Curie's popular international fame rested on the fact that it was she who had discovered radium, the cancer cure. Throughout her life she was to get letters weekly from people she had never met, who personally wanted to thank her for her discovery. One she had from the first woman to be treated with radium acquired by a Gettysburg hospital is typical. Simply and touchingly the woman wrote, 'What it done for me none but God can tell.'[3] And when Baron Henri de Rothschild provided substantial funds for an institution to be called the Curie Foundation for the development of radiotherapy – or Curie-therapy as it was known in France – the use of her and her husband's name in its title was flattering. It was, however, quite logical that this Foundation should be attached to Claude Regaud's Pasteur Institute of biological and medical research rather than to her own laboratory. She had made a formal gift of her radium to her laboratory so that it should not be lost for pure research purposes, but she also made it available to the new Foundation for its cancer treatments.

But flattering as the recognition of her achievements was, the endowment of this new Foundation did nothing to further her own research plans, which were not, and never had been directly related to the medical uses of radium. Her dream was to succour a school of radioactivity which could feed on the laboratory traditions she had built up in the pre-war years. She might never have seen her wish fulfilled had she not, in a moment of weakness and against every prejudice she had against the press, agreed to be interviewed by a journalist.

By now Marie Curie had learnt to make certain accommodations to fame. Dating back to the award of her first Nobel Prize she had been bombarded with requests for public appearances, lectures, autographs and interviews. She was the first scientist in the age of mass communications to become a household name. Her secretary had a standard reply of rejection to commonplace enquiries. Even so, Marie Curie replied personally to most personal letters and meticulously referred those pleading for help in cancer problems, of which there were many, to Regaud. When in doubt she would walk across the garden which separated their two laboratories and consult the doctor himself before making a reply. She even replied to those whom others might have dismissed as obvious cranks, and gave too much of her time to dealing with trivial requests. She thanked the manufacturer of a pipe who wanted to name it after her, but coldly refused his offer: she hated attempts to exploit the name Curie commercially, besides which she disliked the habit of smoking. She spent unnecessary hours checking with English friends that Gorton School was reputable and that she should accede to a house-mistress's request for a signed photograph. She also took trouble to see that there was a reassuring reply to a woman who chose to ask the 'mother of radium' whether there was any danger in accepting the gift of clothes from a friend who had died of cancer.

For the many who asked for an interview, Marie Curie's secretary had a queenly response which told them that her mistress 'received' on Tuesdays and Fridays to discuss 'scientific matters' only. Journalists were sent a stock reply. She did not 'receive press representatives' except 'to give technical information . . . She never speaks of personal questions, her life, her tastes.'[4] She had every reason to feel that journalism had altered the course of her life and had caused her pain, suffering and the abandonment of a relationship with a man which otherwise might have lasted for many years and brought great happiness.

The stock reply was sent off when a woman journalist with the unlikely if alliterative name of Marie Mattingley Meloney, and representing an American magazine with the also somewhat improbable title of *The Delineator* asked for an interview. In spite of Mrs Meloney's rather sweeping claim that, on this visit to inspect the war relief work which her company had sponsored, she was to meet some of the most important people in Europe, Marie Curie saw no reason to vary her rule. It was the sheer persistence of the woman, and the fact that Marie Curie had had a personal approach via Henri-Pierre Roché (the author of the novel *Jules et Jim*) which led her eventually to capitulate and agree to give a short interview.

On a day in mid-1920 Marie Curie opened her office door to Roché and the diminutive dark-haired woman of about forty alongside him, Marie Meloney. Roché had already been captivated by this dynamic little journalist. He now watched with interest as she tackled the reclusive scientist, so well-known among journalists as the fierce guardian of her own privacy. From the start Roché saw there was a sympathy and surprising attraction between the two women whose motivations were so diametrically opposed.

Marie Curie noticed that the woman, whose hat came up only to her own eye-level, had a slight limp and bird-like movements.

Marie Meloney, as her profession demanded, took equal note of her interviewee: 'I saw a pale, timid little woman in a black cotton dress, with the saddest face I had ever looked upon. Her well-formed hands were rough. I noticed a characteristic, nervous little habit of rubbing the tips of her fingers over the pad of her thumb in quick succession.'[5] Roché, who had gone along to act as interpreter soon found his services were superfluous. Marie Curie was obviously quite proud of her Polish-accented English and Mrs Meloney was more than ready to listen to it.

Marie Meloney need have had no fears that Marie Curie had any antipathy to her nationality. For the past two years the Madame had been giving elementary courses in radioactivity at the Sorbonne to American troops. Marie Curie had liked their simplicity. She never found brash straightforwardness offensive. She probably recognised the same characteristics in Marie Meloney, though any brashness in the character of this American had been acquired through her profession and not through her gentle Southern upbringing. Mrs Meloney soon let it be known that all her friends called her 'Missy', a habit which Madame Curie acknowledged, but which she had no intention whatever of adopting.

What was distinctive about Missy was her casual, if not brash, habit of embracing the whole, or almost the whole of 'important' mankind in her ken. It was clear that, although she might have said it to impress, it was true that she had come to Europe to see well-known, if not important people. She had just left England where she had gone to see H. G. Wells, J. M. Barrie, Bertrand Russell and Arnold Bennett. In America she had an immensely wide and influential range of political contacts; Calvin Coolidge's first letter on official Vice-Presidency notepaper was addressed affectionately to Missy.[6] Later neither Mussolini nor Hitler would be outside her range.

On that first visit Missy willingly let Marie Curie practise her English on the subject of America and learnt that there were about fifty grams of radium in her own country, all of whose locations the Frenchwoman could name, and that the only French gram was in the laboratory in which they were then sitting. She also learnt that this laboratory was so short of equipment that, at that time, the chief use to which the gram of radium was being put was to provide radon tubes for cancer therapy.

Missy already had her Madame Curie copy: she could encapsulate it in one sentence: 'She had contributed to the progress of science and the relief of human suffering, and yet, in the prime of her life she was without the tools which would enable her to make further contribution of her genius.'[7]

It was a great story, capable of infinite expansion in the columns of *The Delineator*. However, Missy discovered something else that day: a mission for herself. Madame Curie had clearly liked her and had agreed to have another talk. There was something in Marie Curie – a purity of purpose and a belief in the ultimate goodness which this purpose could achieve – which inspired Missy into the thought that she had discovered something far more important than copy for her magazine. In the sweeping fashion with which she normally viewed life Missy had already conceived a journalistic enterprise with a socially useful goal in which she herself could play an indispensable and dynamic role and of which Marie Curie could be the focus.

Missy visited the Quai de Béthune apartment several times that summer, always impressed by the fact that it was Marie Curie, apparently unable to afford a maid, who opened the door. Each little discovery was fuel to Missy's enterprise.

During these visits Marie Curie learned more of Missy. Marie Mattingley Meloney was no run-of-the-mill reporter. She was in fact the editor of *The Delineator*, a thoroughly respectable women's magazine owned by the Butterick Company. It published tastefully illustrated articles bearing titles such as 'Is something wrong with the American man?' and 'Is friendship possible between a man and a woman, or is it only love in disguise?' It serialised novels by long-since forgotten authors as well as those by the less ephemeral writers among her contacts, such as Arnold Bennett.

Missy had started her journalistic career at the age of sixteen with a series of political scoop interviews with Washington friends of the family. In an age when women reporters were virtually unheard of, she quickly became Washington Bureau

Chief of the *Denver Post*. Her rise to editorship had been rapid. She was still only 39.

She was a staunch Republican and was imbued with a patriotic spirit which showed itself plainly enough in the columns of *The Delineator*. She wrote editorials headlined, 'What it means to be an American', which exhorted her fellow citizens to be generous to less favoured nations. The cable address she had adopted for herself in New York, IDEALISM, was blatantly naïve, but it was her honest aim. Naïvety was a formidable quality when, as in her, it was combined with a solid business sense and a lightning aptitude to deal with figures expressed in dollars.

In spite of her limp, the result of a childhood riding accident, and the fact that she was tubercular, she was an energetic and emotional little woman. 'Life for me,' she once told a friend, 'has become like a highly charged electric wire and I cannot let go.'[8] She had already decided that Marie Curie, if she would co-operate, could be the generator to stimulate the conscience of the American nation.

Missy's initial plan was simple. She had already begun to talk dollars on a scale unimaginable until that time to Marie Curie. She asked the price of radium. Marie Curie told her. Missy converted the figure to 100,000 dollars a gram and announced that in principle there should be no difficulty in persuading wealthy American women to provide the bulk of it: say ten to give 10,000 dollars each. Moreover, she persuaded the Frenchwoman that the name Madame Curie was a publishable commodity; an autobiography, properly promoted in the fashion she, Missy, understood so well could make substantial sums for the laboratory, or for the author herself.

After the Langevin affair Marie Curie gave her intimate trust only to women. She had never given that trust easily, nor formed quick friendships with either sex and the self-protective barrier to intimacy was forever at the ready. But this little dynamo in front of her – 'as busy as a switch engine' was one of Missy's favourite expressions – within the space of a few weeks somehow succeeded in inspiring a rapid and unmatched confidence. Physically the two women had certain common characteristics on which a bond of sympathy could be forged. They were both slight and delicate, both suffered from chronic illnesses and both suffered frequent relapses. Missy normally made light of her lameness, but could suffer fits of bitter depression. Her condition was one with which Marie Curie could empathise. Psychologically, however, they were very different. Marie Curie's reclusiveness contrasted vividly with Missy's extrovert dynamism.

In spite of, or perhaps because of this contrast, Marie Curie felt she could put considerable trust in the woman. She had little to lose from what was being proposed. There was a *quid pro quo* of course. Marie Curie would be expected by her munificent donors to collect the gram of radium in person; but she was not at all averse to a trip to the United States if it could be properly organised. Also, the Butterick Company would expect to publish the first articles about the radium gift since, as Missy said, 'It is not undertaking this work with any selfish motive, but it seems just and fitting that it should have the privilege of publishing the article simultaneously with the gift, so that at least that little bit of credit should come to them.'[9] It was a perfectly agreeable piece of business.

In her own country at this time however, although one leading French newspaper editor called her 'the greatest woman in France',[10] Marie Curie was not what could be described as a popular figure. The *causes célèbres* of 1911 had left Marie Curie's role cloaked in ambivalence; popular understanding of this Polish-born character was still unsure. Missy succeeded in reaching such a degree of understanding in this brief time, that Marie Curie revealed the wounds of the Langevin affair to her. There was a possibility, Marie Curie now feared, that the American visit might provoke American papers into regurgitating the whole of the Langevin story and even inflict more pain. Missy was well-apprised of the situation. She knew how to cope. Before she left she could, if required, cable her progress in the matter to Marie Curie in a code whose key only the two of them shared.

Missy immediately busied herself on Marie Curie's behalf. The minute her boat left Southampton in the late summer, the 'switch engine' was in operation rooting out rich and powerful men. In the first-class section of her liner she found a pair of trustees of the Massachusetts Institute of Technology, one of them P. A. S. Franklin, the President of International Mercantile Marine and the other, 'Mr Stone, the foremost engineer in this country . . . Both of these men have great wealth and influence.'[11] Before her boat passed beneath the welcoming arm of that quarter million dollar symbol of Franco-American amity, the Statue of Liberty, Missy had recruited them both to her cause.

Before Christmas of that year Missy was already sure that, provided she could organise sufficient publicity and turn Marie Curie's visit into an event, she could collect what she needed for the radium purchase. It was obvious to her, however, that she could not gather it from rich women as simply as she had imagined. A wider national campaign would be necessary. Already she had recruited an advisory committee of scientists including the President of the American Medical Association and leading representatives from the Rockefeller Foundation, Harvard, Cornell, Columbia and other universities. To help organise the campaign itself she had recruited Mrs John D. Rockefeller, Mrs Calvin Coolidge, Mrs Robert Mead (the founder of the American Society for the Control of Cancer) and other women with time on their hands and access to substantial bank accounts.

Nor had Missy forgotten to take an interest in the best commercial use of whatever money she could gather. She had discovered that radium costing a hundred thousand dollars a gram in the United States could be had for half that amount in Russia. In spite of the fact that she was in the process of extracting an article from Calvin Coolidge warning American women of the Communist threat, and in particular of the dangers of Reds under women's college beds, she was nevertheless happy for any proper business deal with the Bolshevik State, provided it was to the advantage of her cause.

Marie Curie was unprepared for the speed and the size of the operation. She confirmed that she would be ready to visit the United States, and even agreed, against her own better judgement, to begin to prepare an autobiography which could be published in the States when Missy unleashed her publicity. If Marie Curie had doubts that Missy might not be capable of bringing off her grandiose schemes, then they were now on the point of disappearing. There might, however, still be a misunderstanding. Missy's optimistic barrage of letters during the past weeks had gaily, but indiscriminately, spoken of both 'one gram of radium' and 'one grain of radium'. The time had come when Marie Curie could no longer overlook this ambivalent phrasing.

With the tough pragmatism she could call on at will, she had Pierre Roché cable Missy: 'Madame Curie asks if one grain or gram. Grain insufficient justify absence work here, being one fifteenth of a gram'.[12] Even Madame Curie had her price.

She need never have feared. Grams or grains, it was all the same to Missy. Fifteen or fifty times the cost was not outside her extraordinary grasp. By return she corrected the cable to grams. It was the last of the doubts Marie Curie was to have about Marie Meloney. She now utterly surrendered herself to Missy's care and judgement. When 'The Colony Club' tried to secure for itself some of the cachet of Marie Curie's presence in New York, by inviting her to be its guest, Missy moved to protect her hard-won rights. 'The Colony Club is a very beautiful and luxurious place,' she told Marie Curie, 'yet I am not sure that you would be as quiet there as you might wish. I should of course feel very greatly honoured if you would reside with me the days that you are in New York. My husband and I live very quietly and simply as most literary people here do. I wish you to be my guest while in New York and at no expense to yourself.'[13] Marie Curie deferred. In the same way she accepted every suggestion Missy had to make concerning publishing contacts. 'I hope to make a big material reward for you,' Missy wrote. 'You may receive letters from Macmillan publishing house, Scribner's, Dutton and Houghton Mifflin. These four houses are among the best American publishing companies. I am suggesting that they make definite offers to you. For your own information: the fairest proposition would probably be an advance of a thousand dollars and a royalty. . .Twenty per cent was about the rate given Theodore Roosevelt, and is a really very fine contract.'[14]

Missy equated Marie Curie's importance with that of the US Presidency, or with Royalty if it came to that. When Marie Curie suggested a stay of two weeks Missy replied that 'The King and Queen of Belgium gave six weeks to their visit.'[15]

When Marie Curie demurred and saw rough stretches in the road ahead, Missy steam-rollered them smooth. When Marie Curie tentatively suggested that she might miss her children Missy swept them both into the tour and arranged for the Curie family to take the apartment of her absent neighbour, 'my friend, Mr John R. Crane, Ambassador to China'.[16] There seemed nothing of which she was incapable and nobody she did not know. Marie Curie had already been told that Missy had arranged that her gram of radium would be handed to her personally by the President of the United States.

Most overwhelmingly of all, a cable arrived at the Curie laboratory in early March of 1921 saying simply, 'Cable cost laboratory Midi France. Also please mail new picture yourself and daughters . . . Meloney.'[17]

The scale of the woman's thoughts and the speed of her activity were too much for Marie Curie. Only in passing had she once mentioned to Missy her dream of a private laboratory in some quiet haven in the South of France. She was too staggered to reply at Missy's requested electronic speed.

Your cable in which you ask me the cost of a laboratory in the French Midi really took me by surprise and I was too embarrassed to reply by cable. I suppose that, knowing my wish to have a laboratory in the country and understanding how much I'd love to have it in the Midi, in friendship for me, you've formed a project to help me fulfil this plan, thanks to donations which might be given in America . . .

Indeed, what I would like is a personal laboratory outside Paris where I could live and work. This would certainly be a benefit for my health and for my peace of mind, though these are not my principal reasons for wanting an institution such as this. It's necessary in any case since there are experiments at my Institute which require a total absence of disturbance and which can't actually be carried out in my laboratory in the centre of Paris. Also there's work which requires the treatment of large quantities of minerals and which I absolutely cannot undertake in these conditions here . . . If I also tell you more – that my present laboratory needs enlarging, and that we are short of funds and personnel to such an extent that I have no help at all for my own work and that, at this very moment I am myself typing this letter I'm writing to you – then you will understand without any difficulty that some generous help is very necessary.[18]

However, even if she was content to see Missy rushing on apace, there was one other important matter which had first to be cleared up: she wrote in the same letter:

I want to raise one other question. I would like to ensure that the recipient of the radium you are giving me should be precisely specified. I would like to ask you to compose a text which specifies the conditions of the donation . . . Certain newspapers here have said that the gift is being made to the University of Paris, whilst you have always assured me that it was being made directly to me. You must state your intention on this matter, along with whatever is agreeable to the donors. If the gift is being made to me, it must be stated in the text how I shall be at liberty to dispose of the gift and within what limitations.

Marie Curie never had anything other than a strictly business-like approach to the precious commodity, radium. That it should be for *her* disposal had to be defined before she would proceed further. But again, she need not have feared. Missy was well aware of what her business obligations were. She replied: 'The gram of radium is for you, *for your own personal use* and to be disposed of by you for use after your death. I shall be glad to be of use to the University of Paris if it needs assistance, but for the present my time and energies are concerned only with your personal interests.'[19]

Now that Marie Curie had utter confidence in Missy she was quite happy to accede to Missy's personal *quid pro quo*. Missy wanted to be at the centre of the publicity machine and nowhere else and feared that the control might slip elsewhere if Marie

Curie did not co-operate. But she too need not have feared. Marie Curie told her, 'I won't accept a single proposition without your agreement.'[20]

In her plans for the tour Missy was arranging what she considered a reasonable balance between ceremony and leisure for her distinguished guest. She had set up conferences, honorary degree ceremonies and award-givings. She had been particularly careful to point out tactfully for Marie Curie's benefit which awards carried cash to the recipient along with the usual gold medal.

But the visit was not entirely without hitches in its preparatory stages. Missy told the distinguished ex-President of Harvard, Charles Eliot, that Marie Curie 'might possibly have some good influence while in this country on present discussions of feminism'. Eliot agreed, but he refused either to meet Marie Curie in New York or take part in a formal reception for her.[21] Others felt, as he did, that Missy's zeal was misplaced. Most of these were scientists who believed that Madame Curie had already done quite well for herself by collecting not only two Nobel Prizes, but 50,000 dollars in research fellowships from Andrew Carnegie.

Most American universities were falling over each other to entertain Madame Curie; but not all. Yale, it was true, was proposing to give an honorary degree, but the award was not without opposition from some members of the science faculty. Bertram Boltwood, for one, strongly disapproved, and almost the whole of the Harvard physics department was against the award of the honorary doctorate which was being proposed. Even one of Marie Curie's champions, her former student William Duane of the Harvard Medical School, although in favour of an honorary degree, acknowledged that 'since her husband died in 1906 Mme Curie has done nothing of great importance'.[22] Missy was affronted, but to no avail. In the end the oldest educational institution in the United States, dedicated as it was to 'knowledge and godlynes', withheld its honours.

Press publicity, for the great occasion, however, was mounting phenomenally. On this front a worrying cloud appeared – the first sign of what Marie Curie had most feared. The past was being raked over. In March one newspaper, obviously deriving its information from 1911 cuttings, in which the French nationalist papers had associated Marie Curie with both anti-clericalism and Judaism, reported the fact that Marie Curie was Jewish. Missy immediately rushed to say how distressed she was to hear that 'you were embarrassed by the statement published thoughtlessly in one of our papers, that you were of Jewish nationality. This was corrected the following day. I assure you the papers of this country are exceedingly friendly toward you and have said the finest things in praise of you as a woman and a scientist.'[23]

That the papers did have only friendly things to say was due entirely to Missy. She realised far better than Marie Curie that, quite apart from causing pain, unfavourable press coverage could ruin her whole campaign and put the final result in jeopardy. Missy had already taken the trouble to verify that, ten years earlier, many American papers, particularly in the William Randolph Hearst chain, had given spectacular coverage to the Langevin affair. One Hearst paper, for example had, in 1911, run the head-line, 'Mme Curie Love Mad. "Wife? Fool!" she says'; it was a cruel summary of *L'Oeuvre*'s letters.[24] At all costs Missy had to prevent the re-writing of this kind of story and, if at all possible, stop even a whisper from the past emerging. She fulfilled her promise brilliantly.

She assessed the situation and decided that the only tactic likely to succeed was to visit every leading New York newspaper editor herself and frankly ask for co-operation. To William Randolph Hearst's leading editor, Arthur Brisbane, the Managing Editor of the *New York Evening Journal*, Missy made a special plea. Her charm emerged triumphant. Brisbane, whose salary was linked to the paper's circulation, nevertheless personally handed over to Missy his papers' file on the Langevin affair for her to do with what she willed.

And to crown the achievement she cheerfully extracted from this newspaperman of the most hardened journalistic school 100 dollars for the Marie Curie Radium Fund. Missy never did things by halves.

Chapter 21

America

There was a considerable back-wash to Missy's North American public relations campaign. Surprisingly it spread as far as France. There, national newspapers suddenly awoke to the realisation that in their midst was an international celebrity, shortly to be promoted on one of the most comprehensive press campaigns ever organised in the United States: and they themselves had failed to celebrate her. It was the periodical *Je Sais Tout* which thought up the idea of giving Marie Curie a send-off with dignity.

No less than a gala at the Paris Opera was organised, and a new generation of Parisian reporters who had either forgotten, or did not know of the scandals that once filled the columns they were using, now described the same central character as 'one of the most wonderful figures of French science'. To loud applause she entered the auditorium and sat, the perpetually reticent figure, in the place of honour surrounded by France's most distinguished men of science. Jean Perrin and Claude Regaud stood to give the tributes of friendship and Sarah Bernhardt, now distressingly decrepit, trod the boards to recite an 'Ode to Madame Curie' which, inevitably, dwelt on the soul which burned with a fire of radium. Sacha Guitry organised the entertainment section of the evening which included two acts of his *Pasteur*, gravely performed. For Marie Curie it was a reassuring tribute to which she listened with the same gravity as it was delivered by Paris's most distinguished actors.

Not that she could hear what was being said very clearly. For several months past now she had been suffering from a continuous humming in her ears, and this annoying and tiring symptom, as it worsened, was accompanied by an even more worrying problem: her eyes had begun rapidly to fail her. She could not even see properly what was happening on the stage of the Paris

Opera that evening. Yet she tried to hide the fact from everybody except her close family and intimate friends. It was perhaps vanity which caused her to try to keep up this impossible charade, but more likely it was due to a fear which she did not want to recognise in the hope that she might be mistaken: the fear that her own radium was responsible – that it was affecting her general physical condition, her ears and, most disastrously, her eyes.

Missy was fully aware of the eye problem, and that Marie Curie's sight was likely to disappear altogether unless some rapid action was taken. She had gone to some trouble to see that the US trip included a visit to a leading New York eye-specialist.

Marie Curie's public rehabilitation in France was ritually and successfully performed at the Opera and Missy, whose publicity campaign was responsible for this national about-face, was there to see it happen. It was a triumph. A few days later Missy led her unsure star up the gangway of the S.S. *Olympic*. Following behind was the small party which would share the experience: Irène and Eve, and a young French-speaking American girl, Harriet Eager, whom Marie Curie had met in Paris through Missy, had liked, and had invited along as companion.

Marie Curie was still uncertain about the whole venture. In the first place she was unsure that the motive for the visit was entirely respectable and within the spirit of her scientific traditions. There was an uncomfortable element of begging about it. Although she had gone to such explicit trouble to make sure that the radium should be given to her and to nobody else, for disposal as *she* thought fit, time and again she had insisted to Missy that all publicity should make clear that the radium was being offered at Missy's instigation and that she herself had not asked for it. Then there was the forbidding prospect of days of ceremonial ahead. She genuinely hated and feared these occasions involving crowds she could now no longer even see properly.

Her itinerary, which Marie Curie could examine during the leisure of the trans-Atlantic crossing, as Missy had promised, was arranged to give the maximum amount of rest between official visits, and to give Marie Curie time to see the country. Nevertheless, the sense of foreboding was ever present. She wrote to

Henriette Perrin from aboard the *Olympic*, 'I left France not without a feeling of apprehension for this distant country which offers
so little of my own tastes and habits.'[1]

As a representative of that country Missy was surpassing all
expectations. Her organisation was imperial. She had seen to it
that the President of the 'White Star Line' himself had stood-to
to lead Marie Curie to the ship's bridal suite. Marie Curie worried
herself over whether there was some hidden motive in Missy's
activities, but could find none and now described her with more
fulsome praise than she had used for anybody she had ever met.
'She is more of a friend than I can tell you,' she told Henriette,
'and I don't think she's doing this for any personal advantage; she
is an idealist and seems very disinterested.' Missy had more than
earned the most prized adjective.

During the days at sea Missy did her best to prepare Marie Curie
for what was to come, schooling her in the art of the press conference and in her responses to American habits and familiarities.
But, her experiences in the Great War apart, Marie Curie's life
had been deliberately cloistered. It was too late now to alter a
whole attitude to life. Those who were close to her saw that the
New World would be a surprise, and even a shock to her childlike
sensitivities. The young Harriet Eager watched with some aston-
ishment the naïvety displayed by the distinguished woman twice
her age. One day, in order to discover why Marie Curie had not
put in an appearance at lunch Harriet went down to the bridal
suite and there found Marie Curie standing in front of the open
clothes closet. There was a pained expression on her face. Harriet
could see hanging in the closet, originally intended to hold an
expensive trousseau, three or four small dark dresses, including a
black lace evening gown in which Marie Curie had received her
Nobel Prize and which she intended, these ten years later, to wear
when she met the President of the United States. Harriet asked
what was the trouble. Marie Curie explained that she was delayed
because she had noticed there was a light in the cupboard and she
could not find the switch to turn it off. She did not like to leave
the cabin with this light-bulb secretly wasting its electricity on an
uninhabited wardrobe. Harriet explained that there was a door-

switch which automatically shut off the light when the closet was closed. Since she could see obvious disbelief in Marie Curie's face, Harriet began to look for the switch to prove her point; but she could find nothing. There was an impasse as both women faced the offending light-bulb. Harriet then suggested that Madame Curie might step inside the closet and have the door closed on her. Harriet saw a warm smile appear on the thin face; she had proposed a simple scientific solution which could be tested. Madame Curie slipped inside the closet, Harriet closed it firmly, reopened it, and the Madame emerged. Harriet was vindicated and lunch could now be taken.[2] They went off arm in arm, Marie Curie repeating, 'You are right, Harriet! You are right.'

Missy was also preparing Irène and Eve for the assaults of American inquisitiveness which they would have to endure in a few days' time. The two sisters were very different. Irène, at 23, was grave like her father: raw-boned and solid, she dressed carelessly, and the less charitable of her friends called her peasant-like. She was difficult to approach or to know well, but she was a rock of scientific companionship to her mother. Eve, at sixteen, was mercurial, pretty, attracted attention rather than repulsed it as her sister did, and was sensitive to the fact that she was excluded from the scientific intimacy which her sister shared with her mother. Of the family trio, she was the one whose characteristics were most likely to be understood by the people they were about to visit.

Missy had timed the crescendo of her public campaign to perfection. She herself had planned *The Delineator* issue which would be on sale on their arrival. It was devoted almost entirely to Marie Curie. Missy's article, 'The Greatest Woman in the World', followed her editorial on the same subject, entitled 'That Millions Shall Not Die'.[3] She had stories fed to her newspaper colleagues so that the New York City dailies should have more than adequate copy during the few days before the *Olympic* docked. It was scarcely Missy's fault if the press hyperbole were outrageously to her campaign's advantage. Most newspapers told the Curie radium legend with gross embellishments. Some started Marie Curie's career as a laboratory bottle washer and carried her triumphantly through near starvation to poverty-stricken success. One, quoting 'an authentic source', revealed that during the last winter Marie Curie had not been able to afford any coal until a friend supplied some for her. So the stories went on, with one unlikely tale succeeding another, and with cliché piling on cliché, successfully opening pockets and purses in readiness for the docking of the *Olympic*.

When the day came events were as Missy planned them, and as Marie Curie feared. As the ship berthed, she peered over the ship's rail at a dock-side beehive, crawling with many thousands of sight-seers. Women predominated, ranging from individuals inspired by the Curie legend, to large troops of Girl Scouts, Polish delegations, French contingents, 'The Executive Committee for the Entertainment of Marie Curie', 'The Executive Committee of the Marie Curie Radium Fund', 'The Scientific Committee for Marie Curie', and so on. To add noise and glister to the occasion, brass bands played the French, American and Polish national anthems simultaneously, while two large limousines provided by Mrs Andrew Carnegie purred unheard on the quayside. And of course there were the ubiquitous reporters.

Marie Curie knew that she could not avoid facing them, but she tried to make her own rules about how she did so. She was brought out on to the boatdeck by Missy and allowed herself to be seated in an armchair: a grey head submerged by a sea of felt hats above cameras, notebooks, microphones and every type of threatening equipment. She sat immobile, her grim face hiding the terror she felt of the pressing crowd and misguidedly hoping that the typed statement she had had circulated saying how much she would enjoy being in America would slake the thirst of this formidable corps. The statement passed round unread. Reporters questioned, photographers bellowed, and everywhere screams and waves of American hospitality took on the appearance of hostility. It was an exhausted woman who eventually was led down the gangplank into the welcoming insulation of Mrs Carnegie's limousine.

There had been mutual surprises. Americans were as uncomprehending of Marie Curie's apparent frigidity as she had been of their demonstrativeness. Nor was she quite the commodity Missy had sold in her descriptions of her heroine: this 'woman of rare beauty ... the high broad forehead, the full temples, the generous back, have the lines of an old Greek statue. But the face is not Greek. It is softer, fuller, more human.'[4] This was Missy's vision. The flesh the hardened pressmen had seen had been altogether different. The figure slumped pathetically in the chair had been no Franco-Grecian dream: actuality was much starker, as one reporter wrote: 'Her thin shoulders are bent with much stooping over laboratory tables, the hair brushed back uncompromisingly from her lined forehead, is snow white; there is nothing young about the sharpened contour of her chin, jaw and throat.'[5]

It was the cruel reality for her to read, and see, in large close-up in the next day's papers. She was a white-haired, lined and myopic old woman who had aged drastically in the last ten years.

What hopes she might have entertained that the rest of the tour would be a more gentle version of the reception were soon dashed. On paper the first few days looked relaxing: a quiet lunch with Mrs Carnegie, a degree ceremony at Smith College, a trip to Vassar and West Point, a couple of formal receptions at the Waldorf Astoria and the American Museum of Natural History. But Missy's pre-publicity had been too powerful. Everywhere Marie Curie went she was overwhelmed by speeches, hymn-singing, presentations and specially composed anthems. Within less than a week of her arrival she had her bandaged right arm in a sling to prevent it being shaken and squeezed in the grips of great welcoming masculine fingers.

Even before she reached Washington for the high-point of the visit she was weak and worried and forced into offering up Irène and Eve as substitutes for herself to demanding hostesses who had contributed large sums of money to the fund being gathered in her name.

Reactions to the two girls were as could easily have been predicted. The brusque Irène rebuffed both over-inquisitive reporters and gushing hostesses and, whenever possible, looked for the solitude to which, arm in arm, she could lead her mother.

Newspapermen noted Irène's undisguised yawns of boredom, her black hat and cotton stockings, and contrasted the appearances with Eve's gaiety, her orange-flowered bonnet and silk-covered legs. Irène was scientifically minded and therefore defied description. Eve was pretty and worth news, albeit invented. She had 'radium eyes' and 'preferred jazz to science' so the headlines ran. It was a situation ripe for creating rivalry between the two girls.

But the heat of the public gaze could not be deflected from Marie Curie. Missy had done her work too well. She had succeeded in turning radium into the rage of America. Donations had poured in to such an extent that, not only did she have sufficient funds for a gram of radium but there was likely to be upwards of 50,000 dollars to spare. *In toto* this, in 1921, represented a vast sum of money raised in one quick campaign for a foreign woman of whom America, a few weeks before, had scarcely heard.

May 19th was the day on which the *Kansas City Post* described Marie Curie, at one brilliant reception arranged on her behalf, as looking 'Shy, Weary and Disinterested'. And so she was, as that evening she dragged herself apathetically to her bedroom in Missy's New York apartment. But she was neither so weary nor so disinterested as to forget for one moment the central objective of the mission. Missy, herself physically exhausted by the pace she had set for her retinue, limped into Marie Curie's room carrying the formal document which would give Marie Curie possession of the radium next day. But it was to be no formality for Marie Curie. She had Missy sit and read its contents to her. She was dissatisfied with what she heard. Ever since the death of Pierre when there had been queries raised as to the legal ownership of the radium which she had extracted with the sweat of her own body, she had been obsessed with the rights of succession of her radium on her death. She had Missy redraft the document so that it contained the sentence that the radium was 'for free and un-trammelled use by her in experimentation and in pursuit of knowledge',[6] and so that immediately it would become the property of her laboratory. Although it was late at night Marie Curie insisted that a lawyer be found to process the deed of gift. Missy sought out two of her influential women helpers as witnesses; one of them was Mrs Coolidge, wife of the Vice-President. Marie Curie then had the document translated into French to make sure there was no ambiguity. She had, with Missy's help, exerted her will. But the disposal of the left-over dollars, now that the radium had been dealt with, was still a problem. Marie Curie had no doubts that since the money had been given in her name, it should be disposed of as she thought fit. But the women of Marie Curie's Radium Committee, tough ladies all and recruited by Missy for their competence as well as their wealth, thought differently. The clash of will was to take several years to resolve; but as always Marie Curie's will would emerge dominant.

At four o'clock next day Missy triumphantly led Marie Curie into the White House for the formal presentation ceremony of the mahogany covered, lead-lined 110-pound casket intended to house the gram of radium. Marie Curie, in her ten-year-old black lace dress, stood in yet another sea of faces which on this occasion included the President of the United States, ambassadors, diplomats and as many of the ladies of her committees as Missy had been able to find places for. Warren Harding handed over the casket, and Marie Curie listened to him praise, in what he believed to be an original analogy linking the spiritual and the physical world, her 'radioactive soul'. It was fast becoming the stock cliché of the tour.

The radium was in her hands and the purpose of the trip to the New World was now achieved. But the price she had to pay in return was not yet fully rendered. Before she left Washington Marie Curie had pressed the button starting the engines of the new Low Temperature Laboratory of the Bureau of Mines, gazed solemnly at the instruments of the Bureau of Standards, heard welcoming addresses in halls whose seats had for weeks been over-subscribed, eaten dinners at both the French Embassy and the Polish Legation, as well as lunched with a string of hostesses. She was appalled to discover that, at most of the official receptions, there were invariably as many butlers behind the chairs as guests filling them.

The whole ambiance, the proximity for too much of the time of too many people, was becoming more than she could bear. She was terrified by the crowds, feeling ill, and overcome with boredom at the futility, the purposelessness of ceremony after ceremony.

Within three days of Harding having handed over the mahogany casket, Missy had agreed to cable ahead to the universities and institutions waiting in the queue to entertain radium's Queen, the message, 'Physicians find Marie Curie in a very feeble condition . . . She insists upon trying to carry out the program arranged for her but it is imperative that all unnecessary effort on her part be avoided. Madame Curie has never been strong. The hardships of the war and a serious illness two years ago have left her with little reserve strength. But with care and the laboratory assistance which is now assured her she should be able to continue her important work . . .'[7]

The planned trip to the West Coast was cancelled altogether. Irène and Eve were sent ahead to collect the proxy degrees intended for their mother. Marie Curie meanwhile retired exhausted and unhappy to Missy's apartment in New York. Missy herself was on the verge of tubercular relapse; worse, she had just been told she was suffering from a tumour which might be malignant. She hid the fact from Marie Curie. In the end it was Missy who was first to drop out of what was left of the tour. But the bond between the two women, far from being weakened by the failure to achieve Missy's grand design of a triumphant sequence of appearances in the US, was strengthened, and the last real friendship of Marie Curie's later years prospered.

Missy was determined that her idol, in spite of the problems, should see and admire the country she herself believed to be the most favoured of nations, and the ideal example of democracy in action. She persuaded Marie Curie to take herself and her daughters under the guidance of Harriet Eager on a quiet trip to the Grand Canyon. But even this was doomed to suffer the same failings as the early weeks of the tour. By now the interest in Marie Curie's doings was too great to let her achieve even a passing amount of anonymity. The train compartments the family took to the West gave her some protection, but wherever she emerged to show her face the crowds gathered to stare. Again the tension mounted: again it was too great.

At Santa Fé where travellers to the Canyon had to transfer to a single public diesel car, Harriet found Marie Curie in the empty smoking room at the entrance to the compartment; her head was in her hands and she was trembling in a fashion that reminded Harriet of a hunted animal. It was one of the few times in Marie Curie's life when she was caught with the defences to her inner emotions bare. 'I cannot go in there,' she whispered to Harriet, 'I cannot go in and be stared at like a wild animal.'[8]

She soon took control of herself as the girl watched. And, when Harriet saw that the travellers in the public car had lifted their newspapers and had begun to eat their sandwiches, Marie Curie now once more with the immobile mask on her face, allowed herself to be ushered quietly and unobserved to an inconspicuous seat.

At last it all came to an end and she was back on board the *Olympic*, surrounded by photographers and facing Missy who had never once failed her in any of the promises that were in her power to keep. The 'disinterested' devotion of this small, lame American woman had touched Marie Curie in a way that no other woman's friendship had done. Tears ran down their cheeks as they embraced. Marie Curie, for once uninhibited by curious eyes watching her, was heard to say 'Let me look at your face once more, my dear, dear friend. I may never see you again.' But it was not death that Marie Curie feared at this point. By now she knew that she was suffering from cataracts in both eyes and was convinced that soon she would be blind.

Like so many of the worst fears she had about the fragility of her body, the worst was never to come to pass. Of the two women probably Missy had suffered more in the past few weeks. Marie Curie knew well the price Missy paid. From on board the *Olympic* she wrote a touching letter, not addressed 'Dear Madame' as in all her previous correspondence, but to 'my dear friend' – 'We are worrying very much about your health and I wonder if you have consented to undertake a serious cure. Please let us know as soon as possible. We all love you and want you to be strong and happy.'

But even though the touching human thoughts for her bene-factress were properly expressed, the purpose of the exercise she had just been through was never far out of Marie Curie's mind. In the same letter she took up the subject of the fifty thousand dollars still lying in a New York bank. 'Of course it would be delicate for me,' Marie Curie wrote, 'to discuss the decisions which you and the Committee could take to make life easier for me and my children. ... As far as the general attribution of the fund is concerned, I am sure that the givers who gave money in my cause would desire the money to be used in accordance with my opinion and I feel that I could give good advice.'9

From the financial point of view Marie Curie's visit to the US had been a staggering success. There was a strange paradox in that, although her frigidity and inability to understand American hospitality had confused both her hosts and the journalists who had trailed her on her grand tour, her cold charisma had won not only money, but also scientific materials and equipment on a scale which meant the difference between life and death for her labora-tory. Missy had raised from a publisher a useful 50,000 francs advance of royalties in Marie Curie's autobiography. Marie Curie herself, in visits to American factories and laboratories, had ex-tracted gifts not only of radium, but of mesothorium and other expensive radioactive elements from industrialists touched by her evident frailty, and by hints of poverty. She had also come away with promises of high precision galvanometers, X-ray tubes, electro-magnets, voltmeters and a great deal else she would need to equip a first class physics laboratory capable of competing in a highly skilled international field. She had not set out as a beggar but, respectable as her methods were, that is what she had become, and a most skilled one at that. She had in fact engineered one of the most important contributions to French physics she could possibly have made in those frugal times. The work, and it was work she would continue, would bear rich fruit.

The image of fragility which had so touched hard-hearted

Pittsburgh businessmen even had some effect on her perpetual critic Bertram Boltwood. He wrote to Rutherford,

You must have been amused at all the furor created by the visit of Madame Curie to this country . . . I was appointed for the American Chemical Society to serve on a committee with a number of others. I wrote to the Secretary and respectfully declined the honor (giving a few reasons) but I thought it best to withdraw my resignation later when I found that my action was likely to be misunderstood and to cause some hard feeling . . . I had her for a couple of hours at the Sloane Laboratory and I was quite pleasantly surprised to find that she was quite keen about scientific matters and in an unusually amiable mood, although she is in very poor physical condition and was on the verge of a breakdown all the time she was over here. She has learned a lot of English since we saw her in Brussels and gets along quite well in a conversation. She certainly made a good clean up over here and took back a gram of radium and quite a tidy number of thousands of dollars. But I felt sorry for the poor old girl, she was a distinctly pathetic figure. She was very modest and unassuming, and she seemed frightened at all the fuss the people made over her.[10]

Boltwood was not the only American scientist to be sceptical of her 'clean-up'. During her visit there had been several muffled cries of protest in the American press. One research worker had pointed out that the,

. . . valiant fight for the conquering of a most insidious disease [*cancer*], is transpiring right here in New York City without any knowledge or financial support of any of the great philanthropists. When it is known that the total cost of relieving the average case is only from fifty to one hundred dollars, think what great relief could be given suffering humanity for the cost of a single gram of radium estimated at about $100,000. And for the cost of ten grams of this precious element an institution could be established that would relieve thousands every year.[11]

Meantime, Missy was proudly reporting the full details of the financial success of the whole venture to Dr Anson Stokes, the Secretary of Yale University: 'Madame Curie returned to France with her gram of radium and $22,000 worth of mesothorium and other valuable ores, bringing her precious package up to the value of $162,000. In addition to this she had in cash from awards of scientific societies in this country $6,884.51. There is $52,000 left in the Equitable Trust Company. We are holding this, pending the completion of the fund suggested by a prominent American gentleman, who offered to collect $50,000 for equipment for Madame Curie's laboratory . . .'[12]

Marie Curie had swept the board. She had as many dollars as she needed initially to equip and run the Laboratoire Curie in the way she had in mind. But she was quite unaware that she had left behind an unpleasant taste in some American scientists' mouths.

The boat-train carrying her back to Paris drew into the Gare St Lazare on a warm summer evening. The platform, however, was surprisingly empty. In contrast to the screaming delight of the crowds that had turned out to catch a glimpse of her on every possible occasion in America, here on her home railway station platform she walked towards a reception committee of three: two newspaper reporters and Marcel Laporte, a young research worker from her laboratory.

The whole of Paris's attention was diverted by the Georges Carpentier–Jack Dempsey world heavyweight fight being fought that night. Throughout the city, loudspeakers at road intersections bellowed out round-by-round summaries. The pair of reporters (and there was no reason why they should realise that the gram of radium which Marie Curie was carrying would turn out to be one of the most influential pieces of metal in European scientific-political history) could think of only one question to ask her. 'What do you think,' one ventured, 'of the Carpentier–Dempsey match?' 'I regret,' she replied coldly, 'that I have no opinion on the subject,'[13] and left on the arm of Laporte to try to find a taxi to take the radium casket to the safety of the laboratory. But Laporte could find neither taxi nor bus; every able-bodied man had absented himself from the station's precincts to watch out for aeroplanes which were due to release rockets in celebration of Carpentier's victory. Laporte eventually volunteered to take the radium and its heavy lead case by foot to the laboratory so that the Patronne could make her way back to the Quai de Béthune. In the end he was forced to sit outside the gates of the Laboratoire Curie, his expensive cargo alongside him, until two in the morning when the concierge returned from his evening out.

The radium was safely home. Missy's dream, conceived only a few months earlier in the small office where Laporte deposited his load, had come true. Marie Curie saw to it that France rewarded Marie Mattingley Meloney with the *Légion d'Honneur*. None was more deserved.

Chapter 22

The Suspect

It was a comfort to be back in her own laboratory. She was with people she knew and liked and who liked her. In that intimate atmosphere of family friends and research workers she was not the cold commanding international figure, but still the 'Patronne' who took time to try to understand their personal problems and who was herself a woman with abilities and failings. The failings attracted admiration. One of her failings was to try to keep up the ridiculous charade that her eyesight was as keen as it had always been. During the next few difficult years those who knew the cause was cataract did what they knew she wanted and helped support the pretence. Irène, Eve, or one of the research students who shared the secret would guide her safely through the Paris traffic and up the steps of the laboratory, where, once safely inside, they would see that her equipment was at hand and help her with her secretarial work.

On her laboratory bench she had the dials of her measuring apparatus marked in large black numbers, used lenses for reading whenever she could do so without drawing attention to the fact, and wrote out her lecture notes in big letters. When her sight was at its worst she would walk unaided to her lecture room rostrum as the crowd of students sitting in front of it held a respectful silence, and quietly she would deliver what she had to say without either being able to focus on her audience or properly see the blackboard she was writing on.

She kept up the pretence for the rest of her life, but it took in nobody who had to work with her. One Swedish research student once proudly carried to her office a spectrum for her to admire. He particularly wanted her to inspect a 'doublet' – a pair of vertical lines on the photographic plate which was typical of the element he was working with. It was only when she began to talk about it as a 'singlet' – one line only – that he realised she was pathetically incapable of distinguishing what he had put in front of her.[1]

Neither she nor anybody else was sure whether rays from radium had affected her eyes, though in some research workers' minds the suspicion that the curative wonders of the element could be accompanied by frightful hazards was mounting. Others ignored the warning signs and used it indiscriminately. Worse still, any number of charlatans were already seeing ways of cashing in on radium's mystique without concern for its possible side-effects. During this period Marie Curie, as the acknowledged begetter of the radium industry, was receiving through the mails news, advertising leaflets and sometimes even propositions of co-operation, with free gifts of apparatus and quack medicines containing radium preparations. One of these was sold in the United States for several years in the nineteen twenties under the name of Radiothor. It was a liquid which had in it both radium and meso-thorium; over long periods some Americans each administered 1,000 bottles of the stuff to themselves. Doctors were still dealing with some of its suffering victims and their cancers twenty years later.

One French quack who went by the fortuitous name of Dr Alfred Curie marketed a radium beauty cream and linked the names of the Curies with his in his publicity hand-outs. But although this was a case in which Marie Curie could take legal action, the truth was that, as far as radium was concerned, she, like every other research worker, had access to no experiments which gave a true indication of the effects on the human body of either the ingestion of radium or exposure to its rays. Even in 1920, the year she first had suspicions of her cataracts, some perfectly respectable research workers were using radium to *cure* cataract and saying, 'the application of radium to the eye is harmless'.[2] Today cataract is recognised as one of the possible early signs of exposure to radiation.

That radium did have harmful effects on the body in some circumstances was obvious before 1920; Marie Curie had occasionally suppurating sores on her fingers to prove it and all the workers in her laboratory were aware of the fatiguing effects of

working in an atmosphere of radon. But the radioactive elements
appeared to act differently on different individuals. Her husband
had suffered terrible pains in his legs when she, working under
very similar conditions, had had only a few symptoms of lethargy.
Now, however, she too was beginning to have pains in her arms.
Nevertheless, she still avoided accusing radium. Pierre Curie had
been among the first to show that the cells of animal tissues were
killed by exposure to large doses of radium radiation. But workers
in Marie Curie's laboratory, although they avoided the direct
beam of rays by using metal screens, took no other protective
measures. Amongst her colleagues the attitude persisted that
radium burns on the fingers were medals won on the battlefield of
science, and the older hands carried the most distinguished scars.
She gave no special warnings to any of the young scientists who
came in to her laboratory to learn their trade in radioactivity. One
Englishman attracted to this Mecca of scientific discovery was
taught just one safety precaution: he was advised to change his
laboratory coat frequently![3]

Reports from London in the early nineteen twenties suddenly
set every radium laboratory worker worrying. These suggested
that several deaths in a London hospital had been caused by
radium. Ellen Gleditsch, a gentle and intelligent woman who as a
girl had first worked in the Rue Cuvier in 1907, was one of many
who turned to Marie Curie for advice at the news. In some alarm
she wrote from her laboratory in her native Norway telling the
Patronne, 'They are beginning to talk here about the dangers from
work with penetrating radiations and they have made me a
member of a committee of enquiry. I'm not enamoured by the
idea.'[4] She said that she had heard that, as a result of the English
publications, a French committee of enquiry had been set up, and
she wanted more information. 'I'm certain,' she said to Madame
Curie, 'that you are in touch with the committee in question.' But
the truth of the matter was that, although this was the winter of
1922, two years after the original scare, France had no such committee. All the advice Marie Curie could offer Ellen was the
references of a few inadequate papers on 'protective measures in
radiology'.

There were by now many thousands of radium workers throughout Europe and America who were beginning to suffer dreadfully. It was not until 1924 that a New York dentist began to have deep suspicions about the cause of the cancerous state of the jaws of several of his patients, most of them girls or young women. He was certain that the original diagnoses that had been given to his cases were wrong. One girl had been told that she was suffering from syphilitic osteomyelitis. Only when he realised that most of the people he had been dealing with worked at the same job, did the dentist, Theodore Blum, recognise the true cause of their suffering. They were almost all employed in watch-dial painting 'studios'. For several years they had been painting luminous figures on dials and other instruments. The method they used was to dip camel hair brushes in radium-based paint, lick the brush with their tongues to a fine point, then apply the paint. Blum had discovered 'radium jaw'; the name he gave the ailment left no doubt as to its cause.

Later Marie Curie was to have the extent of the suffering brought home in a letter from a New Jersey journalist who wrote to her,

In Orange, New Jersey, there are five women who are dying from radium necrosis. Twelve women have already died. These women were employed in a factory in the years 1917–20 where they painted luminous dials on watches and clocks. The paint contained radium and mesothorium and in order to apply it the women were instructed to put the paint brushes in their mouths and point them with their lips. . . . No disease showed for several years, but now, as I have said, twelve women have died and five are dying a most horrible and painful death . . : In your wonderful work, I wonder if you have discovered anything which might benefit these women?[5]

She had not; but the fear of cause and effect had now struck her deeply. She had already read reports that she herself was suffering from the effects of radium radiation during her American trip when the *Brooklyn Citizen* ran a headline, 'Mme Curie is made ill by radium'. But the statement had not come from her lips. All that she had allowed to be said to the press at the time of her illness in the US had been that she had low blood pressure and that she was anaemic. Yet it was by this time already suspected that the gamma rays from radioactive elements could destroy red blood corpuscles.

Other events which affected her closely were also causing her much troubled thoughts during these years. If worried friends came into her office with the dreaded word cancer on their lips, she still did not recommend radium treatment, but sent them the few yards across the laboratory garden to Dr Regaud. She herself was optimistic about radium's therapeutic qualities, but the nagging worry that it could be an enemy if misused increased at the same rate as the friends who were looking to her discovery for a magical cure multiplied. She was shocked one day to have to read in a casual letter from Missy that, obviously convinced by her own publicity, Missy had undergone radium treatment for the suspected malignant tumour shortly after Marie's visit to America, but had kept the news from Marie. 'I have not discussed it because they told me frankly it was an experiment,' said Missy.[6]

Marie was equally affected and equally helpless when Loïe Fuller revealed that she had breast-cancer. All the surgeons Loïe had consulted had said the only answer was to cut off the breast. There was one exception. One man had said that radium needles would give Loïe an 8 out of 10 chance of survival. What did Marie Curie recommend, Loïe asked?[7]

It was an agonising personal problem for which Marie Curie had no special knowledge to draw on to give the clear answer expected of her. Loïe, once the confident insouciante with the generous figure and dream-like control over her bodily movements, who had years before danced under the fairy lights in Marie Curie's back garden, was now a frightened middle-aged woman expecting unambiguous guidance from the great scientist. All Marie was able to do was to refer her to Regaud. Loïe, generous in spirit as always tremblingly scrawled a note of thanks to her 'Dear, dear friend. Once again in your debt.'[8]

The problem with radium was simple: it was a double-edged weapon. But the solution to the problem of the harm which might be done by radium and other metallic elements' radioactive rays was far from simple. Even today the physiological effects of radiation are by no means fully understood. In the 1920s it had been clear for almost twenty years that ionising radiations from these metals had a powerful effect on the cells of living tissue. The ability of gamma and other rays to kill cancer cells was why metals like radium were such a hopeful tool in what was, until then, a hopeless war against cancer. The tool was effective because of the powerful influence it has on the nucleus of the cell, and especially so when that nucleus and its surrounding cytoplasm are about to divide and reproduce. There was thus available an excellent method of killing off rapidly dividing cancer cells.

Unhappily the same radiations attack normal cells just as they do cancer cells. The hereditary material of cells, the nucleic acids can be damaged, in some cases, by minute doses of radiation and perfectly healthy cells turned into cancerous ones. Other damage is also possible; for example, irradiated cells are found to be more susceptible to virus infections. Also, as was known in the 1920s, certain radiation causes the number of white cells in the blood to fall. When radium enters the bloodstream a substantial fraction is retained in the bones. Once there, the radium irradiates both the cells on the bone surface, and also the bone marrow itself; it is here that the first stage in the production of the body's blood cells begins. Because of her necessarily primitive way of working Marie Curie must have taken radium into her body. There is no way of estimating how much she absorbed. Today the recommended Maximum Permissible Body Burden of radium-226 for laboratory workers who are continuously exposed to this kind of hazard is 0.1 micrograms.[9] Because of the quantities of radioactive material she handled, it would be surprising if Marie Curie's body was not carrying several times this amount.

In 1922, when hopes for the permanent effects of radiations on cancerous cells were so high, the realisation that there might be equally permanent effects on healthy cells had not yet dawned. However, in that year one event brought the dangers of work in radioactivity very close to Marie Curie's own experience. A woman she had known as a research worker for the Société de Radio-Chimie, who had been involved in using radium and mesothorium in medical preparations, quite suddenly became very ill. No one had any real explanation to offer when this once healthy and intelligent married woman, Madame Artaud, died within a few months. It was said that the cause was anaemia, but no post mortem had been carried out.

It was two years before another tragedy showed the cause with certainty In December 1924 forty-year-old Maurice Demenitroux was admitted to Tenon hospital. Demenitroux was a good-looking man, married with a small child, who had worked with radium for twenty years. His first contact with it had been in the Curie laboratory where he had gone in admiration, to be with the Curies to carry out his first chemical research. His most recent work had been in a factory at Creil where he had worked on an industrial process extracting thorium X.

The symptoms of lassitude and of aching limbs which so many radium workers, including Marie Curie, had felt at some time or other, in his case had suddenly become extreme. Demenitroux had discounted the feeling of fatigue for many weeks before he agreed to be admitted to the hospital. By this time he was a pale and exhausted figure. He died in the first week of the New Year of pernicious anaemia.

The news was sent to Marie Curie immediately by Albert Laborde, one of her scientific colleagues. Laborde had been to see his great friend Demenitroux just before he died. Demenitroux had no doubt as to what was responsible for his pitiable condition. Thorium emanation, Demenitroux had whispered to Laborde, was the killer.

But Laborde, sticking to laboratory tradition, did not blame the radioactive element. 'We are all to blame,' he told Marie Curie,[10] though he made it plain to her that he felt that the methods then being used to ventilate the laboratories of the Pavillon Curie to get rid of radioactive gases from the air, were somewhat inadequate.

But there was worse to come, and Marie Curie had already heard the rumours before she knew of Demenitroux's death. One of his workmates, Marcel Demalander, once her personal assistant, was in the same desperate and frightening state. Within a year of his symptoms first having showed themselves he too was dead. Myeloid leukaemia was diagnosed.

The issue could no longer be avoided. Marie Curie had a report drawn up investigating the deaths of the two chemists. When it was completed this report revealed just how little had been done to investigate the effects of the exposure of the human body to radio-activity during the previous twenty years. It still quoted as one of its authoritative sources the experiments Pierre Curie carried out on guinea pigs in 1904. It concluded that the protective screens of lead and wood used by Marie Curie in her laboratory as a protection against radioactive rays were satisfactory and that the only means of protecting workers from poisonous emanations was by good ventilation. It was a woefully inadequate document.

This report was the first from the Paris laboratory to make an open admission that the hazards of working with radium and other radioactive metals could, under certain circumstances, be great and terrible. And yet, in spite of it, Marie Curie still wanted to shift the burden of blame on to the research workers themselves. She wrote in her own hand at the bottom of the report, 'During the last months of their lives, because they felt so tired and did not want to travel, Demenitroux and Demalander lived at Courbevire in a house very close to the laboratory. They therefore did not take adequate fresh air. Neither of them left the house except ultimately when they had to get out of bed.'[11]

She clearly felt that the onus of self-preservation lay with the men themselves: that they should have cleared their lungs by getting out to the country for long healthy walks or for bicycle rides as she had done. She had never blamed inanimate objects for misfortunes in the past and she was now not willing to do so even under these extreme circumstances. Decisions on matters of self-interest were made by human beings, and not by the things they worked with.

Nevertheless, it was she who led a subscription for Demenitroux and Demalander and gave to the campaign both her name and a thousand francs. But the toll in human life was by no means at an end. During the years that followed there were dozens of painful and unpleasant deaths of workers in radium laboratories and factories in many parts of Europe. The death-roll in Paris was shorter than that in some German cities, though before long Irène was telling her mother about the condition of a brilliant young woman research chemist, Sonia Cotelle, who had been working for some time with polonium. She had had some serious stomach trouble and then her hair had begun to fall out. 'She is very upset, as you can understand,' said Irène. Madame Cotelle, a Warsaw-born girl and the close friend and collaborator of Marie Curie would eventually die from the radioactive exposure she had suffered.

Neither Irène nor her mother were at this stage willing, unambiguously, to link radioactive exposure with these deaths, long after others had reached this unmistakable conclusion. One of the reasons contributing to their stubbornness was that both these women were remarkably resistant to the side-effects of their work. They were careful and cautious workers, but they nevertheless had handled large quantities of the laboratory's most dangerous materials.

Irène was no longer a student. She had been working alongside her mother as a research chemist since the end of the war and was sharing some of the laboratory's teaching. Her students found her as enigmatic a figure as previous generations had found her mother. But the daughter's tough intellect was not covered by as fragile or as feminine a front as the mother. Irène never attempted to disguise her stubbornness any more than she tried to hide her attitude when she felt she could manage quite well without unwanted company. She too had characteristics which could get the best from long hours at the laboratory bench. The ease with which she let herself be drawn into casual conversation had not improved with the years, and many visitors to the laboratory were appalled by the girl's apparent brusqueness, just as they were piqued by the mother's apparent frigidity. It was not unknown for Irène in the middle of a conversation with a stranger to the laboratory to reach down and then up into a hidden pocket under her skirt to extract a large handkerchief and proceed to blow her nose loudly, leaving the visitor non-plussed and his attempted small-talk suspended in mid-flow.

But in spite of Irène's aggressive display of a lack of charm, no scientific visitor to the laboratory had any doubts about her considerable intellectual ability. Marie Curie recognised her daughter's superior qualities, and the scientific companionship Irène was now capable of giving, filled an enormous gap in Marie Curie's life. She adored the girl, loved having her around the laboratory, and missed her badly when she swept away on some masculine pursuit such as mountain climbing or skiing with the Alpine Club.

It was a powerfully emotive day for Marie Curie when in March of 1925 Irène busied herself about the apartment on the Quai de Béthune. She was collecting her papers and notes to take with her to a hall of the Sorbonne where she would present her doctoral thesis. It was more than twenty years since Marie had herself nervously dressed as simply as she could for that same occasion. Now here was her daughter, outwardly confident and calm, dressed as she herself had, in a plain black frock, her hair cut short, preparing to walk the short distance up the hill to the University.

Marie Curie had no intention of accompanying her daughter. She knew full well that, had she put in an appearance in the Sorbonne that day, she would have drawn the focus of attention to herself. Public opinion had by now swung so far in her favour that, had she been present, it would have been impossible for Irène's doctoral day not to be turned into a tribute to the saint-like mother. Marie stayed away and left all honours open to her daughter. Irène swept through the occasion with ease. A thousand people turned out to hear the off-spring of the legendary parents make her first public contribution to science. Not for the first time a member of the Curie family was listened to by a half-comprehending, fashionable crowd. In her flat, uncompromising tones, Irène discussed with competence her research on the alpha rays of polonium, was applauded as she marched from the theatre, and had a bright future predicted for her.

When the affair was over, the laboratory workers, as they did on many similar occasions, gathered in the small garden behind Marie Curie's office and sipped at beakers of champange to celebrate the laboratory's latest academic success. These were quiet protected family celebrations in this sheltered spot; they were among the few celebratory gatherings of which Marie Curie approved. Here she could share the success her daughter had properly earned. When she opened the fly-leaf of Irène's thesis she saw that this success was dedicated to her: it read, 'To Madame Curie by her daughter and pupil.'

Soon afterwards a young woman reporter appeared on the laboratory doorstep to interview Irène. The daughter faced the notebook and pencil with less inhibitions and fears than her mother ever had. The reporter suggested to Irène that perhaps the career she had chosen would be too punishing for a woman. But the mother's attitudes were by now too firmly imprinted on Irène. 'Not at all,' she replied, 'I believe that men and women's scientific aptitudes are exactly the same . . . A woman of science should renounce worldly obligations.' 'And family obligations?' she was asked. 'These are possible,' she answered, 'on condition that they are accepted as additional burdens . . . For my part I consider science to be the primordial interest of my life.'[12]

The reporter also asked about the dangers of radium. Irène swept the question aside. She admitted that she had already had a radium burn, but that it was not serious. Here in the laboratory there were less risks than in industry and 'we know better how to protect ourselves'. Like her mother she had had periodic blood tests but these had shown nothing abnormal. Still the cavalier attitude persisted that a modicum of suffering was a just price to pay for the privilege of working with radium and polonium.

So, a quarter of a century after she had discovered radium, Marie Curie was still not ready openly to admit to her own laboratory workers her worst worries about it. But in private, to a very few of her closest friends, she let slip her fears. One Polish girl who came to work in the new laboratory, Alicja Dorabialska, would on dark winter evenings often see Marie Curie safely from the laboratory to the Quai de Béthune. As they walked hand in hand down to the Seine, Marie would confess that she did not fully understand radium's effects on the human body; she suspected that radium was the real cause of her cataracts, and was the reason why she had to stumble so uncertainly through these streets.

During this period Marie Curie spent many days in total darkness, prostrate on her bed, her eyes bandaged as one cataract operation followed another. In the summer of 1923 the young Eve nursed her mother through the first of these operations and through the haemorrhages and the complications which followed. Four operations were to be performed in the years up to 1930. Eve spent most of her waking hours in the weeks after the surgery, sitting by her mother, reading to her, comforting and reassuring her. Eve had taken over the domestic role in the family. The fact that her mother was dependent on her for support, as Irène was depended on for scientific companionship, drew the family unit closer. It gave Marie Curie the emotional stability missing from so many of the later years of her life.

She emerged from the ordeal with a thick pair of pebble glasses. In spite of the trauma of the operations she was in remarkably good physical shape. As the 1930s approached, it was still not realised that the physiological effects of radioactivity were different for different individuals in apparently similar circumstances. Marie Curie's body had endured punishment which many others could not withstand.

In the late 1930s one physicist tried to buy radium-D from Belgian manufacturers. He was told they could no longer supply it. Reminded that they had previously provided some, the firm replied that their stock 'had been separated by Mme Curie, and that it was too dangerous a process for their men to undertake'.[14]

But the possibility that she might have to give up this work still haunted her. She wrote to Bronia,

Sometimes my courage fails me and I think I ought to stop working, live in the country and devote myself to gardening. But I am held by a thousand bonds, and I don't know when I shall be able to arrange things otherwise. Nor do I know whether, even by writing scientific books, I could live without the laboratory.[15]

Chapter 23

Dignifying Science

In her permanently pessimistic view of her own condition, she never assumed that she would see the end of the decade before her. In her teens it was suicide that would end it all; in her twenties T.B., and later any one of the enfeebling ailments of her kidneys or eyes or blood that would put paid to life. Yet here she was, in the middle of the sixth decade, vigorously alive. Her most creative years were long since past, and she was surprised to find that she was well enough to enjoy some of the fruits of this creativity.

The enjoyment of her daughters was her most passionate indulgence, and as her emotional dependence on them increased, so did her worries over their futures. In the dual role of father and mother she had brought them to premature adulthood and now saw that each had characteristics quite as strong in their way as her own. Eve's was a clear spirit, yet she extracted the usual confused maternal feelings of pride in the girl's obvious attractions, and fear in where these might lead her.

Marie watched with pleasure how, when she took Eve with her to a Geneva conference of brilliant, but elderly physicists, the bright eyes of the tousled haired Einstein twinkled happily in the company of the young girl: and how equally content and at ease the twenty-year-old was in his relaxed company.

Eve's prettiness and outgoing character meant that she was never short of attention, and it was attention from a fresh generation whose moods and morals Marie Curie neither shared nor understood. In particular the outward trappings of the new post-war woman were incomprehensible to Marie Curie. In the evenings when, after dinner, Eve would be dressing to go out, her mother would slip into the girl's bedroom, lie on a divan, and stare with resignation through her thick spectacles at her chick turning herself into a swan:

Oh, my poor darling! What *dreadful* heels! No you'll never make me believe that women are made to walk on stilts . . . And what sort of new style is this, to have the *back* of the dress cut out? Décolletage in front was bearable, just; but these miles and miles of naked back! First of all, it's indecent; secondly, it makes you run the risk of pleurisy; thirdly, it is ugly: the third argument ought to touch you if the others don't.[1]

Nor did Marie Curie know quite how to take the assortment of friends Eve brought back to her small apartment in the Quai de Béthune. They were of a type and character quite different from the repressed little group of scientists she had known in her formative years.

Although Eve spilled over with pride at the scientific achievements of the rest of her family, her reaction against the hard scientific environment of her childhood had not mellowed. She was becoming an accomplished pianist, and beginning to have thoughts about a career in music and, heretically, in journalism. Before the advent of Missy it was a profession of no standing whatever in the Curie household. But this was only one of Marie Curie's views of many aspects of life altered by contact with this American lady's qualities.

There was no hint of heresy in the well-defined sense of purpose in Irène's work. Marie Curie more easily understood the scientific passions and dedication of her elder daughter: there was no confusion here. Just as she had taken pleasure from the effects of Eve's charms on Einstein, so too she wanted the great physicist to appreciate the substantial though less obvious qualities of her other daughter. 'Send me,' wrote the eager mother to Irène from Geneva, 'a reprint of your article on the distribution of alpha rays (from the Journal of Physics) for Monsieur Einstein. If you send it straightaway it will certainly arrive in time.'

Irène, the gauche and plain blue-stocking who had so proudly assured the newspaper reporter that the primordial interest in her life was science, was showing no signs of weakening in this fixation. Of her own admission Irène had the masculine traits of her father, and she always felt that this was why she and her mother were so temperamentally attracted. As Irène grew older she was acting more and more in this husband-companion role. She would get up early, make some breakfast and take it on a plate to her mother's bedroom where they would talk peacefully, about the affairs of the laboratory that was the passion of both. The fashions of the flapper had left Irène untouched, and Marie Curie free in this daughter's case, from complications she did not fully understand.

It was all the more surprising therefore when one day in 1925, Irène appeared at breakfast and unconcernedly reported to her mother that she was engaged to be married. Irène had taken the step with that firm sense of decision learnt from her parents. It was a *fait accompli*, and there was nothing more for Madame Curie to do except learn the name of her future son-in-law.

He was, as everybody else surprised by this piece of information had to admit, both an extraordinary and undeniably attractive young man. His name was Frédéric Joliot.

He had come there, inspired since childhood he said, by the Madame Curie story. In the laboratory which he had rigged up for himself as a student, he had pinned up a photograph of Pierre and Marie as his inspirational icon. One day in 1925 he had arrived in front of Marie Curie's desk and stood nervously in his army officer's uniform; he was still doing military service in the anti-gas corps and now wanted a place in her laboratory. She had already learned that he was strongly recommended by Paul Langevin. Joliot soon found that Marie Curie wasted no words. 'Can you begin work tomorrow?' she asked. He explained that he had three weeks' service yet to complete. 'I will write to your colonel,' she said with an air of already having done so. By the next day he was her assistant.[2]

There were many sceptics to the news of the match between the Patronne's daughter and the Patronne's assistant. To many Irène was a block of ice, and Joliot's extrovert flame was unlikely to mix well with it. Joliot knew their views. Irène neither knew nor cared what others said. But to Marie Curie, Joliot's credentials, both as a physicist and as a life-partner for her daughter, were very acceptable. He was a committed political idealist with a strong impetuous character. He had been Paul Langevin's pupil and had even adopted some of his teacher's mannerisms: habits perhaps likely to endear him to rather than offend Marie Curie. He smoked too much and claimed he was no intellectual: neither was an unforgivable vice.

Yet Marie Curie did worry for the future of Irène. The girl's happiness now meant as much to her as did her own. She did not want to see her suffer as she had herself. Joliot was three years younger than Irène and he had an over-easy charm and a smooth understanding of other people's psychology such as her own husband had never had. Friends who sat at table with them saw how nervously Marie watched over the couple, nervously fidgeting her fingers.

Within a year the couple were married. Fred, as everybody called him, took his place as part of the family in the Quai de Béthune apartment. Familiarity bred tolerance. Fred avoided smoking his cigarettes in his mother-in-law's presence, and she in her turn learnt to live with his non-intellectual pursuits. His craze for Edith Piaf was, after all, no stranger than Irène's infatuation with the imperialist poems of Rudyard Kipling. Marie Curie also learnt to respect Joliot's left-wing political convictions – again strongly influenced by Langevin – and accepted that it was inevitable that her son-in-law should influence her daughter's apolitical inheritance, not necessarily for the worse.

Within weeks the apprehensions of the mother were rapidly evaporating as it became plain that, though human bonds might look weak, the bond provided by science between Irène and Fred had that same strength as the one that had bound herself with Pierre Curie.

One day Marie Curie looked at Frédéric Joliot in her laboratory and said to Jean Perrin who was standing alongside her, 'That boy there is a firework.' And so he was. He had an aesthetic and very acute sense of science. Irène, on the other hand, was no firebrand, but those who worked with her recognised that she was a better chemist than her husband. This combination of brilliance on the one hand, and obsessive skill on the other, was not a very different one from that which had produced radium and polonium.

The brilliance, however, was given freedom to shine in the laboratory created by Marie Curie. Joliot (or Joliot-Curie as he later called himself), unstintingly acknowledged the catalytic effect of his surroundings. He found in that laboratory 'a tradition, which, if we were faced with a phenomenon, could produce in us immediate reflexes, *radioactivists*' reflexes'.[3]

Fred made himself a part of the family tradition of creativity; Marie Curie had provided the means to let that creativity flower. During those years since the war her activities as a scientific beggar had provided 1.5 grams of radium in which had accumulated substantial quantities of radium D and polonium. The highly radioactive polonium source which Fred and Irène were soon to need and set out to prepare together in the laboratory, would be the most intense – and the most dangerous – in the world at that time. They had at their disposal the facilities of an excellent laboratory with materials and equipment, all of which had been provided by the single-minded entrepreneurial efforts of Marie Curie.

What was more, Marie Curie's personal fame and international reputation were sufficiently great for her to go on reaching into the pockets of the rich at a time when the French post-war economy was most unhealthy, and the franc was falling. She carried out her mendicant activities in a queenly fashion which was nothing short of breathtaking. To the President of one American chemical company she wrote pointing out that the free gift of radiothorium he had made to her was inadequate for her needs. Would it be possible, she asked bluntly, for him to supply more of the same without charge and to send it through some intermediary who would avoid customs complications?[4]

Indeed, she seemed so god-like to the President of the Eldorado Gold Mines in the North West Territories, that he wrote to the Bishop of Haileybury, Ontario, assuring the Bishop (who somehow found himself acting as intermediary in the Radium Institute's affairs) that it was a privilege for his mine to send 500 kg.

of pitchblende ore to Madame Curie as a free gift, and added, 'we truly appreciate her attitude in asking for it.'[5]

She was ploughing a very satisfactory furrow indeed for her laboratory. But there was one vital workhorse in this operation: Marie Meloney. The unlikely relationship between the pure scientist and the American journalist, as a result of the successful American tour, had developed into a continuing and deepening friendship. When Missy was not visiting Europe, she and Marie Curie would exchange letters by almost every boat.

Missy's daemonic drive to provide the laboratory with funds never flagged. She would steer rich widows, their cheque books and fat purses at the ready, on to European cruises and in the direction of the small office in the Rue Pierre Curie, where the Madame held her Tuesday and Friday 'receptions'. Modestly Marie Curie would accept what was offered; the very modesty and deference with which the interviews were carried out would engender thoughts of further generosity, and many a dollar passed to France by way of the legacies of women deeply affected by spiritual contact with 'the radium woman'.

But both Missy and Marie Curie had their feet firmly planted not in heaven but in reality. Missy let no chance slip which might benefit Marie personally. When Missy organised the 'Better Homes for America' campaign and the model American house was put on show at a Parisian commercial fair, she immediately saw the possibility of the prototype home and its labour-saving devices, as an ideal gift for Madame Curie to be used as her country home. The scheme only foundered when the manufacturers, as Missy told Marie Curie, decided 'to give this house to the person who is voted in Paris the greatest benefactor to mankind in this generation. I think that is merely a clever scheme to identify you in the public mind with the house they want to use. There is no doubt that the vote they suggest would award the house to you. I have emphatically forbidden their using your name in any way in connection with this thing.'[6]

But later, with that other new labour-saving device, the motor car, Missy achieved her more customary success. She had approached the best man she knew and reported the result to Marie:

'Mr Ford is giving himself the pleasure and the honor of increasing the efficiency of your work by presenting you with a motor car for use in France. Mrs Henry Moses said that she would be very glad to provide the chauffeur.'[7]

Just as Missy's handling of the American tour had taught the withdrawn scientist how to tolerate being a 'personality', so too Missy had taught her protégé a great deal about public relations. Now that Marie Curie saw that her middle years might be less physically restricted than her hypochondriacal prophecies had once led her to believe, she had taken to travelling and to using her new-found skills. During these years she visited Holland, Brazil, Denmark, Czechoslovakia, Spain and many other countries on both official and unofficial scientific missions. A frailer, but still upright figure, she would set off from one of the Paris stations, alone or with one of her daughters, carrying a small bag which she had neatly packed from the handwritten list she prepared for such occasions. When she reached her destination she made quite clear to her hosts what the rules were under which she was making the visit. When she visited Copenhagen, she reminded her host, a professor of physics, that she was not in the habit of making any public speeches other than the lectures which were the purpose of her visit, and that she would accept invitations to dinner only from him and from Niels Bohr; and also, 'I prefer not to have lunch since I need a few minutes' rest in the middle of each day.'[8] And to the Lord Provost of Glasgow, thanking him for his invitation to receive the freedom of his city, she replied, 'I desire, however, that the ceremony should take place in the morning at 11 o'clock (promptly) and that the lunch should be dispensed with. We have already arranged to visit Loch Lomond on that day.'[9]

She was happiest on these occasions when she was accompanied by one of her daughters. Eve or Irène would chivvy the hostess, lucky enough to have the famous personality under her roof for the night, into giving their mother the royal service to which she was by now accustomed. Eve was not beyond removing one unco-operative hostess from her bedroom, and putting her mother in, when it was clearly the best-heated room in the house.

When her daughters were not with her, Marie Curie complained bitterly if they failed to write to her, and was in danger of sinking into her old introspective habits. To Irène she wrote from a luxurious suite of rooms provided for her in Prague during one series of journeyings in 1925,

I am perplexed by the life I am leading and incapable of telling you anything intelligent. I ask myself what fundamental vice there is in human make-up that this form of agitation should, in a certain measure, be necessary. 'Dignifying science' Mrs Melony would say. And what is not deniable is the sincerity of all those people who do this kind of thing and the conviction with which they do it.[10]

But in spite of these bouts of self-examination, and although she was now sixty, she still found something to attract her in these long journeys. It is possible that she realised that the most important contribution she was likely now to make to science, lay in the benefits she could provide for others.

For several years now Marie Curie had been supporting the foundation of an Institute of Radium in Warsaw. Bronia had been the leading light in a campaign organised throughout Poland to try to bring Polish medicine abreast of other European countries in the applications of the science founded by the nation's most famous scientist. Compared with what Missy had organised in America fund-raising had been miniscule. But Bronia, wisely deciding to capitalise on the fame of her younger sister, had promoted the family name, flooded the country with commemorative stamps and publicity posters, and had so successfully organised a 'Buy a brick for the Marie Sklodowska-Curie Institute' campaign that the shell of a building had been built from the innumerable tiny donations collected in this poor country. But the years had passed without sufficient money to equip the Institute with the radium it needed.

Missy, who had provided the means for French science, was the obvious person to turn to now that Poland needed a little help. She had long been interested in the idea and Marie Curie had the chance to moot the subject again when Missy swept into Paris on one of her flying visits early in 1928. In order not to miss her friend, Marie Curie, whose eyes were being troublesome, walked through the Paris streets to the apartment where Missy was staying. Missy scolded her for having made such a demonstrably unnecessary journey when a cab could have taken either one of the two women to the other. But the Missy whom Marie Curie saw during that visit, though as competent and confident as ever in her business affairs, was herself not the same woman Marie Curie had first met. She too was ageing. Her husband had died of tuberculosis and she had good reason to worry about the same condition in herself. Her short bouts of depression were now more frequently observable by her friends; and Marie Curie in particular was touched by the changes she saw. The common situation of the ageing widows drew the pair closer. From here on Marie Curie treated the little American woman with the limp with a more gentle and apprehensive touch, afraid that Missy, the younger of the two, might not outlast her.

But as for the matter in hand and the money for the Polish radium, Missy's confidence in the possibilities were boundless. She was now working as the editor of the Sunday magazine of the *New York Herald Tribune* and was fitting her Parisian trip in to her normal routine of frenetic journalistic editorial administration. She had just left an interview with Mussolini in Italy before dropping in to Paris, but she left no doubt in Marie Curie's mind which part of the whole trip was most valuable. Said Missy, 'I no longer find many things in life worthwhile, but to serve in even this menial way in a great cause is a real compensation for me.'[11] It could well be that this sentence from this hardened journalist was an example of her public relations skill in operation, but it is also true that Marie Curie excited in Missy the same unswerving devotion that she did in so many people who walked in her shadow. Never at any time did Missy ask for any reward – except once. Coyly and surprisingly shamefaced, she reminded Marie Curie, who was signing hundreds of photographs to send to people in America who had contributed to her gram of radium, that she herself, Missy, might also like to have a signed picture.

Once back in the States Missy swung into her usual rapid action. Her confidence, however, suffered a surprising jolt when she discovered that the idea of a gift of radium for Poland in politically isolationist America was not as popular a cause as radium for Marie Curie. Besides which, there was now not so much ready money available. Missy had to admit to Marie Curie that the conditions were not ripe and that her own efforts had failed. She wrote, 'I have hopes of the money for the equipment for your laboratory, but the Polish radium seems still far off. I have not been well and America is in the throes of a terrible political upheaval.'¹²

The only sure way of raising the money was to let the personality cult function again. Marie Curie's personal appearance alone could ensure sufficient cash; the campaign would have to be linked with her name, and not too distinctly with that of Poland.

Marie readily agreed to come and Missy began to prepare the ground. Her foresight and thought for detail were, as usual, outstanding. If Marie Curie were to visit America within the next twelve months, Missy meant to ensure that the most politically influential persons in the nation were operating in the Madame's favour. As the great American election machine of 1928 neared the peak of its emotional momentum, Missy cabled to the Quai de Béthune:

'Herbert Hoover great humanitarian will be next President. He is one of your and Irène's supporters in this country. I hope you will feel free to cable him congratulations.'¹³

Marie Curie did not respond in the top-speed style which was Missy's trade mark. In the first place she never, as she put it, 'interfered' with politics as a matter of principle, and in the second, she could not for the life of her remember whether she had actually met the man. Missy, knowing what Presidential backing for a fund-raising campaign could do, gently insisted. She assured Marie Curie that the tubby gentleman, who had figured large in the sea of faces that had welcomed her to America was none other than Herbert Hoover. Once a mine labourer and subsequently an engineer, he was, repeated Missy, 'a scientist and a humanitarian – and not a politician'.¹⁴ His name, moreover, could be found on the letterhead of the Marie Curie Radium Fund of 1921. Marie Curie did as she was bidden, complete with white lie: 'Remembering the pleasure of having made your acquaintance during my visit to the United States in 1921,'[15] she wrote to the President-elect.

In return Hoover invited Madame Curie to stay at the White House. He was, as Missy said, 'Making an exception which is almost without precedent. Foreigners are not invited there as house-guests . . . because it might easily bring about diplomatic embarrassments.'[16] But Madame Curie had been converted by Missy into a citizen of the world.

However, it was Marie Curie herself who upset Missy's carefully drawn diplomatic plans by casually suggesting that she would like, as before, to be accompanied on the latest trip by a member of her family: her sister Bronia, Madame Dluska, for whom the radium was eventually intended. Missy reacted quickly. Telegrams and letters followed in profusion, all trying as tactfully as possible to head off Bronia's visit. Her undeniable Polish connections might have had a damaging effect on the financial success of the new campaign.

Marie Curie was offended. Warm and motherly Bronia had been promised a visit to the United States, and Marie intended to use every weapon in her armoury to see that she got it. When her first requests to Missy were politely deflected – unusually so, since Missy customarily and proudly never refused a Curie request – Marie brought out her emotional weapons. She wrote to Missy:

> I am almost always ill when I travel in the cold season and the return in November will be dangerous for me. I easily succumb to crisis of fever and of sore throat and bronchia from the middle of October until spring. It's because of this that my doctor has tried to dissuade me from making the journey, and my daughters insist that I either do not go, or I at least should be accompanied by somebody from my family. It would certainly be difficult for me to decide to leave against the formal advice of my doctors. My sister is a doctor and can take care of me.[17]

Under this sort of blackmail Missy had to relent and somehow attempt to rearrange American Presidential protocol. But by this time, it was not necessary. The sensible Bronia had withdrawn her possibly embarrassing presence from the scene and had elected to stay at home. Her sister would make the trip without her. And Marie, in spite of the cold season and her accumulating ailments, set off alone.

This time she was a much more seasoned campaigner. She had made her rules unambiguously clear to all concerned. 'Remember, dear friend,' she told Missy, 'that I must not have in my programme, autographs, portraits and shakehands.'[18] There were to be no interviews, reporters were to be kept at a distance, and she would attend no large dinners or receptions. Missy obliged with the appropriate arrangements and her guest not only survived the two weeks of laboratory visits, scientific conferences and small formal receptions, (including the visit to the White House, where Hoover handed over the money for the gram of radium given to her by the American people); she actually thrived on the experience of being treated like a queen. She even began to admit there was some sense of pleasure to be had from it all. She wrote to Irène,

> They had me come down by the service stairs to avoid sixty reporters who were waiting in front of the main entrance. Then we made a sensational trip from New York to Long Island. In front of us there was a policeman on a motorcycle, sounding blasts on a siren and scattering all the vehicles on our road with an energetic movement of one hand or the other; in this way we carried on like a fire-brigade off to a fire. It was all very amusing.[19]

It was also very profitable. The profits had been assured by Missy's preparations: the campaign fund was again over-subscribed. Yet three days after Marie Curie's joy-ride with motorcycle outriders through the streets of downtown New York, crowds of worried men were gathering on these same streets as panic selling on Wall Street began. Next day was Black Thursday, and cash was all that mattered as stock became worthless. She had scraped home by the skin of her teeth.

The worst financial depression of the century scarcely touched Marie Curie's consciousness. Her cash was well in hand; there was sufficient for the original purpose, as well as money for radium for her laboratory and for the Fondation Curie. To make even better use of what was available Missy had prudently arranged for one of America's most powerful and astute businessmen, Owen D. Young of the General Electric Corporation, to act as the Madame's adviser on both how best to invest her surplus funds, and how to negotiate for a gram of radium from manufacturers at a knock-down charitable price. In addition, Marie Curie could report back to Irène in the laboratory that she was returning to it with a handsome collection of free gifts of radioactive elements, equipment and promises of scholarship endowments for her young laboratory workers. 'You'll see,' she told Irène, 'that I haven't forgotten my laboratory – nor my children in the laboratory.'[20]

As ever, the appeal of the fragile, hush-voiced woman had moved the hearts of industrial giants for the benefit of French radiochemistry, and she returned to her country with money-bags full.

Chapter 24

A New Generation

Everything they had shown her on her trips to America was larger, taller or fatter than anything she had been used to in Europe: the houses, the people, the office blocks, the trees. Even the robins in the trees were bigger and their redbreasts twice as expansive as those at home. They had proudly shown her their vast oaks and tall aspens and asked her to admire the beauty of the leaves' fall colours; though here she had insisted there were just as pretty sights to be seen at home.

During these last few weeks professors of physics who were larger and more prosperous looking than their European counterparts, as well as equally large and prosperous businessmen, had taken the small old woman in the grey coat and black straw hat on their arm and walked her slowly through their laboratories, letting her stare through her thick glasses at their proud possessions. At Columbia University Professor Pegram had taken her at a stately pace past vast banks of high precision instruments and through huge experimental magnets which dwarfed her. It was the biggest university physics laboratory she had ever seen. At the General Electric Corporation's laboratories at Schenectady, this time on the arm of her financial 'protector', as she called Owen D. Young, she had been staggered by the size of his industrial enterprise: great ranges of cathode ray tubes of new design, photoelectric measuring devices by the hundred, apparently endless mass production lines, precious metals and rare gases in profusion – and whole teams of research workers.

She spoke little to them of what she saw, but the overall effect ran deep. She had had a vision of Modern Times and of the new temples of science. It impressed her more profoundly than anything else she had seen on that trip. Since her first visit to the

United States in 1921 the rate of change of science had been phenomenal.

She had never before seen anything to compare with this for the simple reason that, outside the United States, science on this scale did not exist. The American science she had first seen immediately after the Great War had had its base firmly fixed in her own nineteenth-century European heritage. But in the few years that followed, the beginnings of a revolution had taken place; nineteen million dollars, mainly from the Rockefeller fortunes, had been poured into the science departments of key American universities. In industry, the huge profits of mass production were being fed back to the laboratories whose discoveries had created the wealth, in the hope that they would produce more profitable pieces from their cornucopia.

What Marie Curie had seen presaged a new age of fundamental change in the scale of operation of technology throughout the world and its huge impact on society. But although she recognised a few of the portents, her basic view of science and its applications was not changed. In the first place, she was not prepared to accept much of what she had seen as science proper, but something regrettably derived from it. The commercial establishments which she had walked round until she was exhausted, she believed perverted the cause of pure science. A few weeks later, as she walked around the narrow corridors and simple wooden benches of her own establishment in the Rue Pierre Curie, she saw the limitations of both the resources and the scale of her operation, trying to compete in the front-line of modern physics. 'Pure science,' she said, 'needs the complete freedom of a university and of its unconcern for any applications. But how precarious and insufficient are the working conditions given to pure science.'[1]

She still believed that purity, the tradition which she and Pierre Curie had inherited, was still an achievable dream. It was a good dream: but it was no more than that. Marie Curie's generation was one which believed that there existed a definable phenomenon which could be described by the words 'pure science': a generation which saw no reason for doubting that an experiment could be performed for the benefit of science, could remain in isolation, and need have no connection with the fabric of life. Science could be hived off, its external influence restricted, and its joys savoured by the élite few capable of understanding it in the dream-world of a sixth-floor attic.

Marie Curie's 'laboratory children', the lucky few who would benefit from her extraordinary abilities to provide for them, were most of them still young and still influenced by the traditions which had produced the attic dream of scientific insularity and perfection. But within their lifetimes, in many cases before they would even reach middle-age, they would see changes in the world, some of them beautiful, some of them terrible. And these changes would be brought about by men and women whose training and traditions were those of pure science. In 1930 neither Marie Curie nor her 'children' would have dared or wanted to believe that these changes were possible.

Though she was far less active as a laboratory worker these days, she still exerted an enormously powerful influence on the young and intelligent international group she had gathered around her. As ever, newcomers were at first either intimidated or confused by the cold, withdrawn manner with which they were greeted. One twenty-year-old girl mistook the Patronne for the laboratory secretary when she first met her in the waiting-room, and as a result, both the young and the old woman were frozen with embarrassment. But as with all who stayed to experience the old woman's character, the girl found that, once a newcomer was accepted as belonging to the élite, there was revealed behind the cold front a passionately protective and sometimes possessive being.

Many who worked there did so in the hope of emulating the laboratory's founder, ignoring the warning she gave them that 'you can only discover radium once'. Some succeeded brilliantly in following her footsteps. The twenty-year-old girl was one: she was Marguerite Perey, who discovered the radioactive element francium.

Others were taking the laboratory work along some of the new paths of physics. One inventive Jewish scientist in particular, an alive and probing little man called Rosenblum, was carrying out revolutionary work on the spectrography of the alpha rays emitted by the powerful radioactive sources which Madame Curie's laboratory now possessed.

But with undisguised, and to some onlookers, annoying family pride, the apples of her eye were Irène and Fred. At the end of each academic year Marie would sit down and write out a report on the progress of the laboratory. As each year passed, the numbers of papers she herself published diminished as those of Irène and Fred increased. Reluctantly, but gracefully because they stayed in the family, she was handing over the chains of office.

Where she could, she used her skills as a radiochemist to share in some of the undoubted triumphs that were going on around her. Salomon Rosenblum's work on the spectra of alpha rays was in any case a hurried corporate laboratory effort since, in order to compete in the still fierce race to be first to publish, he needed to call on much skilled labour to prepare the strong radioactive sources needed to produce the alpha rays for his work. Marie Curie herself decided to set the rest of the laboratory an example by taking on the role of making a source of radioactinium which Rosenblum could carry with him to Bellevue to use in an experiment with the Academy of Science's new large electro-magnet. As agreed, Rosenblum went to collect his source from her at the Curie Laboratory at eight o'clock one morning. He set out in good time, knowing the Patronne's dislike of unpunctuality. When he arrived, and she handed him the result of her work, he learned that she had already been working there on his behalf since daybreak.

Later that day she heard how, when his experiment with her source succeeded beautifully, the little man had flung himself into a Russian dance round the magnet. Her style was quite different from this. Having listened to the news she immediately sat down at her bench quietly muttering, 'Now I'll make him a really beautiful source.' She was never happier than when she was totally immersed in the chemistry at which her obsessive skills were most useful: when she was cut off from the outside world. What went on at her laboratory bench was, as far as she was concerned, irrelevant to that world. The fine lines which Rosenblum had spotted in his alpha ray spectrum and which had sent him into such paroxysms had told both the young man and the old woman that the new quantum laws could be applied to give more information about the internal structure of the atom. That the work might have implications beyond this simple and beautiful contribution to science was none of their concern.

But although she wanted to keep her science pure she had no intention of opting out of the wider responsibilities which fame and seniority in the ranks of the pure scientists had thrust upon her. In spite of the fact that she was now an old woman she had an unquenchable knack of looking for, and finding work. Still she gave her course of lectures at the Sorbonne, still her sore hands trembled each time she entered the lecture hall, and still the students crowded to hear her, as they had thirty years before. As she used to in the old days, she would shine a light from a projector through her gold-leaf electroscope and project the image of the rising and falling leaves on to a screen as she charged them, then discharged them with a sample of her radium. Sometimes she would walk in front of the lamp and her face would be silhouetted as a vast image on the screen. One student noticed how, in contrast to the lined and emaciated white face looking out at the audience, the sharp profile on the screen was that of a girl.

When necessary in public affairs she could still take even tougher and more uncompromising attitudes than she had when she was in her prime. The woman still existed who had made Bertram Boltwood, Ernest Rutherford, financiers, engineers, architects and many others draw in a quick catch of breath when they knew they would have to do battle with her. One skirmish looked likely as she became increasingly annoyed by the disturbance to the precision instruments of the laboratory caused by heavy motor traffic in the Rue Pierre Curie. She decided that the best solution would be to rearrange the city's one-way street system. The Prefect of Police was poor opposition. Within a month of her putting pen to paper her suggested new system was in operation and Paris's traffic was moving as she had ordained it should.

Although she had accepted the fact that in the creative affairs of the laboratory she had to take a back seat, as always when she moved on to the international scene she was up-front and driving. For several years she played an active role in the League of Nations' International Committee on Intellectual Co-operation. One aspect of the Committee's work to which she applied herself with unexpected and almost perverse fervour was the question of scientific ownership and the rights of the scientist. Considering that it was she who had insisted on renouncing any form of patent rights from radium, it is particularly paradoxical that it was Madame Curie who during the early 1930s took a strong line in insisting that governments should look for some way of rewarding the creative scientist by instituting a form of royalty payment to individuals whose work had been freely applied to benefit society. 'Public opinion does not seem to recognise that Science and Scientists in contemporary society do not enjoy the support to which they have a right because of the services for which the world is indebted to them,'[2] she said. It was however a difficult argument to sustain, at the same time as insisting that science should be pure and free from the responsibilities which go along with the application of science.

It was nevertheless a sign of her changing attitudes. America had influenced those attitudes profoundly. But there was another strong influence from closer at home. Fred Joliot's views of politics were forceful and well known and moving further to the left; already he had shifted Irène's attitudes and moved her far away from her mother's noncommittal position.

During this period French science was indulging in much self-examination and concluding that many of its problems could only be solved by political means. Jean Perrin was one of the most active in this field and Marie Curie was frequently called on for help and moral support. Often the pair of elderly scientists could be seen walking the laboratory precincts, he still the jack-in-the-box, beard bobbing, felt hat pushed to the back of his balding, but still haloed head of hair: she, still dignified, wasting no energy on unnecessary movement, drifting after him. Her formidable presence was more than useful in the offices of Ministers responsible for funding French science; Ministers undoubtedly more susceptible to Marie Curie's undeviating methods of argument than to Perrin's volubility.

Perrin had his eye on the future and sent many of the documents intended to influence governmental policy to Marie Curie for annotation. Yet again she was being presented with more evidence of the interdependence of scientific and political decision. 'France,' said one document he sent her, 'is still no more than in the third rank of European scientific production.' There was no doubt which European country Perrin believed was most successfully harnessing its scientific research effort: Germany. 'We can avoid the decadence which menaces us,' Perrin wrote. 'But there is no time to lose. If the recruitment of our research workers slows down, is interrupted for only a few years, we shall fall into intellectual, then economic dependence on foreign countries.'[3]

These were the documents which eventually led to the formation of the C.N.R.S., the French National Centre for Scientific Research. It would form the nub of French science of the future and Frédéric Joliot would play a leading role in it.

Fred was by now a fully acceptable and accepted member of the family, having tacked on the name Curie to his own (though several observers of the family sensed that Marie Curie felt this was carrying intimacy perhaps too far). Like Irène and Eve, Fred in turn cared for the old lady during her sicknesses and saw to her needs. When her hands were too sore to write letters, he handled her correspondence for her. A granddaughter had arrived. Marie Curie could enjoy the sound of the small voice calling her 'Mé', even though on the surface she was as undemonstrative to the child as she had been to her own offspring. Once more her letters could span within the space of a few sentences, her greatest loves and obsessions: family, health and science:

I think of your little Hélène and I wish her really well. It's so moving to see this little being evolve; she watches you both with limitless confidence, and certainly believes that you can put yourselves between her and all suffering. One day she will realise that your powers aren't quite as great as that . . .

I hope that the dear little thing has a warm cover for her pram since it needs one.

I'm feeling better, but I still have a touch of fever which won't leave me.

The expression $x \cdot \dfrac{dP}{dx}$ is the tangent to the curve $P = $ function $\log_e x$, since

$$x \cdot \frac{dP}{dx} = \frac{dP}{d \cdot \log_e x}.$$

It would be nice if you could send me a note saying whether this is possible.

I embrace all three of you. M. Curie.[4]

A new family was something to which she could attach herself with pleasure. As when her own children were young she could have a vicarious share in the pleasure of a small child splashing at the water's edge at l'Arcouest, collecting crabs and bringing jamjars of shrimps for her to admire. Nor was she just a passive admirer of the new family scene. She still swam and boasted to her children of the three hundred yards she had managed with her respectable and stately breast stroke. She had her physical vanities. Even quite late in life she was capable of standing in front of a mirror and inviting her daughters to admire her slim figure.

And at 65, in spite of the anaemic and worn face, psychologically she was the woman of 40 years earlier. She had always considered herself a weak and permanently vulnerable invalid; yet she had vigorously survived both the ordeals of nature and the self-inflicted wounds from her radioactive work. This paradox could not last forever. Early in 1932 she was walking in her laboratory when she slipped and fell, throwing her right arm out to protect herself. She was picked up, shaken and in pain. The right wrist was broken.

Unlike the other illnesses in her past, this one was obvious and tangible. It was a simple fracture, which once set in plaster should have cleared itself up in a few weeks. Unlike the other illnesses, because it was so definable, she tried to dismiss it and shrug it off. But she could not. Its effects dragged on for weeks, then months. She was confined to bed for long periods. The wound appeared to trigger off other ailments. The radiation burns on her fingers were becoming more sore and the periods when she was free from irritation in her hands, less frequent. And the old maddening drumming in the head, which seemed to centre itself on her eyes and ears, and which she had first suffered during her cataract troubles, had returned again.

Rutherford heard about her fall. For 25 years now he had never managed to look at her face without being convinced that she was at death's door. So certain had he been ten years earlier that she could not be far from the end, that he had agreed to write her obituary for the *Manchester Guardian*. Now he immediately wrote off to tell her how sorry he was to hear of her accident.

Normally a letter from Rutherford would have drawn from her an immediate reply, but she was so shaken by the affair that it was five months before she felt sufficiently recovered to tell him, 'I felt so badly that I even did not have the courage to reply earlier. I am sure you will excuse me. . . . I still remember you saying to me in Brussels, that radioactivity is a splendid subject to work on. To more than one I have repeated this opinion of yours, which surely has not changed.'[5] It had not. As he told her in his bouncing style, things in his laboratory, and in hers – what with the work of Rosenblum and Fred and Irène – were bounding along in 'fine style'.

But although she had avoided writing to her scientific friends during this period, there was one correspondent for whom her letters became more, rather than less demanding. Missy could sense the urgency with which Marie Curie now sought reassurance that the true friendship which they had discovered for one another was as firm and unchanging as ever. Marie Curie, who was planning a rest in the mountains, wrote insistently to Missy, 'You could, I hope, stay with me at Chamonix several days . . . if unhappily you could not do what I ask, then I shall come back to see you in Paris. I count on your friendship that you will not go away so far without taking at least a day with me. Remember I want to see you before you go, and you have promised in your letters that you would join me. So don't change your mind, and keep your promise.'[6]

But again Marie Curie had a task waiting for her old work-horse of a friend. The Madame was, as ever, worried for the safety of her radium, but now the insistence was more pathetic and frightened. Would Missy see that it stayed where it belonged, in her laboratory after her death? And would Missy ensure that there were no loopholes in the legal arrangements allowing Irène to inherit her radium and the rights to continue using it in scientific research, along with the rights to funds provided by the American tour? Missy, though she herself was by this time suffering from peritonitis, was true to her promise.

But she only partly kept another promise. It was one forced on her by Marie Curie in a way that must have told her that her friend was no longer crying wolf when she spoke of approaching death. Marie Curie asked Missy to destroy the letters she had sent her over the years. 'They are part of me,' she said, 'and you know how reserved I am in my feelings.'[7] Her privacy was still her most precious personal possession. Missy burned some, but by no means all, of the letters.

In December of 1933 Marie Curie was taken ill again: this time from an internal illness. X-rays showed she had a large gall-stone in her bladder. She had either to submit to another operation or to a strict diet. She chose the diet, and within a few days was back at her laboratory bench. There were important experiments going on in her laboratory which she did not want to miss. Fred and Irène were doing exciting things.

Her daughter and son-in-law were now the French spearhead in the attack on the nucleus of the atom. Laboratories in Cambridge, Chicago, Göttingen, Rome and many other places were competing with one another, just as they had 35 years ago when radium first presented its challenge. But now this race to lay bare the inner workings of the atom was fiercer than ever. Several workers in the field had glimpsed not just the possibility of great discovery, but of phenomenal applications of this work. In the twenty years since Rutherford and Bohr had thrown up their pictures of the atom, physics had moved at a gallop. In 1919 Rutherford himself had shown that, when alpha particles are fired at nitrogen, it was possible to chip off protons from the nitrogen nucleus, much as a bullet might chip a piece off a stationary cannon-ball. What he had discovered was the first artificial disintegration of the atomic nucleus.

In the few years that followed a new physics had begun to overtake the old. Young men with fresh conceptions of matter and of quantum mechanics moved into the limelight of the international scene. At the Solvay Conference of October 1933, which Marie Curie insisted on attending in spite of her weakened condition, there were, in addition to the old established names of Bohr, Langevin and Rutherford, new names which would eventually become just as famous in the history of physics: Dirac, Fermi, de Broglie and Pauli.

Frédéric and Irène Joliot were also at that meeting and Marie Curie proudly listened to them presenting a paper on their most recent work on the use of alpha rays to bombard atomic nuclei. The paper had a mixed reception, which shook the confidence of the Curie family; the young couple left with the sadly correct feeling that most of the physicists present had not believed in the accuracy of the experimental results.

Already the Joliots had faced one disappointment. In 1931 they had carried out an experiment, noted its unusual result, but had not fully understood it. In the following year James Chadwick, working in Rutherford's laboratory in Cambridge, aimed alpha particles at the element beryllium in order to observe the particles given off after the collision, as the Joliots had done, and correctly interpreted the result – as the Joliots had not. Irène and Fred had missed discovering the neutron by a hairsbreadth.

It was an even more bitter worry for the French pair when Chadwick himself turned up at the Solvay Conference at which their work was having such a disappointing reception. It was a moment of triumph for young Chadwick, so soon after the work which already many physicists acknowledged was of Nobel Prize class, and he was delighted when one day at lunch, he found a place next to Madame Curie. As he sat down, she exchanged a few formal words of greeting with him, then turned away, ate her usual sparse meal, and said not a single word for the rest of the meal. The snubbed young man consoled himself with the fact that the elderly lady seemed to have little wish or energy to speak to anybody that day.

There were many scientists who, during these her autumn years, felt that Marie Curie was more sensitively and more demonstrably proud of her own family's achievements than might have been expected from a woman with such a distinguished past.

Bertram Boltwood, years before, had been bitterly hurt by the fierce possessiveness she felt for anything that belonged, or she felt ought to belong, to her laboratory. Some of these men perhaps forgot, or were too young to know of the anguish she had suffered, the intellectual and social rebuffs she had taken, so soon after her own rise to scientific eminence. This possessiveness was merely a symptom of her own insecurity: a need to have reassurance of her success. But she need not have worried about the eventual success of Fred and Irène.

One day in mid-January of 1934 the young pair carried out a critical experiment, as significant in its way to the history of physics, as had been Marie and Pierre Curie's identification of radium nearly forty years earlier. Fred and Irène's laboratory was in the basement of the Radium Institute. In it there were several tables, and over the tops of these were scattered an untidy assortment of new apparatus, hurriedly thrown together. It was late afternoon. Fred was in full spate. He was, in his commanding fashion, explaining to his friend Pierre Biquard, the details of the experiment he and his wife had carried out only a few hours earlier. In the middle of it all the laboratory door opened. From the gloom of the corridor came the white face and head of Marie Curie. Behind her was Paul Langevin. Fittingly, on hearing the news, she had collected Langevin on her way to the laboratory so that the figure who had played such an important part in her personal history, could be present.

Without wasting time or words, Joliot began his explanation afresh for the two elderly newcomers: 'I irradiate this target with alpha rays from my source: you can hear the Geiger counter crackling.' The four or five people standing between the tables listened, and the sound was clear. 'I remove the source: the crackling ought to stop ...' Joliot moved his source of alpha particles. But the faint noise did not stop. The Geiger counter crackled on for several minutes.[8] It was a simply performed, elegant experiment. And it was almost unbelievable.

Joliot's target was the nucleus of the aluminium atom. What he and Irène had done was to use alpha particles to chip a proton off the nucleus, much as Rutherford had done years before. But the difference here was that, when they stopped bombarding their sheet of aluminium with alpha particles, the substance produced was radioactive; it was giving off the recently discovered particles, positrons. The crucial realisation of the pair was that they had converted their original metal into a radioactive isotope of silicon: they had discovered *artificial radioactivity*. Thus what Frédéric Joliot was now so tensely claiming was that he and his wife had discovered the modern counterpart of the philosopher's stone: the art of being able to change one metal into another at will.

Marie Curie and Paul Langevin quietly asked a few questions and left, fully convinced, with as little fuss as they had arrived. Joliot was ever after well aware that he had successfully elucidated to a historic pair of physicists the correct conclusion from a historic physical experiment. It was a conclusion which won him and Irène the Nobel Prize for 1935: the third to go to the Curie family.

He and Irène were soon able to present to Marie Curie the first sample of an artificially radioactive isotope in a little glass tube, just as she and Pierre used to present little glass tubes of radium to the scientists they admired. As Fred gave his mother-in-law the container, he watched her face light up; then he looked down to the fingers holding it and saw how badly burnt by radium the hands were.[9]

It was plain to everybody that she was ill and that her condition was worsening. That winter Irène and Fred persuaded her to go with them to the mountains for a change of air. They were taking a holiday at Notre Dame-de-Bellecombe and Marie would be able to rest whilst they skied. Nevertheless, she was intent on doing a little skating alongside Irène and seven-year-old Hélène. Irène was worried that her mother, at her age and in her condition, still insisted on physically not merely exercising, but stretching her body. There was momentary alarm when Marie set off alone up the mountain one evening in order to see the sun set over Mont-Blanc. It was well after dark by the time she returned, tired, but proud, as ever, of her achievement, and not so sensitive to her daughter's fears as she might once have been.

Through the weeks that followed her spirits rose and fell, now trying even to plan yet another trip to America under the wing of the ever-ready and faithful Missy, now writing letters obsessively tying up the remaining ends to her life, in the same way as she had neatly tied up the loose pieces after each successful laboratory experiment. From Missy she yet again sought reassurance that her American gram of radium would without fail, 'after I am gone', fall to the possession of Irène 'who is the most qualified person to represent me in this matter, and to follow my views'. She wanted to be assured again and again that there was no legal gap through which her precious metal might slip to some laboratory or function other than the one she ordained.[10]

And to Irène herself she wrote telling her exactly where she could expect to find her instructions: 'I've written a provisional statement which will serve as a will on the subject of the gram of radium and I've put it with the American documents in a packet whose contents are indicated in red. You'll find it all in the drawer of the chest in the restroom, under the locked drawers, in the same place as the dossier which Fred gave back to me, and which has in it some useful letters.'[11]

She had thus made sure that what she considered essential to be seen, should be seen. She ensured that the rest would be lost forever. She removed from her files all, or almost all, the documents which were of a personal nature, and destroyed them. These files now contain nothing from Paul Langevin, and nothing that relates to that time of her middle years that gave her so much intense mental pain. She decided to leave only one set of documents which touched her inner-self for posterity: Pierre Curie's forty-year-old love letters to her, as a young woman. The rest she effaced; that was her privacy, and she intended to take it with her to the grave.

Typically, she had called Bronia to her now that she felt so vulnerable. They had gone off by car together to Cavalaire and to Marie's little flower-surrounded villa with the magnificent view. Instead of the warmth she was looking for, it had been damp and cold. Soon after they arrived she collapsed with a chill. As of old the sixty-six-year-old woman sobbed on the warm bosom of her elder sister.

Bronia guided her back to Paris and a brief recovery. There were some weeks of the Academic year left yet and Marie Curie managed to spend a few of the days in the laboratory.

During this time she set about purifying a radioactive element whose structure she wanted studied by X-ray crystallography. Like most of the work she had been good at, it was exacting, needed great chemical skill, and was dangerous because of the possibilities of exposure to radioactivity. She herself carried the little flask from the Radium Institute, along the Rue Pierre Curie to the Sorbonne X-ray crystallographic department.

A group of young experimental workers was gathered there, all of them keen to get on with the job in hand. But she told them, 'Wait for me a little while. I am going off to rest for a few days and then we can do the thing together.'[12]

She never returned to them. It was mid-May and had become a warm spring, but this change in the weather she had hoped for did not help. She was exhausted. This time the lassitude that had so often dragged her down refused to be appeased when she kept away from the laboratory. She took to bed and doctors diagnosed a recurrence of her old tubercular problem. They recommended a sanatorium and the mountains. Eve, who had acted as nurse and companion to the frequent invalid for so long, now set off with her mother and a nurse by train for Sancellemoz.

Eve ensured that her mother should maintain her privacy and anonymity to the last. The director of the sanatorium was instructed to provide a room which was as quiet as possible with a sunny terrace entirely isolated from the terraces of other patients. Eve told him that it was most important that her mother's presence

at the sanatorium should be kept secret ... At all costs Eve
wanted to avoid any news of this illness being known or com-
municated to the press.[13] Whilst at the sanatorium she was to be
known as 'Madame Pierre'.

The journey was a disaster. Marie Curie's temperature had
already risen and she was gripped by a fever which quickly
weakened her. Her obvious suffering distressed Eve. At Saint-
Gervaise Marie collapsed into the arms of her daughter and the
nurse and had to be rushed the rest of the way to the sanatorium.

Once there Eve, after a fresh X-ray of her mother's lungs, learnt
with some bitterness that the cause of the illness was not tuberculosis; a haematological examination showed both white and
red blood corpuscles to be falling. Pernicious anaemia was
diagnosed; the journey to the mountains had been unnecessary.
Her mother, her face bloodless, was now in a pitiful condition
and Eve had to leave the bedside and go into the corridor to cry
so that her mother should not see her.

The habit of recording every quantifiable event in her life that
had both made her fame and sustained her sanity in the past was
only now abandoned by Marie Curie because she was too weak to
continue. The only figures she could manage to read were those
on her thermometer, held in a hand too weak to write.

Chapter 25

Left in Peace

The last time she was able to hold the thermometer in her fingers was on July 3rd. Her temperature had dropped as she weakened. She was finding speech more exhausting, but she was able to mutter to Eve that she believed the fall in the thermometer was a clear sign of improvement due to the healthy mountain air.

She could do nothing now except lie and listen. There were messages of good wishes from the old and faithful friends to be read to her. One of these was a dim and distant cry from another century. It was a neatly written note from Jacques Curie, Pierre's brother, now himself a feeble old man. He was the only one left of that little band whom she had allowed to use her Christian name, and yet again he wrote it with all the affection he had always felt for her, scolding her like a naughty child.

My dear Marie ... It's my opinion that lately you haven't been caring for yourself sufficiently and that you are not eating properly, in particular in the evening, when your meal is generally a cup of tea. It's manifestly insufficient. It could be the result of this state of things which has made you so feeble and which has compromised your health. You've got an energetic soul; but that isn't enough; it ought to go along with a resistant body in good health. When you are back on your feet you must resolve to follow a more serious and less debilitating regime. Tenderest wishes and affection. J. Curie.[1]

It perhaps made her smile a little she had heard it all before so long ago. Jacques Curie was the last direct link with that dream world where only the great achievements now stayed in her memory. The dream had been created by his brother, Pierre: that tall, strange man with the cropped hair and salt and pepper beard. Pierre had begun to create the dream within a few minutes of their meeting, and no matter what happened to her subsequently, it had been the ideal for her to live by. 'He knew that he had a high mission to fulfil,' Marie Curie once said of him, 'and the mystic dream of his youth pushed him invincibly beyond the usual path of life into a way which he called anti-natural because it signified the renunciation of the pleasures of life. Nevertheless, he resolutely subordinated his thoughts and desires to this dream, adapting himself to it and identifying himself with it more and more completely. Believing only in the pacific might of science and of reason, he lived for the search of truth.'[2]

This man's passion for an ideal had made such a searing impression on her that even towards the end of her life she held up their discovery of radium as a lesson for others to learn by: 'There is no better example,' she said, 'to give us confidence in disinterested scientific research and to inspire both respect and admiration. This new source of light, the fruit of patient efforts of the scientist in the laboratory, will one day throw its rays on humanity and will give it consolation and alleviate its suffering. It will make its contribution to easing life in general and the peaceful progress towards physical, moral and intellectual well-being. Its field of activity spans all known horizons. Every civilised community has the pressing duty to watch over the domain of pure science where ideas and discoveries are made: to protect and encourage the workers in its cause and to give to them every facility. It is only at this price that a nation can grow and pursue a harmonious development towards a distant ideal.'[3]

They were brave words, but they were brave old words: glowing but dying embers which were the expression of impossible nineteenth-century idealism. It was now 1934 and a brave new world was beckoning. It would be an entirely different world from the old. In particular it would be one in which the inevitability that science would solve humanity's problems, as the positivists of her Polish girlhood had never doubted, as Pasteur had assured the world it would, and as Pierre Curie had made her dream it would, had become an open question. The long-lived group of men who, along with her, had swept physics into the twentieth century were many of them still very much alive. Within ten years they would see most of the nineteenth-century scientific ideals which they shared with her, turned, like the world, upside down and shaken.

In only four years' time, in the laboratory of Otto Hahn, a German who had been working on radioactivity almost as long as Marie Curie herself, it would be shown that when uranium is bombarded with neutrons, it is torn apart in a process that would become known as 'nuclear fission'. And then a few months after that, her own son-in-law, Joliot, would publish an article which would show conclusively that uranium bombarded in this way gives off more neutrons, capable of splitting more uranium nuclei. He would show that a chain reaction is possible and that the way was open to releasing the vast amounts of energy stored in the atom.

Joliot, still true to the tradition he had inherited from Marie Curie's laboratory, and to the ideals of 'disinterested' science, would continue to publish his findings until the outbreak of war, so that whoever chose to use them, including his country's enemies, could freely do so. It was work which would lead to the release of the first atomic weapon over the bare Alamagordo desert, and the second over a crowded city in Western Japan.

Marie Curie would not see the event which, more than any other, called into question the role of the disinterested scientist and his responsibility for his creation. Her life had spanned the scientific age of innocence. It was coming to an end with the end of that age.

Neither would Rutherford see this event. But as Marie Curie lay dying in her hospital bed, he was still bounding along on the crest of the wave which, he told everybody, he had made himself, still full of optimism both for himself and for the future of his work, and still telling Marie Curie that life was for living. His life spanned the same age of innocence. Thirty years earlier he had forecast the enormous potential power of atomic energy, jovially praying that it might never be released, and he was to go down in history as the great scientist who, less than five years before the experiment in Hahn's laboratory, had said that atomic power was 'moonshine'. He would die shortly after Marie Curie, from an injury he got falling from a tree in his Cambridge garden where he had been energetically lopping off dead branches.

André Debierne was another man who had kept a special place in her affections since those early days. Debierne, dog-like in his fidelity, was as distressed as he always had been to hear about the now hopeless state of health of his 'dear Madame and friend'. He had worked alongside her in her most back-breaking tasks, had been nursemaid to the children, had acted as her shaggy knight-defender during the worst periods of trial, and had been the one who saw her off at the station whenever she went abroad. 'André,' she used to delight to tell her friends, 'took us – or more correctly, accompanied us – to the station.'[4]

He would, in spite of the fact that he was no leader of men, succeed Marie Curie in the directorship of her laboratory, and spend his last years worrying about the effects of the atomic bomb. And having made next to nothing from his disinterested contributions to science, he would be forced into the humiliating position of nagging the authorities about the inadequate pension of an old man of 72.

Marie Curie's scientist daughter, who in her turn would succeed Debierne in the directorship of the laboratory, was from a generation whose experiences would be forcibly different from those of Rutherford, Debierne and her mother. It would be the generation caught up in the period of scientific involvement in politics and war: the generation which, for the first time, had to acknowledge that this mixture was inevitable and that 'disinterestedness' could not be offered as an excuse for avoiding responsibilities.

Irène accepted this involvement in a way her mother never could have done. Many of the great events of the day appear to have passed Marie Curie by completely, as her letters to Missy show. She was totally unimpressed by the wider repercussions of the collapse of Wall Street and the inevitable depression that would follow, excepting in so far as it affected her laboratory's finances.

The letters which Irène wrote to Missy over the years show the pattern of her developing political maturity. They start in the

1920s, like the letters of her mother to Missy: full of tittle-tattle, health, holidays, the weather and, at their most serious, the financing of the laboratory. But soon she was moved both by the social conditions she saw on her travels and by their political implications. Her letters were to become increasingly socially aware and politically passionate. By 1936 she would be telling Missy that she had committed herself to serving in Léon Blum's Popular Front government as Under-Secretary of State, the main reason for the decision being that, for the first time a woman would have served in a French government, so paving the way for others. It was, said Irène, 'a sacrifice for the feminist cause in France.'[5]

Soon she would be condemning Neville Chamberlain as 'a traitor to every ideal of justice', foreseeing blood on the streets of Paris, and, like her husband, seeing communism and Russia as the hopes for the future. Irène would bitterly criticise the countries which kept out of the war with Germany as those which kept their neutrality 'like an ideal: the beautiful ideal of taking no responsibility'.[6] Though she did not realise it Irène was fiercely criticising those very ideals her mother had lived by. Marie Curie had eschewed any responsibility for the application of her science, had not let herself be used as a figurehead for any feminist cause, and had kept politics far from her life.

Eve, by some paradox, would be attracted to the very profession which had so troubled her mother: journalism. She became a music critic, and writer. Her first full-length work, a biography of her mother, made her realise, in spite of the genuine intimacy of the child with the parent, how little her mother had actually revealed of herself during her lifetime. Eve confessed to Missy that in truth she knew very little about her mother's life.[7]

Eve's rejection of science which had so engrossed and rewarded every other member of her family, had its compensations. It meant that she escaped the tyranny of the laboratory atmosphere and its physiological effects. Irène, however, did not escape. Like her mother, throughout the period that she should have been at the peak of health as a young woman, Irène frequently took to her sickbed with the same symptoms of lassitude and at first inexplicable pains in the limbs. She too, doctors told her, was anaemic. The cause was obvious. From the age of sixteen when she rode with her mother in the radiological cars carrying X-ray machines to the trenches of the Great War, she had been putting her body within range of large doses of ionising radiations; and in the laboratory years that followed she had, with her own hands, prepared many dozens of highly dangerous radioactive sources. In March, 1956, she would die of leukaemia.

Fred would recognise the cause of his wife's death as being due to exposure to radiation, but in the laboratory tradition he had inherited from Marie Curie, he would refuse to admit that he himself had not taken enough protective care. To the end he insisted that the liver disease which killed him two years after his wife's death, was in no way connected with his work on radioactivity.

In their left-wing social and political views the young Fred and Irène were greatly influenced by one of France's most distinguished and revered physicists. He was also the man who had most tumultuously influenced that period of Marie Curie's life from which she had emerged with deep scars: Paul Langevin. Oddly, the political ideals which spurred him on to total involvement with the Communist Party touched Marie Curie not at all. Neither his career nor his private life had ever been other than one of passionate involvement. Bitterly for Marie Curie, he had returned to his wife after years of separation, and then in the 1930s still the dapper, if greyer, moustachioed charmer, had plunged into a deep relationship with a young girl who had been one of his pupils in his Sèvres physics classes, Eliane Montel. As the relationship matured he recommended that Marie Curie should take on the girl as a research worker in the Curie laboratory. He had a son by her.

But whether it was passion, compassion or conscience that had moved him, in 1923 Langevin had made a financial gesture of help to Marie Curie and her daughters by assigning to them a portion of a handsome sum of money he had earned. Ironically, it was the hard cash he had derived from a patent he had shared with Pierre Curie.

Langevin's passionate life had still some storm-tossed distance to ride. As a prominent scientist and left-wing sympathiser he would be an obvious target when the invasion of France began. In October of 1940 he would be taken from his house by two car loads of Gestapo agents and flung into a cell of the Santé Prison, his braces taken from his trousers, and his shoe-laces removed. Eventually he would be put under house arrest and succeed in getting himself smuggled to Switzerland.

The oldest of the friends of Marie Curie, Jean Perrin, would also have to flee the country that meant so much to him. He would die in exile in North America and his ashes, like those of Langevin, would later be ceremonially transferred to rest in the Panthéon and that part of Paris that gave them, and Marie Curie, their most creative years.

Marie Curie's life as a scientist had been one which had flourished because of her ability to observe, deduce and predict, as, in the classical tradition, a good scientist should. And lucky accidents had favoured her, as they do most good scientists, because her mind was well enough prepared to profit from the accidents.

But as she lay isolated, in the shaded room of the mountain sanatorium, her rational habits could have given her no more and no less skill than any other informed woman or man, in predicting the turmoil which the next dozen years would bring to the world. In particular she could have had no inkling of the dramatic future of the group of people with whom she had been most intimately connected. In July of 1934 any accurate prediction of what might happen either politically or scientifically during those years would have been laughed at as too extreme, too revolutionary and too far distant from what looked like the established continuity of political and scientific history.

But Marie Curie's work would influence those years, though that influence had already been delineated several decades before. Her fundamental idea that radioactivity is the consequence of something happening within the atom was a fountainhead in the history of atomic physics. It was a disarmingly simple, but devastatingly important hypothesis. This, combined with the discoveries of radium and polonium, meant that she, along with the Rutherfords, the Einsteins, the Plancks and the Bohrs set physics moving down the avalanche of power that would in the end be so difficult to control.

But it was not this fundamental discovery which gave Marie Curie popular acclaim. Fame came with the application of her work: the use of radium in cancer therapy. She was seen by a grateful public as the bestower of scientific benefits on humanity. And it was Missy, the clever little American journalist, who so dextrously organised this gratitude and turned it to Marie Curie's ends. Marie Curie was proud to acknowledge that she had discovered the element that was to hold out the hope of providing a cure for cancer, but she never claimed the medical applications as being her own. Missy nurtured the myth, built the international fame, and turned the image she had created into hard cash.

Marie Curie found that life, the way she had chosen to lead it, was hard. Some of the suffering she experienced along the way was self-imposed; taken on her own shoulders by her unwavering decision to stick by the ideals of her age: the ideals of 'disinterested' science. It was a conscious decision made in spite of obvious alternatives, and its reward was moral and mystical satisfaction.

And because of these attitudes she was to spend the greater part, and certainly the most important part of her later years, not as a scientist innovator, but looking for money to provide the means for other scientists. Whereas it is true to say that she did nothing whatever of importance scientifically after 1902, what she did in the years that followed was to make possible the work of the Joliots, Rosenblum and many others in a spate of discovery in the laboratory of her making: the thing she had created from a plan on paper and had turned into a living tradition. She had become the first in the long line of laboratory chiefs who, in order to see their laboratories survive and flourish, had to turn themselves into a new breed of fund-raisers. Unquestionably she was one of the most successful.

Her uniqueness during her creative years lay in the simple fact of her sex. Until the name Marie Curie reached the headlines of popular newspapers there had been no woman who had made a significant contribution to science. Yet she resisted every attempt to draw her into the feminist movement, which she saw as political involvement and with which, as a scientist, she so strongly believed her life should have no connection.

As a woman scientist she *was* liberated because she had created the conditions for her own liberation. She had tackled her profession's problems as an equal to all the rest involved; and all the rest happened to be men. She had expected no concessions and none had been made. She had survived because she had made men believe that they were not just dealing with an equal, but with an insensitive equal. They were wrong about her feelings, and she suffered; but always she hid the suffering behind the barrier of her privacy.

She also had an unparalleled physical toughness, disguised by a frail-looking body and a ready hypochondria. Throughout life she submitted herself unknowingly to dangers which other bodies could not, and did not resist. At 66 she was dying from the same cause that had brought her husband's body to a standstill, and that would ravage two more members of her family. The aplastic pernicious anaemia that was drawing away her life would be readily diagnosed by the sanatorium's director as being due to the long accumulation of radiations to which she had exposed herself.

As her conversation became more feeble and then at times incoherent, Eve Curie, sitting alongside the bed in the otherwise still and silent room, took a pencil and began to write down her mother's mutterings.

'I can't express myself properly.'

'My head's turning.'

She tried feebly to turn a spoon in a glass cup as though it were perhaps a glass rod in a beaker on her laboratory bench.

'Yoghurt: has it been made with radium or mesothorium?'

'You know, it was wrong to accept that vice-presidency . . . We must tell them . . .'

'I've drunk too much water. I've drunk too much water.'

'38°! I don't know if it's right: I'm trembling so . . .'

'I'd like to put myself straight. My head's turning.'

'What are you going to do to me . . .'

320

'I don't want it.'
'I want to be left in peace.'
They were her last words – her lifetime's cry.

When they came to bury her at Sceaux cemetery in the private little ceremony she asked for, just a few of the family and friends gathered round Pierre Curie's grave. She had asked that her body should be put above his in the simple family plot at the bottom of the graveyard's slope.

As the small group gathered round the grave a crowd of journalists, kept out by the locked iron gates, climbed noisily up the cemetery wall to get a better view. Fred Joliot walked over to ask them to give her, in burial at least, the privacy she had always yearned for. But they would not.

Notes

The following abbreviations are used;

B.N.   Curie Papers, Bibliothèque Nationale, Paris.

E.C.   Letters quoted in *Madame Curie* by Eve Curie (Heinemann, 1938). The original letters were destroyed during fighting in Warsaw in the Second World War.

L.C.   Curie Papers, Laboratoire Curie, Paris. Since this book was completed some papers from the Laboratoire Curie have been transferred to the Bibliothèque Nationale.

M.C.   *Pierre Curie* and *Autobiographical Notes* by Marie Curie (The Macmillan Company, New York, 1923). These were published in the United States in one volume. Subsequently Marie Curie refused the authorisation for publication of her *Autobiographical Notes* in any other country.

Chapter 1. Polish Childhood

1 Richter, W., *Bismarck* (Macdonald, London, 1962), p. 101.
2 Syrop, K., *Poland* (Robert Hale, London, 1968), p. 125.
3 Welna-Adrianek, M., *Annales Universitatis Mariae Curie-Sklodowska*, Lublin, *XII Sectio AA*, 1967, p. 16.
4 *M.C.*, p. 163.   5 *E.C.*, p. 40

Chapter 2. Positivist Girlhood

1 *E.C.*, p. 52.
2 Ziemecki, S. *Annales Universitatis Mariae Curie-Sklodowska*, Lublin, *XII Sectio AA*, 1967, p. 35.

3 Reddaway, W. F., *et al.* (editors), *The Cambridge History of Poland* (Cambridge University Press, 1950), p. 388.

Chapter 3.   Breaking the Bonds

1 *E.C.*, p. 61.	6 *E.C.*, p. 75.	11 *M.C.*, p. 168.
2 *E.C.*, p. 65.	7 *E.C.*, p. 80.	12 *E.C.*, p. 82.
3 *E.C.*, p. 68.	8 *E.C.*, p. 81.	13 *M.C.*, p. 167.
4 *E.C.*, p. 68.	9 *E.C.*, p. 81.	14 *E.C.*, p. 92.
5 *E.C.*, p. 74.	10 *E.C.*, p. 83.	15 *E.C.*, p. 78.

Chapter 4.   Paris

1 James, H., *Parisian Sketches* (Hart-Davis, London, 1958), p. 41.
2 However, to be fair on French scientists of the late nineteenth century an addendum should be made: they were by no means the last of their breed to defend Lamarck's fourth law: nor are his champions restricted to Frenchmen. His adherents could still be found in Soviet Russia in the nineteen-fifties and in England and other places in the nineteen-seventies.
3 Bertaut, J., *Paris* (L'Opinion et les Moeurs sous la troisième République), (Eyre and Spottiswoode, London, 1936), p. 107.

4 *M.C.*, p. 171.	6 *M.C.*, p. 71.	8 *M.C.*, p. 173.
5 *M.C.*, p. 171.	7 *E.C.*, p. 107.	9 *E.C.*, p. 119.

10 *E.C.*, p. 120.
11 Reuben, B. G., in 'Humane education for the Industrial Chemist', *New Scientist*, November 5th, 1970, p. 282.
12 Cuny, H., *Louis Pasteur* (Souvenir Press, London, 1963), p. 18.
13 *Ibid.*, p. 19.

Chapter 5.   Pierre

1 *B.N.*, M. Lamotte to Maria Sklodowska, July 10th, 1895.
2 *M.C.*, p. 173.
3 Cotton, E., *Horizons*, 59, 1956, p. 34.
4 *B.N.*, Pierre Curie to Maria Sklodowska, August 14th, 1894.

5 *M.C.*, p. 44.
6 *B.N.*, Pierre Curie to Maria Sklodowska, July 29th, 1897.
7 Curie, J. and P., *Compt. rend.*, *91*, 1880, p. 294.

Chapter 6. A Sense of Values

1 *B.N.*, Pierre Curie to Maria Sklodowska, August 10th, 1894.
2 *B.N.*, Pierre Curie to Maria Sklodowska, August 14th, 1894.
3 *B.N.*, Pierre Curie to Maria Sklodowska, September 7th, 1894.
4 *M.C.*, p. 31.   5 *M.C.*, p. 77.   6 *M.C.*, p. 67.
7 *B.N.*, Pierre Curie to Maria Sklodowska, September 17th, 1894.
8 *M.C.*, p. 70.   9 *B.N.*
10 *B.N.*, M. Lamotte to Maria Sklodowska, July 10th, 1895.
11 *E.C.*, p. 142.

Chapter 7. Discovery

1 Bertaut, J., *loc. cit.*, p. 177.   2 *Ibid.*, p. 179.
3 Curie, M., Bul. de la Sté. d'Encouragement à l'Industrie Nationale, 1898.
4 *E.C.*, p. 153.   5 *B.N.*, Pierre Curie to Marie Curie, July 29th, 1897.
6 Glasser, O., *Dr W. C. Röntgen* (Thomas, Springfield, Illinois, 1945).
7 Thompson, J. S. and H. G., *Silvanus Phillips Thompson, his Life and Letters* (Fisher Unwin, London, 1920), p. 185.
8 Eve, A. S., *Rutherford* (Cambridge University Press, 1939), p. 26.
9 Thompson, S. P., *Phil. Mag.*, *42* (5), 1896, p. 104.
10 Thompson, J. S., and H. G., *loc. cit.*, p. 186.
    See also Badash, L., *Am. J. Phys.*, *33*(2), February, 1965, p. 129, for an interesting account of radioactivity before the Curies.
11 Badash, L., *Isis*, *57*(2), *no. 188*, 1966, p. 267, gives a summary of these events.
12 Becquerel, H., *Compt. rend.*, *122*, 1896, p. 501.
13 *M.C.*, p. 94.   14 *M.C.*, p. 97 and p. 182.
15 Curie, M., *Compt. rend.*, *126*, 1898, p. 1101.
16 Schmidt, G. C., *Verhandl. Physik. Ges. Berlin*, *17*, 1898, p. 14.
17 *M.C.*, p. 97.

Chapter 8. Fruitful Years

1 *B.N.*
2 Weill, A., *Revue de l'alliance Française, 16,* 1943, p. 6.
3 Curie, P. and Curie, M. S., *Compt. rend., 127,* 1898, p. 175.
4 *B.N.,* Eugène Demarçay to Marie Curie, October 4th, 1902.
5 Demarçay, E., *Compt. rend., 127,* 1898, p. 1218.
6 Curie, P., Curie, Mme P. and Bémont, G., *Compt. rend., 127,* 1898, p. 1215.
7 Curie, E., *Madame Curie* (Heinemann, London, 1938).
8 Jaffé, G., *J. Chem. Ed., 29,* 1952; p. 238.
9 *L.C.,* S. Henson to Pierre Curie, August 4th, 1898.
10 *L.C.,* Undated draft letter, probably to Vienna Academy of Science.
11 *M.C.,* p. 186.
12 Ostwald, W., *Lebenslinien, eine Selbstbiographie,* (Klasing, Berlin, 1927), Vol. 3, p. 158.
13 Urbain, G., 'Discours sur les Eléments Chimiques et sur les Atomes, Hommage au Professeur Bohuslav Brauner,' *Rec. trav. chim., 44,* 1925, p. 285.
14 *M.C.,* p. 187.   15 *M.C.,* p. 186.
16 Cotton, E., *Les Curie* (Seghers, Paris, 1963), p. 142.   17 *M.C.,* p.104.

Chapter 9. Competition

1 Thomson, J. J., *Recollections and Reflections* (Bell, London, 1936), p. 413.
2 *B.N.,* Pierre Curie to Marie Curie, July 19th, 1897.
3 Jaffé, G., *loc. cit.*   4 *M.C.,* p. 109.
5 *B.N.,* Pierre Curie to Edouard Guillaume, December 30th, 1898.
6 Eve, A. S., *loc. cit.,* p. 80.   7 *E.C.,* p. 189.
8 Romer, A., *Radiochemistry and the Discovery of Isotopes* (Dover, New York, 1970), p. 11.
9 *M.C.,* p. 188.

Chapter 10. All the Rage

1 Eve, A. S., *loc. cit.*, p. 129.
2 Cotton, E., *Horizons, 59,* 1956, p. 36.
3 *B.N.,* Paul Appell to Pierre Curie, May 2nd, 1903.
4 Eve, A. S., *loc. cit.*, p. 261. 5 *Ibid.*, p. 109.
6 Curie, P., *Compt. rend., 130,* 1900, p. 73, and Curie P. and Curie, M. S., *Ibid.*, p. 647.
7 Rutherford, E., *Phil. Mag.,* 47[5], 1899, p. 109.
8 Soddy, F., *Interpretation of Radium* (Murray, London, 1920), p. 169.
9 Curie, M. S., *Revue Générale des Sciences,* 10, 1899, p. 41, and *Revue Scientifique (Revue Rose),* 4th series, *14,* 1900, p. 65.
10 Howorth, M., *Pioneer Research on the Atom* (New World Publications, London, 1958), p. 81.
11 Riley, J. F., *The Lancet,* November 21st, 1970, p. 1076.
12 *L.C.,* Marie Curie to Ernest Rutherford, September 12th, 1932.
13 Curie, P., and Curie, M. S., *Compt. rend., 134,* 1902, p. 85.
14 Rutherford, E., *Radioactivity* (Cambridge, 1905), p. 439.
15 Eve, A. S., *loc. cit.*, p. 91.
16 Royal Institution, London. Pierre Curie to James Dewar, June 26th, 1903.

Chapter 11. The Prize

1 *The Archives of the Royal Institution of Great Britain* (Scholar Press, Ilkley), Vol. 1, p. 132.
2 Curie, P., *Proc. Royal Institution, 17,* 1903, p. 389.
3 Becquerel, H., and Curie, P., *Compt. rend., 132,* 1901, p. 1289.
4 Marbo, C., *Souvenirs et Rencontres* (Grasset, Paris, 1968).
5 Rutherford, E., *Radioactivity* (Cambridge, 1905), p. 217.
6 Royal Institution, London, Pierre Curie to James Dewar, January 8th, 1903.
7 *B.N.,* Georges Sagnac to Pierre Curie, April 23rd, 1903.
8 *E.C.,* p. 220.
9 This estimate is based on the following assumptions;
   On several occasions in the early years of the twentieth century Marie

Curie produced quantities of purified radium salts weighing as much as 0.1 gm. To produce these amounts would have involved her in many weeks of repeated purification processes. Her notebooks suggest that it would not be unreasonable to estimate that she worked at least a 50-hour week. For the purposes of a calculation it might be assumed that she kept the radium salt in aqueous solution in a stoppered litre flask. It is difficult to guess a distance separating her body from the radium: sometimes she would hold the flask, sometimes she would be at the far end of the shed well separated from it: two metres would seem to be a not unreasonable figure in order to arrive at a quantitative result.

Using these assumptions, for which I am entirely responsible, Dr J. Vennart of the Medical Research Council Radiobiology Unit, Harwell, has most kindly calculated for me that, with a fully stoppered flask, the dose in a working week would be 1 *rem*. (1 *rem*. is the unit of Dose Equivalent of ionising radiation which gives the same biological effect as an absorbed dose of 1 *rad* of X-rays or gamma-rays.)

If the flask were leaking radon to the air the dose would be correspondingly less, but the operator would be exposed to the risk of breathing radon. In a room of 3m cube with a typical ventilation rate of 2 changes per hour Dr Vennart calculates that, if all the radon escapes from the flask, the equilibrium concentration of radon in the room would be approximately 10^{-5} Ci/cm^3. The Maximum Permissible Concentration of radon for workplaces recommended by the International Commission on Radiological Protection is 3×10^{-8} Ci/cm^3. (1 Ci, or 1 Curie, is the quantity of radioactive isotope which decays at the rate of 3.7×10^{10} disintegrations per second.)

10 *E.C.*, p. 199.
11 Schück, *et al.*, *Nobel, the Man and his Prizes* (Elsevier, Amsterdam, 1962), p. 34.
12 *Nobel Lectures, Physics, 1901–21* (Elsevier, Amsterdam, 1967).
13 *M.C.*, p. 190.   15 *E.C.*, p. 221.
14 *Echo de Paris*, December 30th, 1903.   16. *M.C.*, p. 126.

Chapter 12. The Spirit of a Whipped Dog

1 *B.N.*, E. Mascart to Pierre Curie, May 22nd, 1905.
2 *B.N.*, E. Mascart to Pierre Curie, May 25th, 1905.

3 Cotton, E., *Les Curie* (Seghers, Paris, 1963), p. 47.
4 Bertaut, J., *loc. cit.*, p. 198.   5 *E.C.*, p. 238.
6 Curie, P., Nobel Lecture, June 6th, 1905.
7 *Danrit* (Èmile Driant), *La Guerre de Demain* (Fayard, Paris, 1890).
8 *B.N.*, Captain Ferrié to Pierre Curie, January 29th, 1900.
9 *B.N.*, Pierre Curie to an un-named woman, February 6th, 1906.
10 *L.C.*, Austro-Hungarian Ambassador in Paris to Pierre Curie, March 3rd, 1905.
11 Bicquard, P., *Frédéric Joliot-Curie* (Souvenir Press, London, 1965, p. 182).
12 Bouchard, C., Balthazard, V. and Curie, P., *Compt. rend.*, *138*, 1904, p. 1385.
13 Lot, F., *Jean Perrin* (Seghers, Paris, 1963), p. 101.
14 *B.N.*, Pierre Curie to Maria Sklodowska, September 17th, 1894.
15 *M.C.*, p. 177.

Chapter 13.   Death in the Family

1 *Le Journal*, April 20th, 1906.
2 *E.C.*, p. 261. This extract is from the English translation of the Heine-mann edition of Eve Curie's biography.
3 Lapique-Perrin, A., *Heures Claires, 130*, 1956, p. 6.
4 *B.N.*, Georges Gouy to Marie Curie, May 8th, 1906.
5 *Le Journal*, July 12th, 1906.
6 *B.N.*, Georges Gouy to Marie Curie, May 8th, 1906.
7 Schulhof, C., *Cinquantenaire du premier cours de Marie Curie à la Sorbonne* (Coueslant, Cahors).
8 *Le Journal*, November 6th, 1906.

Chapter 14.   The Widow

1 Personal communication, Mrs M. W. Davis, November, 1971.
2 Joliot-Curie, I., *Europe, 108*, 1954, p. 109.
3 *Ibid.*, p. 94.   4 *E.C.*, p. 284.
5 Carnegie Corporation of New York, Andrew Carnegie to L. Liard, November 9th, 1906.
6 Rutherford, E., *Nature, 74*, 1906, p. 634.
7 Curie, M., Nobel Lecture, December 11th, 1911.

8   Curie, M., *Compt. rend., 145,* 1907, p. 422.
9   Curie, M., *Phys. Z., 4,* 1902–03, p. 234. See also Romer, A., *Radiochemistry and the Discovery of Isotopes* (Dover, New York, 1970), for an excellent summary.
10 Marckwald, W., *Phys. Z., 7,* 1906, p. 369.
11 Curie, M., and Debierne, A., *Compt. rend., 151,* 1910, p. 523.
12 Personal communication, E. N. da C. Andrade, August, 1970.
13 Cambridge University Library, Bertram Boltwood to Ernest Rutherford, October 11th, 1908.
14 Cambridge University Library, Henry Bumstead to Ernest Rutherford.
15 Yale University Library, Ernest Rutherford to Bertram Boltwood, December 14th, 1910.
16 Eve, A. S., *loc. cit.,* p. 190.
17 Cambridge University Library, undated note.
18 *L.C.,* Irène Curie to Marie Curie, August 6th, 1910.
19 *E.C.,* p. 277.

Chapter 15.   Academic Miscalculation

1   *A History of the Cavendish Laboratory, 1871–1910,* (Longmans Green, London, 1910)
2   Marbo, C., *loc. cit.,* p. 105.   3   *Ibid.,* p. 106.
4   Daudet, L., *Souvenirs* (Nouvelle Librairie Nationale, Paris, 1926).
5   *La Patrie,* July 4th and 5th, 1905.   6   *M.C.,* p. 202.
7   *Le Figaro,* November 24th, 1910.   8   *Le Temps,* December 2nd, 1910.
9   *Le Temps,* December 31st, 1910.
10 Curie, E., *Madame Curie* (Heinemann, London, 1938), Terrat-Branly, J., *Mon Père, Edouard Branly* (Corréa, Paris, 1946).
11 de Cassagnac, P., in *L'Autorité.* Quoted by Terrat-Branly, J., *loc. cit.,* p. 211.
12 *B.N.,* Edouard Guillaume to Marie Curie, January 26th, 1911.
13 *B.N.,* Georges Gouy to Marie Curie, January 24th, 1911.
14 Yale University Library, Ernest Rutherford to Bertram Boltwood, February 1st, 1911.

Chapter 16. The Breath of Scandal

1 Rutherford, E., and Soddy, F., *Phil. Mag.,* 5, 1903, p. 576.
2 Andrade, E. N. da C., *Rutherford and the Nature of the Atom* (Heinemann, London, 1964), p. 111.
3 Marbo, C., *loc. cit.,* p. 109.
4 Cambridge University Library, Ernest Rutherford to Stefan Meyer, November 8th, 1911.
5 Cambridge University Library, Marie Curie to Ernest Rutherford. Undated letter.
6 Cambridge University Library, Ernest Rutherford to Stefan Meyer, November 8th, 1911.
7 Yale University Library, Ernest Rutherford to Bertram Boltwood, November 20th, 1911.

Chapter 17. The Terrible Year

1 *Le Temps,* November 5th, 1911.
2 *L'Intransigeant,* November 6th, 1911.
3 *Le Temps,* November 8th, 1911. Hauser's letter is dated November 5th.
4 *Le Journal,* November 5th, 1911.
5 *L'Action Française,* November 17th, 1911.
6 *L'Oeuvre,* 47, 1911, p. 11.
7 Marbo, C., *loc. cit.,* p. 111.   8 *Ibid.,* p. 117.
9 Baldrick, R., *The Duel* (Chapman and Hall, London, 1965), p. 188.
10 *L'Oeuvre,* 48, 1911, p. 4.   11 *E.C.,* p. 292.
12 Marbo, C., *loc. cit.,* p. 112.
13 Schück, H., *et al., Nobel, the Man and his Prizes* (Elsevier, Amsterdam, 1962), p. 371.
14 *B.N.,* Ernest Rutherford to Marie Curie, November 8th, 1911.
15 Cambridge University Library, Bertram Boltwood to Ernest Rutherford, December 5th, 1911.
16 Curie, M., Nobel Lecture, December 11th, 1911.

Chapter 18.   Recovery

1   Cambridge University Library, Jean Perrin to Ernest Rutherford. Undated letter.
2   *B.N.*   3   *L.C.*, Irène Curie to Marie Curie, July 19th, 1912.
4   *L.C.*, Irène Curie to Marie Curie, July 2nd, 1912.
5   Sharp, E., *Hertha Ayrton* (Arnold, London, 1926).
6   *Ibid.*, p. 161.   7   *Ibid.*, p. 246.
8   *Westminster Gazette*, March 14th, 1909.
9   *B.N.*, Hertha Ayrton to Bronia Dluska, January 7th, 1912.
10 Cambridge University Library, Marie Curie to Ernest Rutherford, October 17th, 1912. The letter is torn and a few words are missing.
11 Yale University Library, Ernest Rutherford to Bertram Boltwood, April 22nd, 1912.
12 *L.C.*, Marie Curie to Irène Curie, September 15th, 1913.
13 *L.C.*, Marie Curie to Irène Curie, September 10th, 1913.
14 Eve, A. S., *Rutherford* (Cambridge, 1939), p. 223.
15 *B.N.*, Ernest Rutherford to Marie Curie, October 4th, 1912.
16 Lacassagne, A., *Bulletin du Cancer*, 1967, *54*, p. 257.

Chapter 19.   War

1   *L.C.*, Marie Curie to Irène Curie, August 1st, 1914.
2   *L.C.*, Irène Curie to Marie Curie, August 2nd, 1914.
3   *L.C.*, Irène Curie to Marie Curie, August 3rd, 1914.
4   *L.C.*, Marie Curie to Irène Curie, September 6th, 1914.
5   *M.C.*, p. 206.
6   *B.N.*, Henriette Perrin to Marie Curie, September 23rd, 1914.
7   *B.N.*, The document is dated August 12th, 1914.
8   Charlier, A., *Arch. Med. Pharm. milit.*, 67, 1917, p. 643.
9   *B.N.* From the case-book of Radiological car 'E'.
10 Churchill, W. S., *The World Crisis* (Odhams, London, 1938), Vol. II, p. 769.
11 *B.N.*, undated document. Quoted in Marie Curie's *Autobiographical Notes*, p. 216.
12 Joliot-Curie, I., *Europe, 108*, 1954, p. 103.

13 Curie, M., *La Radiologie et la Guerre* (Alcan, Paris, 1921), p. 107.
14 Letter in possession of M. André Langevin. Jean Perrin and Marie Curie to Paul Langevin, January 22nd, 1915.
15 Rutherford, E., *Proc. Roy. Soc.*, A., *93*, 1917, p. xii.
16 *B.N.*, Maurice Curie to Marie Curie, February 23rd, 1915.
17 *B.N.*, Maurice Curie to Marie Curie, June 11th, 1915.
18 *B.N.*, Dr Theveuin to Marie Curie, August 5th, 1916.
19 *B.N.* 20 Laborde, Mme A., *Paris Medical, 24*, 1916, p. 555.
21 Professor John Joly in Dublin was the first man to use radon in this fashion. He drew off radon into glass capillaries, sealed them electrically, and inserted them into platinum tubes for medical use.
22 Eve, A. S., *loc. cit.*, p. 256.
23 *L.C.*, Irène Curie to Marie Curie, June 1st, 1918.
24 *L.C.*, Irène Curie to Marie Curie, August 12th, 1918.

Chapter 20. Missy

1   *L.C.*, Marie Curie to Irène Curie, September 3rd, 1919.
2   *B.N.*, J. L. Breton to Marie Curie, November 24th, 1919.
3   *L.C.*, Mrs S. E. Swoper to Marie Curie, October 22nd, 1929.
4   *L.C.* Mme L. Razet was Marie Curie's secretary for many years.
5   *M.C.*, p. 16.   6 Columbia University Library.   7 *M.C.*, p. 18.
8   Personal communication, Mrs M. W. Davis, October, 1972.
9   *L.C.*, Marie Meloney to Marie Curie, September 16th, 1920.
10 Stephane Lauzanne, editor-in-chief of *Le Matin*. *M.C.*, p. 22.
11 *L.C.*, Marie Meloney to Marie Curie, September 16th, 1920.
12 Columbia University Library, Pierre Roché to Marie Meloney, January 8th, 1921.
13 *L.C.*, Marie Meloney to Marie Curie, December 28th, 1920.
14 *L.C.*, Marie Meloney to Marie Curie, September 16th, 1920.
15 *L.C.*, Marie Meloney to Marie Curie, February 17th, 1921.
16 *L.C.*, Marie Meloney to Marie Curie, March 19th, 1921.
17 *L.C.*, Marie Meloney to Marie Curie, March 5th, 1921.
18 *L.C.*, Marie Curie to Marie Meloney, March 9th, 1921.
19 *L.C.*, Marie Meloney to Marie Curie, March 23rd, 1921.
20 *L.C.*, Marie Curie to Marie Meloney, March 4th, 1921.
21 Columbia University Library, Charles W. Eliot to Marie Meloney, December 18th, 1920.

22 *Ibid.*   23   L.C., Marie Meloney to Marie Curie, March 19th, 1921.
24   *San Francisco Examiner*, November 26th, 1911.

Chapter 21. America

1   B.N., Marie Curie to Henriette Perrin, May 10th, 1921.
2   Personal communication, Mrs M. W. Davis, October 1971.
3   *The Delineator*, April, 1921.   4   *Ibid.*
5   *New York City Evening World*, May 12th, 1921.
6   B.N., document dated May 19th, 1921.
7   L.C., Marie Meloney to Dr Mary Thomas, May 22nd, 1921.
8   Personal communication, Mrs M. W. Davis, October, 1971.
9   Columbia University Library, Marie Curie to Marie Meloney, July 1st, 1921.
10   Cambridge University Library, Bertram Boltwood to Ernest Rutherford, July 14th, 1921.
11   Letter to *New York Evening Journal*, May 23rd, 1921.
12   Yale University Library, Marie Meloney to Anson Stokes, July 27th, 1921.
13   Laporte, M., Interview with Paul Bordry for a UNESCO radio broadcast on the hundredth anniversary of Marie Curie's birth.

Chapter 22. The Suspect

1   Personal communication, T. Graf, June, 1970.
2   *Radium*, 15, 1920, p. 12.
3   Personal communication, M. Francis, September, 1969.
4   L.C., Ellen Gleditsch to Marie Curie, November 20th, 1922.
5   L.C., Florence Pfalzgraph to Marie Curie, May 25th, 1928.
6   L.C., Marie Meloney to Marie Curie, July 9th, 1923.
7   L.C., Gay Bloch to Marie Curie, undated letter.
8   L.C., Loïe Fuller to Marie Curie, December 23rd, 1922.
9   This is the amount recommended by the International Commission on Radiological protection.
10   L.C., Albert Laborde to Marie Curie, January 7th, 1925.
11   L.C., undated report.   12   *Le Quotidien*, March 30th, 1925.

13 Personal communication, Alicja Dorabialska, September, 1971.
14 Eve, A. S., *loc. cit.*, p. 388.   15 *E.C.*, p. 388.

Chapter 23.   Dignifying Science

1 *E.C.*, p. 373.
2 Interview with F. Joliot-Curie in *Gazette de Lausanne*, June 29th, 1957.
3 *Ibid.*   4 *L.C.*, Marie Curie to Harlan S. Miner, July 13th, 1922.
5 *L.C.*, President of Eldorado Gold Mines to Bishop of Haileybury, September 12th, 1932.
6 *L.C.*, Marie Meloney to Marie Curie, May 18th, 1925.
7 *L.C.*, Marie Meloney to Marie Curie, January 15th, 1930.
8 *L.C.*, Marie Curie to Martin Knudsen, October 1st, 1926.
9 *L.C.*, Marie Curie to Lord Provost of Glasgow, June 14th, 1929.
10 *L.C.*, Marie Curie to Irène Curie, June 14th, 1925.
11 *L.C.*, Marie Meloney to Marie Curie, January 18th, 1928.
12 *L.C.*, Marie Meloney to Marie Curie, April 20th, 1928.
13 *L.C.*, Marie Meloney to Marie Curie, June 16th, 1928.
14 *L.C.*, Marie Meloney to Marie Curie, July 27th, 1928.
15 *L.C.*, Marie Curie to Herbert Hoover, August 21st, 1928, unsigned draft letter.
16 *L.C.*, Marie Meloney to Marie Curie, August 22nd, 1929.
17 *L.C.*, Marie Curie to Marie Meloney, August 19th, 1929.
18 *L.C.*, Marie Curie to Marie Meloney, August 19th, 1929, draft letter.
19 *L.C.*, Marie Curie to Irène Curie, October 20th, 1929.
20 *L.C.*, Marie Curie to Irène Curie, November 5th, 1929.

Chapter 24.   A New Generation

1 *L.C.*, Report to the Dean of the Faculty of Science of Paris University, 1929.
2 *L.C.*, Curie, M., Report to L'Académie de Medécine, June 13th, 1931. Marie Curie was elected to the Academy of Medicine in 1922 as an associate member as a spontaneous gesture by the Academy. She thus successfully won her entry into the Institut de France without having to submit her own candidacy.

3   *B.N.,* undated document.
4   *L.C.,* Marie Curie to Frédéric and Irène Joliot-Curie, December 29th, 1928.
5   *L.C.,* Marie Curie to Ernest Rutherford, September 12th, 1932.
6   *L.C.,* Marie Curie to Marie Meloney, August 2nd, 1933.
7   Columbia University Library, Marie Curie to Marie Meloney, August 28th, 1932.
8   Biquard, P., *loc. cit.,* p. 41.
9   From a talk prepared by Frédéric Joliot-Curie for Radiodiffusion-Télévision Française in 1957, but banned by the government and subsequently published in *La Nef.*
10 Columbia University Library, Marie Curie to Marie Meloney, July 18th, 1932.
11 *L.C.,* Marie Curie to Irène Joliot-Curie, March 26th, 1934.
12 Weil, E., *Revue de l'Alliance Française, 16,* 1943, p. 10.
13 *B.N.,* Eve Curie to Clinic Director, Sancellemoz, June 22nd, 1934.

Chapter 25.   Left in Peace

1   *B.N.,* Jacques Curie to Marie Curie, June 19th, 1934.
2   *M.C.,* p. 143.
3   Curie, M., *La Radiologie et la Guerre* (Alcan, Paris, 1921), p. 143.
4   *L.C.,* Marie Curie to Irène Joliot-Curie, April 22nd, 1931.
5   Columbia University Library. Irène Joliot-Curie to Marie Meloney, June 19th, 1936.
6   Columbia University Library, Irène Joliot-Curie to Marie Meloney, February 26th, 1940.
7   Columbia University Library, Eve Curie to Marie Meloney, February 9th, 1937.

Selected Bibliography

Andrade, E. N. da C., *Rutherford and the Nature of the Atom* (William Heinemann, London, 1964).

Annales. Universitatis Mariae Curie-Sklodowska, Sectio AA, Physica et Chemia, vol. XXII, 1967 (Lublin, 1967).

Arnold, S., and Zychowski, M., *Outline History of Poland* (Polonia Publishing House, Warsaw, 1962).

Badash, L. (editor), *Rutherford and Boltwood* (Yale University Press, New Haven and London, 1969).

Baldrick, R., *The Duel* (Chapman and Hall, London, 1965).

Bertaut, J., *Paris, L'Opinion et les Moeurs sous la Troisième République* (Eyre and Spottiswoode, London, 1936).

Biquard, P., *Frédéric Joliot-Curie* (Souvenir Press, London, 1965).

Biquard, P., *Paul Langevin* (Seghers, Paris, 1969).

Born, M., *The Born–Einstein Letters* (Macmillan, London, 1971).

Boyd, J. P., *The Paris Exposition of 1900* (Boyd, 1900).

Churchill, W. S., *The World Crisis* (Odhams, London, 1938).

Cotton, E., *Les Curie* (Seghers, Paris, 1963).

Crowther, J. G., *British Scientists of the Nineteenth Century* (Routledge, London, 1962).

Crowther, J. G., *Fifty Years With Science* (Barrie and Jenkins, London, 1970).

Cuny, H., *Louis Pasteur* (Souvenir Press, London, 1965).

Curie, E., *Madame Curie* (William Heinemann, London, 1938).

Curie, M., *Oeuvres* (Polish Academy of Sciences, Warsaw, 1954).

Curie, M., *La Radiologie et la Guerre* (Libraire Félix Alcan, 1921).

Curie, M., *Pierre Curie* with *Autobiographical Notes* (Macmillan, New York, 1923).

Danrit (Émile Driant), *La Guerre de Demain* (Fayard, Paris, 1890).

Daudet, L., *Souvenirs* (Nouvelle Librairie Nationale, Paris, 1926).

Eve, A. S., *Rutherford* (Cambridge University Press, 1939).

Feather, N., *Lord Rutherford* (Blackie, London, 1940).

Gieysztor, A., *et al.*, *History of Poland* (Polish Scientific Publishers, Warsaw, 1968).

Glasser, O., *Dr W. C. Röntgen* (Thomas, Springfield, Illinois, 1945).

Griffiths, R., *The Reactionary Revolution* (Constable, London, 1966).

Selected Bibliography

Haber, L. F., *The Chemical Industry, 1900–1930* (Oxford University Press, London, 1971).

Hahn, O., *My Life* (Macdonald, London, 1970).

Harding, J., *General Boulanger* (W. H. Allen, London, 1971).

Howorth, M., *Pioneer Research on the Atom* (New World Publications, London, 1958).

Jennings, W. A., and Russ, S., *Radon* (John Murray, London, 1948).

Joliot-Curie, I., *Marie Curie, Ma Mère* in *Europe, 108*, 1954, p. 89 (Les Éditeurs Français Rèunis).

Langevin, A., *Paul Langevin, Mon Père* (Les Éditeurs Français Réunis).

de Livois, R., *Histoire de la Presse Française* (Spes, Lausanne, 1965).

Lot, F., *Jean Perrin* (Seghers, Paris, 1963).

Marbo, C., *Souvenirs et Rencontres* (Grasset, Paris, 1968).

Medical Research Council, *The Hazards to Man of Nuclear and Allied Radiations* (H.M. Stationery Office, London, 1956, 1960).

Nettl, J. P., *Rosa Luxemburg* (Oxford University Press, London, 1966).

Nicolle, J., *Louis Pasteur* (Fawcett, New York, 1966).

Pierre et Marie Curie (Bibliothèque Nationale, Paris, 1967).

Poynter, F. N. L., *Medicine and Surgery in the Great War* (Wellcome Institute, London, 1968).

Reddaway, W. F. *et al., The Cambridge History of Poland*, (Cambridge University Press, 1950).

Regaud, C., *Marie Sklodowska Curie* (Fondation Curie, Paris, 1934).

Richter, W., *Bismarck* (Macdonald, London, 1962).

Romer, A. (editor), *Radioactivity and the Discovery of Isotopes* (Dover, New York, 1970).

Romer, A. (editor), *The Discovery of Radioactivity and Transmutation* (Dover, New York, 1964).

Rose, W. J., *Poland Old and New* (Bell, London, 1948).

Rutherford, E., *Radio-activity* (Cambridge University Press, 1905).

Schück, H., *et al., Nobel, The Man and his Prizes* (Elsevier, Amsterdam, 1962).

Sharp, E., *Hertha Ayrton* (Edward Arnold, London, 1926).

Soddy, F., *The Interpretation of Radium* (Murray, London, 1920).

Steed, H. W., *Through Thirty Years* (William Heinemann, London, 1924).

Terrat-Branly, J., *Mon Père, Edouard Branly* (Corréa, Paris, 1946).

Thompson, J. S., and H. G., *Silvanus Phillips Thompson* (Fisher Unwin, London, 1920).

Thompson, S. P., *The Life of Lord Kelvin* (Macmillan, London, 1910).

Weeks, M. E., *Discovery of the Elements* (Journal of Chemical Education, Easton, Pa. 1967).

Index